I0131002

M. Diderot

Literature on the Blind

Volume 1

M. Diderot

Literature on the Blind
Volume 1

ISBN/EAN: 9783742833761

Manufactured in Europe, USA, Canada, Australia, Japa

Cover: Foto ©Thomas Meinert / pixelio.de

Manufactured and distributed by brebook publishing software
(www.brebook.com)

M. Diderot

Literature on the Blind

AN ESSAY ON BLINDNESS

IN

A LETTER

TO

A PERSON OF DISTINCTION

RECITING THE MOST INTERESTING PARTICULARS RELATIVE
TO PERSONS BORN BLIND AND THOSE WHO HAVE
LOST THEIR SIGHT

BEING

AN ENQUIRY INTO THE NATURE OF THEIR IDEAS,
KNOWLEDGE OF SOUNDS, OPINIONS CONCERNING
MORALITY AND RELIGION, &c.

INTERSPERSED WITH SEVERAL ANECDOTES OF SAUNDERSON, MILTON,
AND OTHERS

WITH COPPER-PLATES

ELUCIDATING DR. SAUNDERSON'S METHOD OF WORKING
GEOMETRICAL PROBLEMS

Translated from the French of

M. DIDEROT

PHYSICIAN TO HIS MOST CHRISTIAN MAJESTY

LONDON
PRINTED FOR RICHARD DYMOTT, OPPOSITE SOMERSET HOUSE,
IN THE STRAND
MDCCLXXIII.

[Price 1s. 6d.]

LONDON
SAMPSON LOW, MARSTON, AND COMPANY
LIMITED
St. Dunstan's House
FETTER LANE, FLEET STREET, E.C.
1895

LONDON :

PRINTED BY WILLIAM CLOWES AND SONS, LIMITED,

STAMFORD STREET AND CHARING CROSS.

THE PREFACE.

It is proper the public should be informed of the author's motive for writing the following letter. A foreign physician of some reputation had bills put up at the corners of all the streets at Paris, that on such a day he would give sight to a girl who was born blind. The philosophers were one and all stricken at the confidence with which this kind of prodigy was thus published : and the celebrated Mr. Diderot desired the physician to allow him the favour of being present at the operation. It was answered that his presence would, to be sure, be a great honour ; however, dreading the philosopher's keen eye, he performed the operation in private ; but, at the same time, was willing to make the honour of it as public as possible. On this, the philosopher determined to lay open the fraud, which he did very ingeniously in this letter ; a letter stored with such refined ideas, and such profound investigations, that it may well be accounted the standard of human wit and penetration. The impostor stoutly maintained his point, in which he was so seconded by the monastic Phalanx, that, as proves but too commonly the case, he got the better, and the philosopher was sent to Vincennes castle.

But the truth came at length to light, and falsity was exploded with ignominy. Mr. Diderot's letter could not be sufficiently extolled, and, as a complete crown of its glory, Mr. d'Alembert has given a most judicious extract of it in the Encyclopedia, with observations, omitted here purely to avoid swelling the price of

this admirable composition, but which throw great light on the
work itself, and may serve as a model to reviewers and others,
whose business is to select the plan, ground-work, and essence of
books. I have added a few remarks of my own, which arose in
me as I perused the book, humbly offering them to the reader's
notice.

TABLE OF CONTENTS.

LETTER ON THE BLIND.

MADAM,—It was no more than what I apprehended, that the blind girl, whom Mr. Reaumur had couched for a cataract, would not inform you of what you was curious to know; but I little thought that it would neither be her fault nor yours. I have, in person, and by means of his best friends, and by paying him many compliments, applied to her benefactor, but without the least success; and the first dressing will be taken off, without your being admitted to see it. Some persons of the first distinction have had the honour of being put on a level with philosophers in this sense: in a word, it was only before some eyes of no consequence he would remove the veil. If you would know why that wonderful operator makes such a secret of experiments, at which you think too great a number of intelligent witnesses cannot be present, my answer is, that the observations of such a celebrated person do not so much stand in need of spectators, whilst making, as of hearers, when made. Thus disappointed, Madam, I betook myself to my first intention, and, being obliged to go without an experiment, in which I saw but little to be gained, either for my own instruction, or yours, but which Mr. Reaumur will doubtless improve to a much higher purpose, I fell to philosophizing with my friend on the important matter which is the object of it. Happy, if you will be pleased to accept the narrative of one of our conversations, instead of the sight which I had too hastily promised you.

On the very day that the Prussian performed the operation of the cataract on Simoneau's daughter, we went to have some talk with the Puiseaux man who had been born blind. He is possessed of good solid sense, is known to great numbers of creditable persons, understands something of chemistry, and has attended

the courses of botany in the king's garden with tolerable
improvement. His father was an eminent professor of philosophy
in the University of Paris, and left him such a fortune, as would
have very well sufficed for the senses remaining to him; but in
his youth he was carried away by love of pleasure, which, with
the dishonesty of some others, so reduced his domestic affairs,
that he retired into a little town in Provence, from whence every
year he takes a journey to Paris, bringing with him liquors of
his own distilling, and which give great satisfaction. These,
Madam, are circumstances, indeed, not very philosophical; but,
on that very account, the fitter to make you conclude, that the
person I am speaking of is not imaginary.

It was about five in the afternoon when we came to the blind
man's house, where we found him hearing his son read with
raised characters: he had not been up above an hour; for you
must know that his morning is our evening; carrying on his
domestic affairs, and working while others are asleep. At mid-
night he is free from disturbance himself, and is not troublesome
to others. His first care is to put in its place every thing that
has been displaced during the day; that his wife, at her getting
up, commonly finds the house set to rights. The difficulty which
blind persons have in finding things mislaid, makes them love
regularity and exactness; and I have observed, that those about
them imbibe that quality, whether from the good example set
them by the blind, or from an humane concern for them. The
blind would, indeed, be very unhappy, without such regard from
those about them, nay, we ourselves would feel the want of it.
Great services are like large pieces of gold or silver, which we
seldom have occasion to make use of; but little complaisances
are as current cash, which we are continually either receiving or
paying away.

This blind man judges very well of symmetries. Symmetry,
which perhaps is no more than a matter of mere compact among
us, is certainly such in many respects between a blind man and
those who have their sight. A blind man studies, by his touch,
that disposition required between the parts of a whole, to entitle

it to be called fine; and thus, at length, attains to a just application of that term. But in saying *that is fine*, he does not judge ; it is no more than repeating the judgment of those who see ; and is not this the case of three-fourths of those who give their verdict on a play or a book ? Beauty, to a blind man, is but a word when abstracted from utility ; and wanting an organ, how many things are there, the utility of which lies out of his verge ? Are not the blind extremely to be pitied in accounting nothing fine unless it be likewise good ? How many admirable things are lost to them ? The only compensation is, their having ideas of the beautiful, which, if less extensive, are more clear than those of many keen-sighted philosophers, who have composed prolix dissertations on it.

He is continually talking of looking-glasses. You are sensible that he does not know what the word looking-glass means, yet is he never known to put a glass in a wrong light. He expresses himself as sensibly as we on the qualities and the defects of the organ which is wanting in him. If he annexes no idea to the terms he makes use of, yet has he this advantage over most other men, that he never uses them improperly. He discourses so well and so justly of so many things absolutely unknown to him, that his conversation would considerably lessen the weight of that inference which, without knowing wherefore, we all draw from what passes in ourselves to what passes within others.

I asked him what he meant by a looking-glass ? "A machine," answered he, "which puts relievo things at a distance from themselves, if when properly placed with regard to it : it is like my hand, which, to feel an object, I must not put on one side of it." Had Descartes been born blind, he might, in my opinion, have hugged himself for such a definition. Do but consider, I beg of you, what an ingenious combination of ideas it implies. This blind man has no other object but by the touch. He knows, from the account of others, that objects are known by means of the sight as to him by the touch ; at least, it is the only notion he can form of them. He farther knows that there is no seeing one's own face, though it may be touched.

He must therefore conclude sight to be a kind of touch, reaching only to objects' different from our face and at a distance from us. The touch gives him an idea only of relief : " therefore," adds he, " a looking-glass is a machine representing us in relief out of ourselves." How many famous philosophers have laboured with less subtility in the pursuit of notions as false ? But how surprising must a looking-glass be to this blind man ? How much must his amazement have increased on our informing him that there are some of those machines which magnify objects, others which, without duplicating them, put them out of their place, bring them nearer, remove them farther, cause them to be perceived, and lay open the most minute parts to the eyes of the naturalists ; that some again multiply them by thousands, and that some appear totally to change the figure of objects ? Concerning these phenomena, he asked us abundance of strange questions ; as, " Whether none but those called naturalists saw with the microscope, and whether astronomers alone saw with the telescope ? Whether the machine which magnifies objects be larger than that which lessens them ? Whether that which brings them nearer was shorter than that which removes them farther off ? " And not conceiving how that other self, which, according to him, the looking-glass represents in relief, should not be tactile, " So," said he, " there's two of our senses set at variance by a little machine : a more perfect machine might possibly reconcile them, without the object's being ever the more real for that ; and perhaps a third, still more complete, and less illusory, would make them vanish and show us our mistake."

And what do you take eyes to be ? said M. D. " They are," says the blind man, " an organ, on which the air has the effect which my stick has on my hand." This answer amazed us, and whilst we were looking at one another, wrapped in admiration, " So true is this," continued he, " that on my putting my hand between your eyes and an object, my hand is present to you, but the object absent. It is the same with me when I am seeking one thing with my stick and meet another."

Madam, only turn to Descartes' Dioptics, and there you will

see the phenomena of sight illustrated by those of the touch, and optic plates full of men busied in seeing with sticks. Descartes and all his successors have not been able to give us clearer ideas of vision ; and that great philosopher was, in this respect, no farther superior to the blind man than a common man who has the use of his eyes.

None of us thought of questioning him concerning painting and writing ; but it is evident that there are no questions in which his comparisons would not have borne him out, and I make no doubt but he would have said that to go about reading or seeing without eyes was like seeking after a pin with a faggot stick. We only talked to him of those kinds of glasses which exhibit objects in relief, and are both so very similar to, and so very different from, our looking-glasses ; but these we perceived rather contradicted than coincided with his idea of a looking-glass, and he was apt to think that a painter might perhaps paint a looking-glass, and thus it came to represent objects in colours.

We afterwards saw him thread very small needles. May I beg the favour of you, Madam, here to suspend your reading, and think how you would go about it, were you in his case ? Should no expedient offer itself, I will tell you that of the blind man's. He places the needle's eye transversally between his lips, and in the same direction as his mouth ; then, by the help of his tongue and suction, he draws in the thread, which follows his breath, unless it be much too large for the eye ; but, in that case, he who has his sight is little better off.

He has a prodigious remembrance of sounds ; and the infinite diversity we perceive in faces, he perceives in voices, with number-less minute gradations which escape us, as not so much con-cerned to observe them. Those gradations are, to us, like our own face ; as of all the men that we have ever seen, he whom we should least recollect is our very self. We take notice of faces only for better knowing the persons, and that we do not remember our own is because we shall never be liable to take ourself for another person, or another for ourself ; then, the

helps which our senses reciprocally afford to each other hinder
their improvement.   It is not here only that I shall have occasion
to make this remark.

   On this head our blind man said, "That he should think
himself a pitiable object in wanting those advantages which we
enjoy; and that he should have been apt to consider us as
superior intelligences, had he not a hundred times found us very
much inferior to him in other respects." This reflection gave
rise to another in us. This blind man, said we, values himself
as much, and perhaps more, than we who see. Why, then, if
the brute reasons, and it is scarce to be doubted, why, on
weighing its advantages over man as better known to it than
those of man over it, should it not make a like inference ? He
has arms, perhaps says the gnat, but I have wings. If he has
weapons, says the lion, have we not claws ? The elephant will
look on us as insects ; and all the animals, very readily allowing
us a reason, with which we should at the same time stand in
great need of their instinct, will set up to be endued with an
instinct by means of which they do very well without our
reason.

   One of our company asked the blind man whether he should
not be very glad to have eyes ? "Were it not for curiosity,"
said he, "I would full as lieve have long arms. My hands, I
think, would inform me better of what is doing in the moon
than your eyes or your telescopes. Besides, the eyes sooner
cease to see than the hands to touch, that to improve the organ
which I have would be as good as to give me that which is
wanting in me."

   This blind man points with such exactness at the place whence
a noise comes that I make no doubt the blind may, by practice,
become very dexterous and very dangerous. Here is a passage
which will show you how imprudent it would be to stand the
throwing of a stone or discharging of a pistol by him, were he
in the least used to that weapon. He had, in his youth, a
quarrel with one of his brothers, who came off but badly.
Provoked at some insulting language, he laid hold of the first

PLATE I.

object which came to hand, threw it at him, and hit him directly on the forehead, so as to lay him flat on the ground.

This, with some other adventures of the like kind, caused him to be brought before the police. The blind are proof against all those ensigns of power which make such strong impressions on us. He made his appearance before the magistrate as his equal, and without being in the least intimidated by any of his threats. "What would you do to me?" said he to M. Herault. "I will commit you to the dungeon," answered the magistrate. "As to that, Sir," replied the blind man, "I have been in one these twenty-five years." There was an answer, Madam; and what a text for one who is so fond of moralizing as your humble servant! We go out of life as from a splendid entertainment, the blind man as out of a dungeon. We may possibly have more pleasure in living than he, but certainly death to him is a much less disagreeable affair.

The blind man judges of the nearness of fire by the degrees of heat, of the fulness of vessels from the noise made by liquors which he decants into them, and of the proximity of bodies by the action of the air on his face. So sensible is he of the least change in the atmosphere, that he can distinguish a street from a turn-again. He has a wonderful faculty in determining the weights of bodies and the capacities of vessels; and of his arms he has made such exact balances, and his fingers are compasses so well known to him from numberless experiments, that in this kind of statics I will always wager on our blind man's head against twenty persons with all their eyes about them. The polish of bodies has scarce fewer gradations to him than the sound of voices; and there is no danger of his mistaking another for his wife, unless he was to be a gainer by the exchange. Yet is it very probable that, among blind people, wives would be in common, or their laws against the adulteress must be severe indeed, so very easy would it be for wives to deceive their husbands by concerting a sign with their gallants.

He judges of beauty by the touch: in this, however, there is no great mystery; but what is not so easy to be comprehended is, that he includes in this conjecture, pronunciation and the sound of the voice. I wish anatomists would inform us whether there is any relation between the parts of the mouth and the palate and the external form of the face. He turns very neatly, does pretty pieces of needlework, levels with a square, and makes up and takes to pieces common machines. He is so far skilled in music as to perform a piece after being told the notes and their value. He estimates the duration of time much more precisely than we, by the succession of actions and thoughts. A smooth skin, firm flesh, an elegant shape, a sweet breath, a mellow voice, a graceful pronunciation, are qualities on which he sets a great value.

He married to have eyes of his own, which superseded a former intention of taking into partnership with him a deaf man, to find eyes, as he, in return, would contribute ears. I could not sufficiently wonder at his singular address in a great many things ; and on our expressing our surprise, " I perceive, gentlemen," says he, " that you are not blind : you are astonished at what I do, and why not as much at my speaking ? " I believe there is more philosophy in this answer than what he himself dreamed of. The facility with which we all are brought to speak is not a little surprising. It is only by a series of ingenious and profound combinations of the analogies observed between objects out of the verge of sense, and the ideas they raise, that we come to annex an idea to many terms not represented by sensible objects ; and, consequently, learning to speak should be more difficult to a blind man than to any other, the number of objects without the verge of his senses being much greater, and thus his field for comparing and combining much more limited. How, for instance, can the word physiognomy imprint itself on his memory ? It is a kind of comeliness, consisting in objects so little sensible to a blind person, that for want of its being sufficiently so even to us who see, we should be at no little loss to explain very precisely what physiognomy is. If the eyes be the parts in which it chiefly resides, then the touch can give us no information ; and, besides, what does a blind man know of dead eyes, languishing eyes, brisk eyes, expressive eyes, &c. ?

I infer from thence that we unquestionably derive great advantages from the concurrence of our senses and our organs; still would it be quite another thing did we use them separately, and never employ two where one alone would suffice. To add the touch to the sight, when our eyes will do the business, is like putting to a carriage with two horses, already sufficiently stout, a third, which will draw one way while the others draw another.

As to me it has always been very clear that the state of our organs and our senses has a great influence on our metaphysics and our morality, and that our most intellectual ideas, in a great measure, depend on the conformation and texture of our bodies. I put some questions to the blind man concerning the vices and virtues. I immediately perceived that he had a violent aversion to theft; possibly for two reasons—it being an easy matter to steal from him without his perceiving it, and still more, perhaps, that he could be immediately seen were he to go about filching. Not that he is at any loss to secure himself against that sense which he knows we have above him, or that he is but awkward at hiding what he might steal. Modesty he makes no great account of. He would scarce understand the use of apparel, were it not for the weather; and he frankly owns he cannot think why one part of the body is covered more than another, and still less how, among those parts, the preference is given to some which, from their use, and the indispositions to which they are subject, ought rather to be kept free. Though living in an age when philosophy has rid us of a great number of prejudices, I don't think we shall ever go such a length as to set aside the prerogatives of modesty so absolutely as this blind man. Diogenes would have been no philosopher in his account.

As of all the external signs which raise our pity and ideas of pain the blind are affected only by complaint, I have, in general, no high thoughts of their sympathy and tenderness. What difference is there to a blind man between him who is making water and him whose blood is gushing out, but makes no complaint? And we ourselves—where is our compassion, when distance, or the smallness of objects, render them the same to us, as the want of sight does to the blind? So near akin are our virtues to our manner of sensation, and the degree in which external things affect us! Nay, I make no doubt but that, setting the law aside, many could sooner kill a man at such a distance as to seem no bigger than a swallow, than cut an ox's throat with their own hands. We pity a horse in pain, and we make nothing of crushing an ant; and still is it not by the same principle that we are moved? Ah, Madam, how different is the morality of the blind from ours! How different would that of a deaf man likewise be from his! And how deficient, to say nothing more, would our morality appear to one with a sense more than we have!

Our metaphysics and theirs agree no better. How many of their principles are mere absurdities to us, and *vice versâ!* Concerning this, I might enter into a detail, which I am pretty certain would entertain you, but which a set of exceptious men exclaim against, as profaneness and infidelity, as if it was in my power to make the blind perceive things otherwise than they do. I shall therefore only observe one thing, and that, I believe, every one must allow: it is, that the mighty argument drawn from the wonders of nature, is a very weak one to the blind. The facility with which we, as it were, create fresh objects, by means of a small glass, is something more incomprehensible to them than constellations, from the sight of which they are totally excluded. That lucid globe, moving from east to west, astonishes them less than a small fire, which they are able to make greater or less: seeing matter in a much more abstract manner than we, they are less indisposed to believe that it thinks.

A man who has seen but a day or two must, among a blind people, either be silent, or be looked upon as brain-sick. He would be every day acquainting them with some new mystery, which would be such only to them, and thus free-thinkers would oppose it tooth and nail. Might not the champions of religion greatly avail themselves of such a stubborn infidelity, which, however just in some respects, is yet so very ill grounded? Be

pleased only to dwell a little upon this supposition. It will
bring to your mind, under a borrowed imagery, the history and
persecutions of those whose misfortune it has been to find out
truth in an age of darkness, and who imprudently made it their
business to spread it among their blind cotemporaries ; and their
most envenomed enemies were those who, from their class and
education, one would have thought least remote from such
opinions.

So much for the morality and metaphysics of the blind : I
proceed to things less important, but more nearly connected with
the end of the various observations everywhere made here since
the Prussian's arrival.

Question I. How can one born blind form to himself ideas of
figures ?

I believe that the motions of his body, the successive existence
of his hands in several places, the continuous feeling of a body
passing between his fingers, give him the notion of direction.
In sliding them along a thread tightly stretched, he has the idea
of a straight line ; in following the bending of a slack thread, he
gets that of a curve line : he has, by repeated experiments of the
touch, a remembrance of sensations felt in different points.
These sensations, or points, he is able to combine, and form
figures by them. A straight line is to a blind man, who is no
geometrician, only the remembrance of a series of sensations
placed in the direction of a tight thread ; a curve line the
remembrance of a series of tactile sensations referred to the
surface of some solid body, concave or convex. Study rectifies
the geometrician's notions of these lines by the properties he
discovers in them ; but he who was born blind, whether he
understands geometry, or not, refers all to his fingers' ends. We
combine coloured points, he combines only palpable points ; or,
to speak more precisely, only such tactile sensations which he
remembers. The operations in his head have little analogy with
ours ; he cannot imagine, as imagination implies a coloured
ground and points detached from that ground, by supposing
them differing in colour from that ground : make those points

of the same colour as the ground, and they are instantly lost in it, and the figure disappears : at least, that is the case in my imagination ; and I suppose imaginations are alike. Thus, when I purpose to perceive in my head a straight line otherwise than by its properties, my first step is to spread in it a white canvas, detaching from the ground a continuous series of black points in the like direction. The stronger the colours of the ground and points, the clearer my perception of the points. To view in my imagination a figure of a colour very nearly bordering on that of the ground, puts me to no less trouble than if out of myself and on a canvas.

You see then, Madam, that laws might be given for imagining with ease various objects, variously coloured ; but such laws are by no means calculated for one born blind, who not being able to colour, and consequently not to imagine, in our way, remembers only such sensations as are derived from the touch ; and which he refers to different points, places and distances, and of which he forms figures. So certain is it that there is no figuring in fancy without colouring, that if little balls, to the colour and matter of which we are strangers, be given us to touch in the dark, we shall immediately suppose them white or black, or of some other colour ; and that if we do not annex a colour to them, we, like the blind man, shall have the remembrance only of little sensations excited at our fingers' ends, and such as little round bodies may occasion. If this remembrance be very fleeting in us, if we have but little conception how one born blind fixes, recalls, and combines the sensations of the touch, it is owing to the custom we derive from our eyes, of performing everything in our imagination with colours. It has, however, been my own case, under the agitation of a violent passion, to feel a thrilling throughout one of my hands, and the impression of bodies, which it was some time since I had touched, renewed as strongly as if still actually under my touch : the limits of the sensation likewise precisely corresponding with those absent bodies. Though sensation be of itself indivisible, it takes up, if I may be allowed the term, a large space, which

the person blind from his birth can increase or contract by
thought, enlarging or diminishing the part affected. Thus he
composes points, surfaces, and solids : he will even have a solid
large as the terraqueous globe, by supposing his fingers' ends
as large as the globe, and everywhere in length, breadth, and
depth, taken up by the sensation.

I do not know anything which better demonstrates the reality
of internal sensation than this faculty, so weak in us, but so
strong in those who are born blind, of feeling or calling to mind
the sensation of bodies, even when absent, and no longer acting
on us. We cannot bring one born blind to understand how
imagination exhibits absent objects to us as if present ; but we
easily perceive in us the same faculty of feeling at the fingers'
ends a body when no longer there, as in one born blind. In
order to this, squeeze your fore-finger against your thumb, shut
your eyes, spread your fingers, and immediately after they are
separated, look into yourself, and tell me, whether the sensation
does not last a considerable time after the compression has
ceased ? whether if, during the compression, your soul appears
to you to be rather more in your head than at your fingers'
ends ? and whether this compression does not, by the space
which the sensation fills, give you the idea of a surface ? We
distinguish the presence of beings out of us, from the imagery
of them in our imagination, only through the force or weakness
of the impression. So he, who is born blind, discerns the
sensation from the real presence of an object at his fingers' ends,
only by the force or weakness of that very sensation. Should a
philosopher, who has been blind and deaf from his birth, ever
make a man in imitation of that of Descartes, I dare affirm,
Madam, that he will place the soul at the fingers' ends ; as from
thence deriving his principal sensations, and all his lights. And
who will put him in mind, that his head is the residence of his
thoughts ? If the labours of imagination impair our brain, it is
because our effort in imagining is pretty similar to that which
we exert in perceiving very near or very small objects. But it
will not be so with him who has been blind and deaf from his

birth : the sensations which he has derived from the touch will be, as it were, the mould of all his ideas ; and I should not be surprised that, after a deep and close meditation, his finger should be as much tired as our head. It would give me no apprehension, were a philosopher to object to him, that the nerves are the causes of our sensations, and that all nerves have their origin in the brain. Were these two propositions fully demonstrated, which is very far from being the case, especially the former, an exposition of all the dreams of naturalists on this head would be sufficient to confirm him in his opinion.

But if the imagination of a blind person be no more than the faculty of calling to mind, and combining sensations of palpable points ; and that of a man who sees, the faculty of combining and calling to mind visible or coloured points : the person born blind consequently perceives things in a much more abstract manner than we ; and in questions merely speculative, he is, perhaps, less liable to be deceived. For abstraction is only separating the sensible qualities of bodies, either from one another, or from the body itself in which they are inherent ; and from this being wrong or improper, springs error, wrong in metaphysical questions, and improper in physico-mathematical questions. A way, in which one can scarce avoid being mistaken in metaphysics, is not sufficiently simplifying the objects under investigation ; and an infallible secret for coming to false conclusions in physico-mathematics, is to suppose them less compounded than they are.

There is a kind of abstraction, of which so very few are capable, that it seems reserved to pure intelligences : the reducing everything to numerical unities. It must be allowed, that the results of this geometry would be very exact, and its formulas very general, there being no objects, either actually existing or possible, which these simple unities could not represent, by points, lines, surfaces, solids, thoughts, ideas, sensations, &c. ; and if this should prove to be the foundation of Pythagoras's doctrine, he might be said to have failed in his plan, his mode of philosophizing being too much above us, and too near that of the Supreme Being, who, according to the ingenious expression of an English geometrician, is perpetually geometrising in the universe.

Unity, pure and simple, is too vague and general a symbol for us. Our senses bring us back to signs more analogous to the extent of our intellects, and the conformation of our organs. We have even brought those signs to be in common among us, and to serve, as it were, for the staple, in the mutual commerce of our ideas : some we have appointed for the eye, as characters ; some for the ear, as articulate sounds ; but for the touch we have none, though there is a proper way of speaking to that sense, and getting answers from it. The want of this language precludes all conversation between us and those who are born deaf, blind, and dumb. They grow up, but still in a state of imbecility ; whereas they might, perhaps, acquire ideas, were they, from their childhood, trained in a fixed, determinate, constant, and uniform manner to understand us : in a word, by tracing on their hand the same characters which we delineate on paper, with the same signification unalterably annexed to them.

Now, Madam, does not this language appear to you as convenient as another ; and is it not even ready invented ? And would you take upon you to affirm, that you never have been brought to understand anything in the like manner ? All that remains then is to fix it, and make a grammar and dictionaries of it, should the expression, by the common characters of writing, be thought too slow for this purpose.

There are three avenues for knowledge ; but one, from the want of signs, is kept barricaded : had the two others been neglected, we should be little better than brutes ; as the touch understands only by compression, so would it have been the only means of speaking to the ear. Madam, it is only the want of one sense can make us thoroughly acquainted with the advantages of the symbols appointed for those which we enjoy ; and what a consolation would it be to those, whose misfortune it is to be deaf, blind, and dumb, or who should lose those three senses

by any accident, were there a clear and precise language for
the touch.

It is much shorter to use symbols ready invented, than to

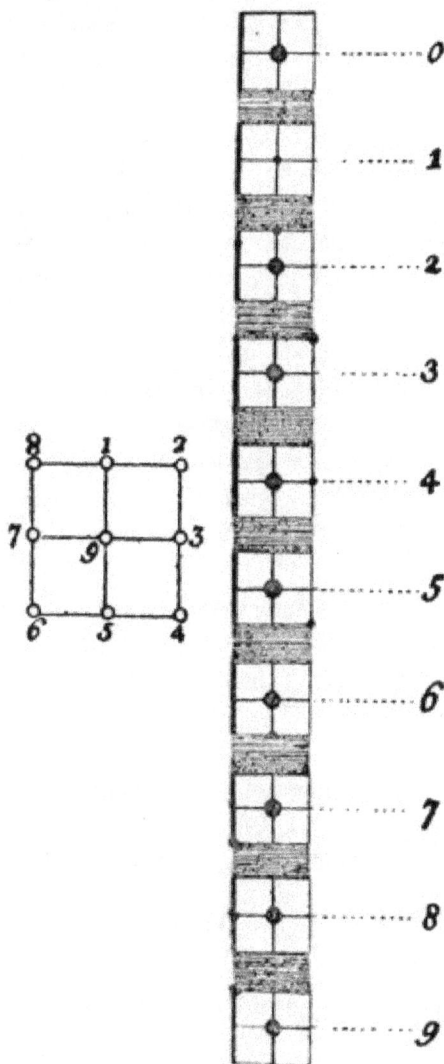

PLATE II.

invent them, which yet must be done when taken unprepared.
What an advantage would it not have been for Saunderson, to

find in his sixth year a tangible arithmetic ready to his hands, instead of being put to contrive one when he was twenty-five. This Saunderson, Madam, is another blind man, with whom it will not be foreign from my purpose to make you acquainted. Wonderful things, indeed, are told of him ; and yet there is not one to which, from his improvements in literature, and his skill in mathematical sciences, we may not safely give credit.

The same machine served him for algebraical calculations, and for the description of rectilineal figures. You would like to have this explained to you, did it come within your understanding ; and now you shall see that it supposes no farther knowledge than what you are mistress of, and that it would be very useful to you, should you ever take it into your head to work long calculations *by feeling*.

Suppose a square, as Plate II. Divide it into four equal parts by perpendicular lines at the sides, so as to form the nine points, 1, 2, 3, 4, 5, 6, 7, 8, 9. In this square are nine holes, capable of admitting two kinds of pins, all of the same length and bigness, except the heads of some being a little bigger than others.

The large-headed pins were never placed but in the centre of the square ; and the small-headed always on the sides, except only in the single case of a nought, and this was marked by a large-headed pin placed in the centre of the little square, without any other pin on the sides. The cypher 1 was represented by a small-headed pin in the centre of the square, without any other pin on the sides. Cypher 2, by a large-headed pin placed in the centre of the square, and a small-headed pin placed on one of the sides at point 1. Cypher 3, by a large-headed pin placed in the centre of the square, and a small-headed pin placed on one of the sides at point 2. Cypher 4, by a large-headed pin placed in the centre of the square, and by a small-headed pin placed on one of the sides at point 3. Cypher 5, by a large-headed pin in the centre of the square, and a small-headed one in one of the sides at point 4. Cypher 6, by a large-headed pin in the centre of the square, and a small-headed pin on one of the sides at

point 5.   Cypher 7, by a large-headed pin placed in the centre of
the square, and a small-headed pin placed on one of the sides at
point 6.   Cypher 8, by a large-headed pin placed in the centre of

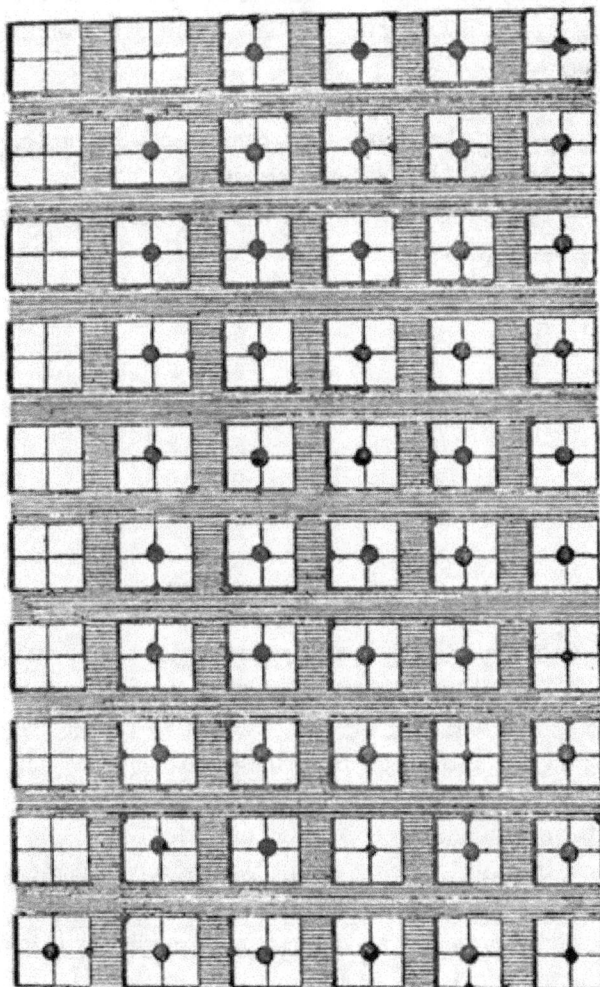

PLATE III.

the square, and a small-headed pin placed on one of the sides at
point 7.   Cypher 9, by a large-headed pin placed in the centre of
the square, and a small-headed pin placed on one of the sides of
the square at point 8

Here are ten different expressions for the touch, each answering to one of our ten arithmetical characters. Now fancy a table as large as you please ; divide it into little squares horizontally disposed, and separated one from another at the same distance, as in Plate III., and this gives you Saunderson's machine.

You readily conceive, that there are no numbers which may not be written on that table ; and, consequently, no arithmetical operation but what may be performed by it.

Let it be proposed, for instance, to find the sum of the nine following numbers :—

1	2	3	4	5
2	3	4	5	6
3	4	5	6	7
4	5	6	7	8
5	6	7	8	9
6	7	8	9	0
7	8	9	0	1
8	9	0	1	2
9	0	1	2	3

I write them on the table as they are named to me. The first cypher at the left of the first number, on the first square to the left of the first line ; the second cypher at the left of the first number, on the second square, at the left of the same line ; and so on. The second number I place on the second row of squares, the units under units, the tens under tens, &c.

I place the third number on the third row of squares, and so on, as you see, Plate III. Then, with my fingers going over every vertical row from the top to the bottom, beginning by that which is most to my left, I add up the numbers expressed in that row, writing the surplus of the tens at the end of the column. I go on to the second column, proceeding towards the left, which I work in the same way. From that to the third ; and thus successively go through my addition.

How the same table served him for demonstrating the

PLATE IV.

properties of rectilineal figures was thus : supposing he was to demonstrate, that parallelograms of the like base and height have equal surfaces ; he placed his pins as you see, Plate IV., annexing names to the angular points, and performed the demonstrations with his fingers.

Had Saunderson made use of only large-headed pins to denote the limits of his figures, he could place round them small-headed pins disposed in nine different manners, all quite plain and familiar to him ; so that he was never at a stand, but when the great number of angular points to be named in his demonstration, laid him under a necessity of recurring to the letters of the alphabet ; and how he made use of them, we are not informed.

All we know is, that his fingers ran over his table with surprising dispatch ; entering on the longest calculations, breaking off, and perceiving when he was out, that he easily proved them, and so convenient was the arrangement of his table, that this operation did not take him up anything of the time which we should conceive.

This arrangement consisted in placing large-headed pins in the centre of all the squares ; after which, all he had to do, was determining their value by the small-headed pins, except in the case of a nought. Then, instead of the large-headed pin, he placed in the centre of the square a small-headed one. Sometimes, instead of forming a whole line with his pins, he only placed them at all the angular or intersecting points, with silken threads round them, which completed the limits of his figures. See Plate V.

He has left some other machines, which made the study of geometry easier to him. His particular way of using them is not known ; and, perhaps, the finding it out would require more sagacity than to solve a problem of integral calculation. I wish some geometrician would find out what use he made of four solid pieces of wood in the form of rectangular parallelopipedes, each eleven inches in length, to a breadth of five and a half, and little more than half an inch in thickness, with the two thick

PLATE V.

opposite surfaces divided into small squares, like that of the abacus, before described, with this difference, that they were perforated only in some places where the pins were thrust in up to the head. Every surface represented nine small arithmetical tables, each of ten numbers ; and each of those ten numbers was composed of ten cyphers. Plate VI. exhibits one of these little tables, with its numbers.

9	4	0	8	4
2	4	1	8	6
4	1	7	9	2
5	4	2	8	4
6	3	9	8	6
7	1	8	8	0
7	8	5	6	8
8	4	3	5	8
8	9	4	6	4
9	4	0	3	0

He wrote *The Elements of Geometry*, a very complete work in its kind, and which bears no other marks of his blindness, than the singularity of some demonstrations, which a man with his eyes would perhaps not have hit on. He first found out the division of the cube into six equal pyramids, with their summits in the centre of the cube, and their bases each of its faces. It is used in a very plain demonstration, to show that every pyramid is the third of a prism of the same base and height.

His own taste led him to the study of the mathematics, and the smallness of his fortune, but chiefly the encouragement of his friends, put him on holding public lectures. They made no question of his succeeding beyond his hopes, by his wonderful facility in making himself understood. Saunderson, indeed, used to speak to his pupils as if they had lost their sight ; but that blind man, who speaks so as to be clearly understood by the blind, must go a great way with those who have their sight : it is a telescope the more. They who have written his life say, that he abounded in happy expressions ; and that

PLATE VI.

C

is very probable. But, perhaps, you will ask me, what do you mean by happy expressions? I answer, Madam, that they are such which are proper to one sense, as to the touch, and, at the same time, metaphorical to another sense, as the sight; a circumstance, from which the person spoken to receives a double light, the real and direct light of the expression, and the reflected light of the metaphor. It is evident, that on these occasions, Saunderson understood himself only by halves, as perceiving only half the ideas annexed to the terms he used. But who is not now and then in the like case? Many a smart jest shall come from idiots, and persons of the best sense drop a silly thing without either being aware of it.

I have observed the want of words produce the like effect in foreigners, who, in our language, are obliged to say everything in very few words, some of which they unknowingly place very happily. But every language being to writers of a lively fancy deficient in fit words, they are in the same case as foreigners of wit; the situations invented by them, the delicate gradations they perceive in characters, the natural pictures which they draw, are continually leading them from the common ways of speaking into terms and phrases, which never fail to charm, when neither obscure nor affected; and these faults are dealt with according to the reader's own wit, and his little acquaintance with the language. Hence it is that, of all French writers, M. de M—— is best liked by the English; and Tacitus, of all the classics, bears the bell among *thinkers :* they do not attend to the licences of the style, it is only the truth of the expression which strikes them.

Saunderson was Professor of Mathematics at the University of Cambridge. He read lectures on optics, the nature of light and colours; he explained the theory of vision, the effects of glasses, the phenomena of the rainbow, and several other points relating to sight, and its organ.

The marvellous of these things, Madam, will be found considerably to abate, on your taking into consideration, that there are three things to be distinguished in every physico-geometrical question ; the phenomenon to be explained, the geometrician's suppositions, and the calculation resulting from the suppositions. Now, it is manifest, that to a blind person, how great soever his penetration be, the phenomena of light and of colours are unknown. The suppositions he will understand, as all of them relate to palpable causes ; but the geometer's reason for preferring them to others, will be out of his verge, as in order to that, he must be able to compare the suppositions themselves with the phenomena : therefore, the blind man takes the suppositions for what they are given him ; a ray of light for an elastic and fine thread, or for a series of minute bodies striking our eyes with incredible velocity ; and he calculates accordingly. The transition from physics to geometry is now got over, and the question becomes simply mathematical.

But what are we to think of the results of the calculation ? 1. That the coming at them is sometimes extremely difficult, and that it would be to little purpose that a naturalist could form the most plausible hypotheses, were he not able to verify them by geometry : accordingly, the greatest natural philosophers, as Galileo, Descartes, and Newton, were great geometricians. 2. That these results are more or less certain, as the hypotheses on which they are built are more or less complicated. When the calculation is founded on a simple hypothesis, the conclusions acquire the force of geometrical demonstrations. When the suppositions are multifarious, the probability of each hypothesis being true diminishes in proportion to the number of the hypotheses ; but, on the other hand, increases from the little probability, that so many false hypotheses would exactly correct each other, and produce a result confirmed by the phenomena. This would be like an addition, the result of which was right, though the partial sum of the numbers added had been all miscounted. The possibility of such an operation cannot be denied ; but, at the same time, you see that it would very seldom prove so. The more numbers are to be added, the greater the probability of a mistake in the addition of each ; but this probability is likewise lessened, if the result of the operation be right : so that there is a number of hypotheses, the certainty resulting from which would be the least possible. If I make A, plus B, plus C, equal to 50, am I to conclude from 50 being the real quantity of the phenomena that the suppositions represented by the letters A, B, C, are true, there being number-less ways of taking from one of those two letters, and adding to the other, and 50 to prove always the result ? But the case of three combined hypotheses is, perhaps, one of the most dis-favourable.

One advantage of calculation, which I must not omit, is, that the contrariety found between the result and the phenomenon excludes false hypotheses. A naturalist, to find the curve formed by a ray of light in the atmosphere, is obliged to regulate himself by the density of the strata of the air, the law of refraction, the nature and figure of the luminous corpuscle, and, perhaps, by other essential elements which he does not bring into account, either as voluntarily neglecting them, or being unknown to him. At length he determines the curvature of the ray. If it be otherwise in nature than his calculation makes it, his suppositions are deficient or false ; if the determination agrees with the natural curvature of the ray, it follows either that some suppositions have corrected others, or that they are all exact : but which of the two, he knows not ; yet that is the certitude to which he can attain.

I have carefully perused Saunderson's *Elements of Algebra*, in hopes of meeting with what I was desirous of knowing from those who familiarly conversed with him, and who have made us acquainted with some particulars of his life ; but my curiosity has been disappointed, and I thought that elements of geometry from him would have been a work both more singular in itself, and much more useful to us. We should there have been let into his definitions of point, line, surface, solid, angle, intersections of lines and planes, in which I make no question but he would have proceeded on principles of very abstract metaphysics, and near akin to that of the idealists. Idealists, Madam, are those philosophers who, being

conscious only of their existence and a succession of internal
sensations, admit nothing else. A system of such extrava-
gancy, that I should think it must have been the offspring of
blindness itself; and yet, to the disgrace of the human mind
and of philosophy, is the most difficult to combat, though the
most absurd. Dr. Berkeley, Bishop of Cloyne, in Ireland, has set
it forth, with great candour and perspicuity, in three dialogues.
It were to be wished, that the author of the *Essay on our Knowledge*, would take this work into examination; he would there
find matter for useful, agreeable, and ingenious observations; for
such as, in a word, no person has a better talent. Idealism
deserves very well to be reported to him; and this hypothesis is
as a double incentive for him, its singularity, and much more the
difficulty of refuting its principles, they being precisely the same
as those of Berkeley. According to both, and according to
reason, the terms, essence, matter, substance, agent, &c., of
themselves, convey very little light to the mind. Besides, as
the author of *The Essay on the Origin of Human Knowledge*
judiciously observes, whether we ascend up to the heavens, or go
down into the abysses of the earth, we never go out of ourselves,
and what we perceive is only our own thoughts: now this is the
very result of Berkeley's first dialogue, and the foundation of his
whole system. Would it not highly delight you, Madam, to see
two enemies engaged, whose weapons are so much alike? If
either got the better, it must be he who should manage them
with the greater dexterity; and the author of *The Essay on the
Origin of Human Knowledge* has lately, in a treatise on systems,
given fresh proofs of his adroitness, and how much he is to be
redoubted by systematics.

Here, you will say, this is quite losing sight of the blind. True,
Madam; but you must be so good as to allow me all these digres-
sions. I promised you a conversation, and, without this indulgence,
I cannot keep my word.

I have perused, with the utmost stretch of my attention, what
Saunderson has said concerning infinitude: and I can assure you
that he had such very just and very clear ideas on this head, that,

in his account, most of our infinitarians would have been looked
on but as blind.   You yourself shall be judge : though this
matter be somewhat difficult, and a little beyond your mathematical knowledge, I trust to bring it within your compass, and
initiate you into this infinitesimal logic.

This celebrated blind man proves that touch, when improved
by exercise, may become more precise than sight ; for, in handling
a series of medals, he could distinguish the genuine from the
spurious,* though the imitation was such as might have deceived
a clear-sighted connoisseur ; and he judged of the exactness of a
mathematical instrument, by drawing his fingers' ends along its
divisions. These are certainly things of another kind of difficulty,
than forming a judgment by the touch of the likeness of a bust
to the person it represents.   This shows that a blind people
might have sculptors, and put statues to the same use as among
us, to perpetuate the memory of glorious actions, and of persons
dear to them ; and, in my opinion, feeling such statues would give
them a more lively pleasure than we have in seeing them.   What
a delight to a passionate lover, in gently drawing his hand over
beauties which he would know again, when illusion, which would
act more strongly on the blind than in those who see, should
come to re-animate them ; but likewise, the more pleasure such
remembrance gave him, the less, perhaps, would his grief be for
the loss of the original.

Saunderson, like the Puiseaux blind man, was affected on the
least alteration in the atmosphere, and sensible, especially in calm
weather, of any objects being near him.   It is related of him,
that being present at the making some astronomical observations
in a garden, the clouds, which now and then intercepted the sun's
disk, at the same time occasioned such a change in the action of
the rays on his face, as signified to him the intervals which
favoured or impeded the observations.   You may, perhaps, think
that there was some agitation in his eyes, which apprised him of

---

* The roughness of those new cast is thought to have assisted him in this
distinction.

the presence of light, but not of that of objects. So I should have thought, too, were it not certain that Saunderson was not only blind, but without the very organ of sight.

Thus Saunderson saw, by means of a pellicle; and of such an exquisite sensibility was this tegument, that a little practice would have brought him to have known an acquaintance by having his portrait delineated on his hand, and that, by the succession of the sensations excited by the pencil, he would have confidently said, "Oh! this is Mr. Such-a-one." Thus the blind have likewise a painting, in which their own skin serves for the canvas. These ideas are so far from the chimera, that I make no question, were somebody to draw on your hand Mr. ——'s little mouth, you would immediately know it; yet, you must allow, that this would be much easier to one born blind than to you, though so accustomed to see it and to think it so wonderfully pretty. For your decision implies two or three circumstances : the comparison of the delineation made on your hand, with the picture of it on the ground of your eye; the remembrance of the manner in which we are affected by things felt, and of that with which we are affected by things which we have only seen and admired; lastly, the application of these data to the designer's question, who asks you, with the point of his pencil on the skin of your hand, "Whose mouth is this which I am drawing?" Whereas the sum of the sensations excited by a mouth on the hand of a blind man is the same as the sum of the successive sensations excited by a designer's pencil.

To this account of the Puiseaux blind man and Saunderson, may be added Didymus of Alexandria, Eusebius the Asiatic, and Nicaise of Mechlin, with some others, who appeared so superior to other men, though with one sense less, that the poets might, without exaggeration, have feigned the gods to have deprived them of it from a jealousy lest mortals should equal them. For Tiresius, who had seen into the secrets of the gods, and had the gift of prediction, what was he but a blind philosopher, whose memory had been preserved by fable? But we will keep to the wonderful Saunderson, and follow this extraordinary person to his grave.

When drawing near to his end, Mr. Jervis Holmes, a clergyman of great abilities, was desired to attend him. They had a
conversation together on the existence of God, some fragments
of which are remaining, which I will translate, as well as I can,
it being not a little curious.

The clergyman began with haranguing on the wonders of
nature. " Ah, Sir," said the blind philosopher to him, " what
is all that grand spectacle to me ? I have been condemned to
spend my life in darkness: you mention wonders quite out of
my understanding, and which are proofs only to you, and those
who, like you, have their sight. If you would have me believe
in God, you must make me feel Him."

" Sir," replied the clergyman, very appositely, "feel yourself,
and you will meet with the Deity in the admirable mechanism
of your organs."

" Mr. Holmes," replied Saunderson, " I must repeat it, all that
may be very fine to you, yet is not so to me ; but were the
animal mechanism as perfect as you make it, and I believe it to
be so, for you are a worthy man, and would scorn to impose on
me, what relation is there between such mechanism and a
supremely intelligent Being ? If it amazes you, it is, perhaps,
from your being used to call everything you cannot directly comprehend, a wonder. I myself have so often been an object of
wonder to the world, that I have but a very slender opinion of
its wonders. People have come from the farthest part of
England to see me, not conceiving how I could perform geometrical operations. You must allow those people not to have
been very exact in their notions of the possibility of things. If
a phenomenon appears to us above human comprehension, we
immediately say it is the work of God ; nothing less will satisfy
our vanity. Would not a little less pride, and a little more
philosophy, do better in our conversations ? If in nature we
meet with a difficult knot, let us leave it as it is, and not call in
to cut it the hand of a being which afterwards becomes a fresh
knot more difficult for us to untie than the former. Ask an
Indian how the world remains suspended in the air ? He will

answer, that it is carried on the back of an elephant. And on
what does the elephant bear ? On a tortoise. And what supports the tortoise ?—You pity the Indian, and one might say to
yourself as to him, My good friend Holmes, acknowledge your
ignorance, and forgive me the elephant and the tortoise."

Here Saunderson made a little pause, probably expecting an
answer from the clergyman ; but on which side is a blind man
to be attacked ? Mr. Holmes availed himself of Saunderson's
good opinion of his probity, and of the abilities of Newton,
Leibnitz, Clarke, and some others of his countrymen, possibly the
first geniuses of the world, who all had been stricken with the
wonders of nature, and acknowledged an intelligent Being as its
Author. This was undoubtedly the most forcible objection which
the clergyman could offer to Saunderson. Accordingly, the
good blind man allowed that it would be something pre-
sumptuous to deny what such a man as Newton had acquiesced
in : yet he represented to the clergyman that Newton's testimony
was not of that weight to him, as that of all nature must be to
Newton ; and that it was on God's word that Newton believed ;
whereas he was reduced to believe on Newton's word.

"Consider, Mr. Holmes," added he, "what a confidence I
must have in your word and in Newton's. Though I see
nothing, I admit that there is in everything an admirable order ;
but I promise myself, that you will not require anything farther.
Concerning the present state of the universe, I yield to you ; and
in return, you will allow me the liberty of thinking as I please on
its ancient and primitive state, with relation to which you are as
blind as myself. In this you will have no witnesses to bring
against me, and your eyes are out of the question. You are
therefore welcome to imagine that the order which you so highly
admire has ever subsisted ; but allow me to think that it is otherwise, and that if we recurred to the origin of things and times,
and that we perceived matter actuated, and the chaos unfolding
itself, we should meet with a multitude of informous for a few
well-organized beings. If I have nothing to object to you concerning the present condition of things, I may at least question
you concerning their past conditions. I may, for instance, ask

you who told you, who told Leibnitz, Clarke, and Newton, that at the primordial formation of animals, some were not without a head, others without legs ? I might affirm that some had no stomach, others no bowels ; that some species, which, having a stomach, a palate and teeth, seemed likely to last, have failed through some defect in the heart or the lungs. That monsters have successively destroyed each other, that all the faulty combinations of matter have disappeared, only those remaining, the mechanism of which was no important contradiction, and which could subsist and perpetuate themselves.

" On this supposition, if in the first man the larynx had been closed, if he had wanted proper aliments, if the generative parts had been defectuous, if he had not met with his mate, or had mingled within another species, pray, Mr. Holmes, where would the human species have been ? It would have been involved in the general depuration of the universe, and that haughty being called man, thus dissolved and scattered among the moleculæ of matter, would have remained perhaps for ever in the class of possibility.

" Had there never been any informous beings, you would not fail affirming that there never will be any, and that I run into chimerical hypotheses ; but," continued Saunderson, "amidst all this so perfect order, monstrous productions come forth now and then." Then, facing the minister, he said, " Behold me, Mr. Holmes, I have no eyes. What had either you or I done to God, that one should have that organ, and the other be without it ? "

Saunderson pronounced these words with a countenance so earnest and so expressive of deep concern, that the clergyman and the rest of the company could not forbear participating in his grief, even to tears. The blind man perceiving it, said to the clergyman, "Mr. Holmes, the goodness of your heart was well known to me, and I am very sensible of this fresh proof of it in these my last moments ; but if you have any concern for me, do not grudge me the comfort of dying without having ever caused affliction to any one."

Then, with something of a more resolute voice, he continued, " It is therefore my conjecture, that at the beginning, when the fermentation of matter disclosed the universe, such as I were very common. But why should not I affirm of worlds what I believe of animals? How many maimed, abortive worlds have been destroyed, or perhaps are continually amended and destroyed, in those remote spaces which I cannot reach, and you do not see; but in which motion continues and will continue to combine masses, till brought to some proper disposition for duration? Come, philosophers, accompany me then to the confines of that universe, beyond that point within which I touch, and you see organized beings; range that new ocean, and amidst its irregular agitations seek some vestiges of that intelligent Being, whose wisdom you here so much admire.

"But there's no need of taking you out of your element. Pray, Mr. Holmes, what is this world? Is it not a compound subject to revolutions, all indicating a continual verging to destruction; a rapid succession of beings following and propelling one another, and disappearing; a transient symmetry, a momentary order? I was just now taxing you with estimating the perfection of things by your capacity; and here I may find fault with you for measuring the duration of them by that of your life: you judge of the world's successive existence as the ephemeron-fly of yours. This world is eternal to you, just as you are eternal to the being who lives but an instant; and still the insect shows more reason than you. What prodigious series of ephemerons, what immense traditions, bear witness to your eternity! We shall all, however, pass away, without a possibility of denoting the real extent which we took up, or the precise time of our duration. Time, matter, and space are perhaps but a point."

During this conversation, Saunderson became moved something beyond what his condition would bear, that he was seized with a delirium, which lasted for some hours, and on coming to himself he only cried out, "O thou God of Clarke and Newton, have mercy on me!" and expired.*

---

* The professor, however, had, according to his life prefixed to his *Algebra*, been so far brought to a sense of Christianity, that a time had been appointed for his receiving the Sacrament.

Thus died Saunderson. You see, Madam, that all the reasonings which he objected to the clergyman were not able so much
as to fix a blind man. What a shame for those who see, and
have no better reasons than he, and to whom the wonderful
spectacle of nature, from the rising of the sun to the setting of
the smallest stars, declares the existence and glory of its Author!
They have eyes, which Saunderson wanted; but Saunderson had
a purity of manners, a candour and openness, which they have
not. Accordingly, they live as if blind, and Saunderson died as
if he had had his sight. The voice of nature made itself sufficiently understood by him through his remaining organs; and
this indeed adds to the force of his testimony against those who
obstinately shut their eyes and ears. I would fain ask, whether
the darkness of paganism did not shroud the true God from
Socrates, more than did the loss of sight, and of the grand
spectacle of nature, from Saunderson?

I am very sorry, Madam, that, both for your satisfaction and
mine, other interesting particulars of this celebrated blind man
have not been transmitted to us. His answers would perhaps
have afforded more light than all the experiments proposed to be
made. Those about him must have had very little of the philosopher in them, with exception, however, of Mr. William Inchclif,
who was with Saunderson only in his last hours, and has preserved for us his last sayings, on account of which I would advise
all who have any acquaintance with the English to read a work
printed at Dublin in 1747, under the title of *The Life and
Character of Dr. Nicholas Saunderson, late Lucasian Professor
of the Mathematics in the University of Cambridge. By his
Disciple and Friend, William Inchclif, Esq.* They will find in
it a beauty, a force, and a variety, scarce ever paralleled, but
which, with all my care, I do not presume to think my translation
has preserved.

In 1713 he married the daughter of Mr. Dickons, rector of
Boxworth in Cambridgeshire, by whom he had a son and
daughter, still living. His last farewell to his family is very
moving. "I am going," said he, "where we shall all go; spare

me your lamentations—they affect me too much; your expressions
of grief for me sharpen those which escaped me. It is no uneasiness to me to leave a world which has been only a long desire
and one continued deprivation. I wish you all happiness ; live
virtuously, and learn in me to die quietly." Then taking his
wife by the hand, he squeezed it a while between his ; he turned
his face towards her, as if desirous of seeing her : after giving his
children his blessing, he embraced all his family, and desired them
to withdraw, their lamentations being more uneasy to him than
the approaches of death.

England is the country of philosophers, virtuosi, and system-
makers ; yet, had it not been for Mr. Inchclif, we should have
known no more of the celebrated Saunderson than what any
common man could have told us, as that he knew again such
places where he had once been by the noise which the walls and
the floor reflected, amongst a hundred other such things, all
equally common to most blind persons. Are Saundersons then
so very common in England ? Does every town there produce
persons, who, without ever having their sight, read lectures on
optics ?

We are curious of seeing sight given to those who were born
blind ; but, on farther consideration, philosophy, I believe, would
be found rather a greater gainer by questioning a sensible blind
man. We should learn the state of things in him, and could
compare them with the state of things within ourselves ; and
perhaps we might from this comparison come at the solution of
the difficulties which make the theory of vision and of the senses
so intricate and so uncertain. But I own I cannot conceive
what is to be hoped for from a man who has just undergone a
painful operation on a very tender organ, which the slightest
accident disorders, and which, when sound, is known to deceive
those who had for a long time enjoyed its advantages. For my
part, as to the theory of the senses, I had much rather hear a
metaphysician, well acquainted with the principles of natural
philosophy, the elements of mathematics, and the conformation
of the parts, than a man of no education, and void of learning,

who has had his sight restored to him by the cataract operation. I should lay less stress on the answers of a person seeing for the first time than on the discoveries of a philosopher who had thoroughly digested his subject in the dark, or, to speak practically, had put out his eyes to be the better acquainted with vision.

In order to give some certainty to experiments, the subject must at least have been prepared long before, been well educated, and the better if made a philosopher; but even for a philosopher to make a philosopher is not the work of an hour; and what will it be if he be not one? And it is still much worse if he conceits himself such. The observations should by no means be commenced till long after the operation. In order to this, the patient ought to go through his cure in the dark, till his wound be thoroughly healed and his eyes entirely sound. I would not have him at first exposed to open day. If our own sight is disordered by the glare of a strong light, what effect will it not have on an organ which cannot but be extremely tender and sensible, having never yet felt any impression to blunt it?

But farther, it would still be a very nice point to reap any benefit even from a subject thus prepared, and to adapt our questions so that he may precisely say only what passes in himself. This interrogatory should likewise be before the Academy; or rather, for avoiding a superfluity of spectators, only such as deserve that distinction by their knowledge in philosophy, anatomy, &c., should be invited to such a meeting. It would be no disparagement to the most profound scholars or to men of the finest intellects. To prepare and question one born blind would not have been beneath the combined talents of Newton, Descartes, Locke, Leibnitz.

I shall conclude this letter, which I own is already too long, with a question which was proposed some time ago, and which my reflections on Saunderson's singular condition have shown me to have never been absolutely solved. Suppose one blind from his birth, and grown up to manhood, and who has been taught to distinguish by his touch a cube and a globe of the same metal, and nearly of the same bigness, so that when he touches either he can tell which is the cube and which the globe. Again, suppose the cube and the globe put on a table, and this blind person is made to see; and the question is, if by seeing them without touching them, he will be able to distinguish them, and tell which is the cube and which the globe?

This question was first proposed by M. Molineux, who likewise set about solving it. The decision was, that the person would not distinguish the globe from the cube; for, said he, though experience has taught him how the globe and the cube affect his touch, he does not yet know that what affects his touch in such and such a manner must affect his sight thus or thus, nor that the same angle of the cube which presses on his hand unequally must appear to his eyes as in the cube.

Locke, being consulted, said, "I am entirely of M. Molineux's mind. The blind man could not at first sight be able to affirm with any certainty which was the globe and which the cube, if he only viewed them; though by handling them he might confidently name and distinguish them by the difference of their figures, his touch bringing them to his remembrance."

Concerning this question, the Abbé de Condillac, whose *Essay on the Origin of Human Knowledge* you read with so much pleasure and improvement, and whose excellent *Treatise on Systems* accompanies this letter, has a particular opinion. To lay before you the reasons on which he bottoms, would be both needless, and envying you the pleasure of reading over again that work, in which they are set forth in a manner so entertaining and yet so philosophical, as forbids my displacing them. I shall only observe that they all tend to demonstrate that the person born blind sees not anything, or sees the sphere and the cube as different; and that the conditions of these two bodies being of the same metal, and nearly of the same bigness, inserted in the state of the question, are superfluous, which cannot be disputed; for, he might have said, if there be no essential connection between the sensation of the sight and the touch, as Messrs. Locke and Molineux pretend, they must allow that a body may

to the eye appear to have two feet diameter, which yet would
vanish on being touched. The Abbé however adds, that if the
person born blind sees bodies, discerns their figures, and still
hesitates what to think of them, it must be from metaphysical
reasons, and those not a little subtile, as you shall presently see.

Thus here are two different opinions on the same question, and
between first-rate philosophers. One would think that, after
being canvassed by such men as Molineux, Locke and Condillac,
nothing more could be said ; but so many are the faces in which
the same thing may be viewed, that it is not in the least strange
if they have not drained the subject.

They who declare for the blind man's distinguishing the cube
from the sphere have set out with supposing a fact, which perhaps
ought to have been examined ; that is, whether a person born
blind would be able to make use of his eyes immediately after
being couched ? All they have said is, " A person blind from his
birth, by comparing the ideas of the sphere and cube which he has
received from the touch with those received from sight, will necessarily know them to be the same ; that it would be very odd for
him to say that the cube gives his sight the idea of a sphere, and
the sphere that of a cube ; that what by the touch he called
sphere and cube he from the sight will call cube and sphere."

But how do their antagonists argue ? They have in like
manner supposed that the person born blind could see immediately after his organ's being restored. They supposed that an
eye couched for a cataract was like an arm recovered from the
palsy. "This," say they, "feels without any previous exercise,
and consequently the other requires none to see." And they
have added, "Let us allow the person who was born blind a
little more philosophy than you afford him ; and after carrying
his reasoning where you left him, he will go on thus : But still,
who has assured me, that when I have come near to those bodies,
and have laid my hands on them, they will not on a sudden
deceive my expectation ; the cube imparting to me the sensation
of the sphere, and the sphere that of the cube ? Experience alone
can teach me whether there be an analogy between the sight and

the touch. These reports of the two senses may be contradictory without my knowing it ; nay, I should perhaps believe what is actually before my sight to be only a mere appearance, had I not been informed that they are the very same bodies which I had touched. This, indeed, seems to be the body which I called cube, and this the sphere ; but I am not asked about what they seem, but what they are ? and that is a question which I am in no wise able to answer."

"This reasoning," says the author of the *Essay on the Origin of Human Knowledge*, "would be very perplexing to him who had been born blind ; and I see nothing under experience which can furnish an answer to it." The Abbé, in all likelihood, means only that experience which the blind man himself would repeat on the bodies by a second handling. You will soon perceive why I make this remark. That able metaphysician might likewise have farther added, that in one born blind the supposing two senses to be contradictory should be the less absurd, as he conceives that a speculum makes them in reality contradictory, as I have noticed above.

The Abbé proceeds to observe that M. Molineux has perplexed the question with several conditions, which neither obviate nor remove the difficulties metaphysics would form in one who had been blind from his birth : this observation is the more just, the supposing the blind man acquainted with metaphysics being not at all out of the way ; as the experiment in all philosophical questions should be accounted to be made on a philosopher, that is, on a person who, in the questions proposed to him, perceives all that reasoning and the state of his organs allow him to perceive.

This, Madam, is in brief what has been said *pro* and *con* on this question ; and you shall now see, by my examination of it, how very far they, who determined that the man born blind would see the figures and distinguish the bodies, were from perceiving that they were in the right, and what great reason they who denied it had to think that they were not in the wrong.

The question about the man born blind being taken a little more generally than M. Molineux has proposed it, includes two others,

D

which we shall separately consider. It may be asked :
(1) Whether he who was born blind will see immediately after
his cataracts are couched ? (2) Whether, in case he does see,
his sight will be such as to distinguish figures ; whether, in
seeing them, he will be able to give them, with certainty, the
same names which he gave them by the touch, and whether he
will have any demonstration that these names suit them ?

Will he who was born blind see immediately after the cure of
the organ ? They who hold the affirmative say, " As soon as the
blind man comes to the use of his eyes, all the scene before
him becomes painted at the bottom of his eye. This image, as
consisting of an infinite number of objects concentred within a
very small space, is but a confused heap of forms, which he will
not be able to distinguish from one another. Both sides are
nearly agreed that experience alone can teach him to judge of the
distance of objects, and that he is even under a necessity of
drawing near to them, handling them, removing farther off from
them, approaching them, and handling them again, before he
is assured that they are not a part of himself, that they are
foreign from his essence, and that he is sometimes near and
sometimes at a distance from them. And why should not
experience be likewise necessary to him for perceiving them ?
Without experience, he who perceives objects for the first time
should imagine, as they are going out of his sight, or he is
going from them, that they no longer exist ; for it is only
experience on permanent objects, and such which we find again
in the same place where we left them, which evidences and con-
firms to us the continuance of their existence when out of our
sight. It may be for this reason that children become so soon
easy about their playthings being taken away from them. It
cannot be said that they quickly forget them, for some children,
at the age of only two years or two years and a half, know a
considerable part of the words of a language, and they are more
at a loss to conceive them than retain them : now this is a proof
of childhood's being the very season of memory. Would it not
be more natural to suppose that children at that time imagine

what they no longer see exists no longer, and the rather, as their joy shows a great mixture of wonder on seeing again the objects which had been taken from them? Their nurses help them in the notion of the continuance of absent things, by a play, in suddenly hiding one's face and showing it again. Thus they experience a hundred times in a quarter of an hour, that what ceases to appear does not therefore cease to exist. Whence it follows that to experience, and experience only, we owe the notion of the continued existence of objects; that it is by the touch we acquire that of their distance ; that the eye perhaps learns to see, as the tongue to speak ; that it would not be strange, should the assistance of one of the senses be necessary to another, and that the touch, which ascertains the existence of objects without us, when present to our eyes, is likewise the sense to which the confirmation, not only of their figures and other modifications, but even of their presence, is reserved."

To these reasonings are added Cheselden's famous experiments.[*] The youth whose cataracts were couched by that eminent surgeon, could not for a long time distinguish either dimensions, distances, situations, or even figures. An object not above an inch square, being put before his eye, so as to hide a house from him, seemed to him as large as the house itself. All objects seemed close to his eyes, as the objects of touch to the skin. He could not distinguish what, by means of his hands, he had judged to be round, from what he had conceived to be angular ; nor discern with his eyes whether what he had felt to be either above or below him was really above or below. He at length, but not without great trouble, came to perceive that his house was larger than his room, but how the eye gave him that idea he could not conceive. It was not till after many repeated experiments that he became assured of paintings representing solid bodies ; and when, by viewing of pictures, he was certain that what he saw was not bare surfaces, on putting his hand to a picture he stood quite amazed at finding only a flat plane without any prominence. He then asked

---

[*] See *The Elements of Newton's Philosophy*, by M. Voltaire.

where the deception lay, in the sight or the touch ? Painting likewise had the same effect on savages. They took the figures for living men, asked them questions, and were both surprised and affronted at receiving no answer. Now this error in them certainly did not proceed from their not being accustomed to see.

But what can be answered to the other difficulties ? That a man's experienced eye does, in reality, show the objects better than the weak and recent organ of a child, or one born blind, whose cataracts have been just couched. Please, Madam, to consult all the proofs which the Abbé de Condillac adduces at the conclusion of his *Essay on the Origin of Human Knowledge*, against the objections of Mr. Cheselden's experiments, as related by Voltaire. The effects of light on an eye, the first time it is affected with it, and the conditions required in the humours of that organ, the cornea, the crystalline, &c., are specified with great perspicuity and exactness, and leave little doubt but that vision is performed very imperfectly in a child opening its eyes for the first time, or in a blind person just couched.

It must therefore be granted, that we should perceive an infinity of things in objects which are unperceived by an infant or one born blind, though these objects be equally painted at the bottom of their eyes ; that for objects to strike us is not enough, we must farther attend to their impressions ; that consequently, at first using the eyes, one sees nothing ; that in the first instants of vision we feel only a multitude of confused sensations, to the proper discernment of which we are brought only by length of time, and habitual reflection on what passes in us ; that it is experience alone which teaches us to compare the sensations with what occasions them ; that sensations having no essential resemblance with the objects, it is from experience that we are to inform ourselves concerning analogies, which seem to be merely positive. In a word, that the touch contributes greatly to give the eye an exact knowledge of the conformity of the objects with the representation it receives from it, is unquestionable ; and I am inclined to think that were not everything in nature done by laws infinitely general,—if, for instance, the puncture of some hard bodies were painful, and that of other bodies attended with pleasure,—we should die before we had collected the hundred-millionth part of the experiments necessary for the preservation of our body and our well-being.

It is, however, by no means my opinion that the eye cannot instruct itself, or, if I may be allowed the expression, make experiments with itself. For the touch to ascertain to us the existence and the figure of objects, there is no necessity of seeing : and why must we touch to be assured of the same things by sight ? I am no stranger to all the advantages of feeling, nor have I concealed them in these observations on Saunderson or the blind man of Puiseaux, but I cannot allow it that prerogative. That the use of one of the senses may be improved and quickened by the observations of the other is easily conceived, but not that there is an essential dependence between their functions. There are certainly qualities in bodies that we never should perceive without the touch : by the touch we become acquainted with the presence of certain modifications insensible to the eyes, or not perceiving them till informed by that sense ; but these services are mutual, and in those whose sight is more sensible than the touch it is the former of those senses which notifies to the other the existence of objects and modifications, the minuteness of which would escape it. Were a piece of paper, or some other smooth, thin, and flexible substance, put without your knowledge between your thumb and fore-finger, it is only your eye which could inform you that the contact of those fingers would not be immediate. Let me cursorily observe, that to deceive a blind man in this would be infinitely more difficult than imposing upon a person used to see.

A person brought to his sight would certainly be put to no small trouble in acquiring a certainty that external objects are not a part of himself, that he is sometimes near and sometimes far from them, that they have forms, that some are larger than others, that they have depth, &c. ; still I make no doubt that at length he will come to see them, and to see them so distinctly as to discern, at least, their more obvious limits. To deny this would be setting aside the destination of the organs ; it would be forgetting the principal phenomena of vision : it would be concealing from one's self that there is no painter of such skill as to come near the beauty and accuracy of the miniatures painted in the bottom of our eyes ; that there is nothing more exact than the likeness of the representation to the object represented ; that the canvas of this portraiture is not so very small ; that there is no confusion among the figures ; that they take up about half an inch square ; and farther, that nothing is more difficult than to explain how the touch would go about teaching the eye to perceive, were the use of this latter organ absolutely impossible without the assistance of the former.

But I, instead of bare presumptions, ask whether it is the touch which teaches the eye to distinguish colours ? I do not think the touch will be allowed so extraordinary a privilege ; as granting that, the consequence will be that one born blind and just brought to sight, on being shown a black cube with a red sphere on a large white ground, will immediately discern the several limits of those figures.

It may be answered, not before the time necessary to a suitable arrangement of the humours of the eye, for the cornea to mould itself into the convexity requisite for vision, for the pupil to be susceptible of the dilatation and contraction proper to it, for the reticles of the retina to become of a sensibility adapted to the action of light, for the crystalline to exercise itself in its forward and backward motions, for the muscles to perform their functions well, for the optic nerves to be habituated in transmitting sensations, for the whole ball of the eye to accommodate itself to all the necessary dispositions, and for all the parts composing it to concur in the execution of that miniature which so much illustrates the demonstration, that the eye will bring itself to the requisite experience.

I own that, plain as the picture is which I have now represented to the eye of one born blind, he will not be able thoroughly to distinguish its parts till the organ comes to have all the preceding conditions ; that this possibly may be instantaneous ; and by applying the reasoning objected to me, to a machine a little complicated, as a watch, it would not be difficult to demonstrate by the detail of the several motions in the drum, the fuzee, the wheels, the pallats, the balance, &c., that the hand would take up a fortnight in moving the space of a second. If it be answered that these motions are simultaneous, I reply that possibly it may be the same with those of the eye when opened for the first time, and of most of the consecutive judgments. Whatever conditions be required in the eye to be fit for vision, it must be granted that it is not the touch which imparts them to it, that the organ acquires them of itself, and consequently will come to distinguish the figures painted in it without the assistance of any other sense.

But it will be farther said, when will it attain such improvement ? Perhaps much sooner than is thought. Do you remember, Madam, the experiment of the concave speculum, when I had the honour of attending you to the museum in the king's garden, and the fright you was in at seeing the point of a sword making at you with the same swiftness as the point of that which you pushed towards the surface of the speculum ? and yet you was sufficiently accustomed to refer objects painted in the speculums to something beyond them. Experience, therefore, is not so very necessary, nor even so infallible as imagined, for perceiving objects or their images where they are. Your very parrot affords me a proof of it. The first time he saw himself in a glass, he stretched his head towards it, and not meeting with himself, whom he took for his representation, he went round the glass. Though I am not for laying greater weight on the instance of the parrot than it will really bear, still is it an animal experiment, in which prepossession cannot be supposed to have any share.

Yet were it affirmed to me, that one born blind is not able to distinguish anything for the space of two months, I should not wonder at it. I shall only infer from it the necessity of the organs being experienced ; but not at all that the touch is necessary to that experience. It will only give me the better to see the propriety of letting such a person remain for some time in the dark, when it is intended he should make observations ; of giving

his eyes a freedom of exercise, which will be done more con-
veniently in the dark than in a full light ; of showing him the
experiments only in a kind of twilight ; or at least of procuring,
in the place for making the experiments, the advantage of increasing or diminishing the light at pleasure. I shall only be
the more inclined to agree that these kinds of experiments will be
always very difficult, or very uncertain ; and that the shortest way
to rectify them, though in appearance the longest, is to furnish
the subject with so much philosophy as to be able to compare the
two conditions through which he has passed, and to acquaint us
with the difference between the state of a blind person and of
him who has his sight. Once more, what precision is to be
expected from one not at all accustomed to reflect and look into
himself, and who, like Cheselden's blind man, is so ignorant of
the advantages of sight as to have no sense of his misfortune, not
conceiving that the loss of that sense very much impairs his
gratifications ? Saunderson, who must be allowed to have been
a philosopher, certainly was not thus indifferent ; and I doubt
much whether he would have agreed with the author of the excellent *Treatise on Systems.* I am apt to think the latter of these
philosophers has himself slipped into a little system in advancing,
" That had the life of man been only an uninterrupted sensation
of pleasure or of pain, happy without any idea of calamity, or
wretched without any idea of happiness, he would have enjoyed
or suffered ; and that, as if such had been his nature, he would
not have looked around to discover whether any being super-
intended his preservation or strove to hurt him. So that it is
the alternative transition from one to the other of these states
which puts him on reflecting, &c."

Can you believe, Madam, that by a progression from clear perceptions to clear perceptions (for that is the author's method of
philosophizing, and it is the best) he would have ever been led to
this conclusion ? It is not with happiness and misery as with
darkness and light ; one does not consist in a total and absolute
privation of the other. Perhaps we should have entertained a
persuasion of happiness being no less essential to us than existence

and thought, had we enjoyed it pure and without restraint ; but I cannot say so much of wretchedness. It would have been very natural to look on it as a forced state, to feel one's self innocent, yet to believe one's self guilty, and to accuse or excuse nature as at present.

Does the Abbé think that a child in intense pain cries only from his pain not having been without intermission since his birth ? If he answers me, " That to exist and suffer would be the same thing to one who had always suffered, and that his pain allowed of intermission without destroying his existence would never have come into his thoughts," I reply : The man living in continual misery possibly might not have said, What have I done, that I should suffer thus ? But why might he not have said, What have I done, that I should be brought into being ? Yet I see not why he might not have made use of the two verbs, *I exist* and *I suffer*, as synonymous, one for prose and the other for poetry, like *I live* and *I breathe.* You will, moreover, Madam, observe better than I that this passage of the Abbé's book is so admirably beautiful, and I am very much afraid that, on comparing my criticism with his reflection, you will say, you like Montaigne in the wrong better than Charon in the right.

What, ever digressing ! you cry out. Yes, Madam, our treaty allows it. Now my opinion on the two foregoing questions is this : the first time the eyes of one born blind open to the light, he will have no perception of anything ; his eye will require some time for experience, but that it will acquire of itself, and without any help from the touch ; and it will come not only to distinguish colours, but discern, at least, the grosser limits of objects. Let us now see whether, supposing he acquired this aptitude in a very short time, or arrived at it by moving his eyes in the dark apartment to which he had been prudently confined, and desired to use that exercise for some time after the operation, as preparatively to the experiments ; let us, I say, see whether his sight would indicate to him the bodies which he had touched, so as to give them their proper appellations ? This is the final question.

That my manner of performing it may please you, as you love method, I will distinguish several sorts of persons on whom the experiments may be tried. If they are dullards, without education, void of knowledge, and unprepared, I hold, that on the organ being rectified by the cataract operation, and the eye healed, the portraiture of objects in it will be very distinct ; but such persons not being used to any kind of reasoning, and not knowing anything of sensation or idea, and unable to compare the representations received by feeling with those which the eye conveys to them, will at once say, that is round, that is square, so that their judgment is not to be rested on ; or even they will frankly own that they do not perceive anything in the objects before their eyes like what they have handled.

Others there are, who, comparing the apparent figures of bodies with the impressed ones made on their hands, will, by an ideal application of their feeling to those bodies before them, say of one, that it is a square, and of another, that it is a circle, without well knowing why, their comparison of the ideas which they have received from the touch, with those given them by the light, not being clear and distinct enough to convince their judgment.

I shall now, Madam, without any digression, suppose the experiment made on a Metaphysician. He, I make no doubt, would, from the very first instant of his perceiving objects distinctly, reason as if he had seen them all his life ; and after comparing the idea received from his sight with those he had imbibed from feeling, he would declare, as positively as you or I, " I am very much inclined to think this the body which I have always called a circle, and that again what I named a square, but will not assert it to be really so. Who has revealed to me, that if I laid my hands on them, they would not vanish ? How do I know whether the objects of my sight are intended to be likewise objects of my feeling ? I know not whether what is visible be palpable ; but were I not under this uncertainty, and did I firmly believe on the word of those about me, that what I see is really what I touched, I should be little the better. They may change in my hands, and thus the ideas by feeling be quite opposite to those resulting from sight. Gentlemen," would he add, "this body appears to me the square, this the circle ; but that they are to the feeling as to the sight, is what I have no knowledge of."

If to the Metaphysician we substitute a Geometrician, as Saunderson to Locke, he will, like him, say, "That if his eyes may be relied on, of the two figures before him, this is what he called a square, and this a circle ; for I perceive," would he add, "that it is only in the first I can dispose the threads and place the large-headed pins which denoted the angular points of the square ; and it is only the round which admits of the arrangement of my threads, used in demonstrating the properties of my circle : so, therefore, that is a circle, and that is a square ; but would he with Locke have proceeded ? On my beginning to feel these figures, they may perhaps transform themselves into each other, so that the same figure would serve me in demonstrating to the blind the properties of a circle, and to those who have their sight the properties of a square. I might possibly see a square, and at the same time feel a circle. They, to whom I demonstrated the properties of a circle and of a square, had not their hands on my *Abacus*, nor did they touch the threads which I had stretched along as the limits of my figures, yet did they comprehend me ; they therefore did not see a square, when I felt a circle, otherwise we should never have understood one another : I should have been delineating one figure, and demonstrating the properties of another ; I should have given them a straight line for the arch of a circle, and an arch of a circle for a straight line ; but as they all understand me, all men then see alike ; therefore, what they saw square, I saw such, and circular what they saw circular ; so, that is what I have always named a square, and that is what I have always named a circle."

I have instead of a sphere put a circle, and a square instead of a cube ; because, in all appearance, it is only by experiment that we come to judge of distances, and, of course, he who uses his eyes for the first time sees only surfaces, without knowing anything of projecture ; the projecture of a body to the sight, consisting in some of its points, appearing more to us than the other.

But could a person born blind determine concerning the projecture and solidity of bodies at the first view of his eyes, and be able to distinguish not only the circle from the square, but likewise the sphere from the cube ; yet do I not therefore think that this will hold good with regard to more complicated objects. M. de Reaumur's girl, who had been born blind, did very probably distinguish colours ; but it is great odds that her judgment of the sphere and the cube was purely guesswork ; and I am firmly persuaded, that without a revelation, it was not possible for her to know her gloves, her bed-gown, and shoes. The modifications are so multifarious, and the total form of them so little agreeing with that of the parts which they cover, that Saunderson would have been infinitely more puzzled to find out the use of his square than M. d'Alembert, or M. Clairaut, in deciphering the use of his tables.

Saunderson would infallibly have supposed a geometrical relation between things, and the use of them ; and in consequence have perceived in two or three analogies that his cap was made for his head. But what would he have thought of the angles and tuft of his trencher cap? What can this tuft be for? Why four angles rather than six ? And those two modifications, which to me are matters of ornament, would to him have been the source of a multitude of absurd reasonings, or rather an occasion of excellent satire on what we term good taste.

Things duly considered, it will be owned that the difference between a person who has always seen, but to whom the use of an object is unknown, and one who knows the use of an object, but who has never seen, is not on the side of the latter. Yet, do you think, Madam, that were a head-dress to be shown you to-day for the first time, you would ever guess it to be a part of dress, and particularly intended for the head ? But if it be the more difficult for one born blind, and seeing for the first time, to judge rightly of objects, the more forms and modifications they have, why might he not take a spectator quite dressed, and sitting motionless in an elbow chair, for a piece of furniture or a machine; and a tree, with its boughs and leaves shaken by the wind, for a self-moving, animated, and thinking being? How many things our senses suggest to us, Madam; and were it not for our eyes, how apt should we be to suppose that a block of marble thinks and feels!

It remains then to be proved, that Saunderson would have been certain of his not being mistaken in the judgment he had just given only of the circle and the square; and that there are cases when the reasoning and experience of others may assist sight concerning the relation of the touch, and convince it, that what a thing is to the eye, it is likewise so to the touch.

It would, however, be not the less essential in the demonstration of some propositions of eternal Truth, as they are termed, to try one's demonstration by depriving it of the testimony of the senses; for you are very well aware, Madam, that would anyone go about proving to you that the projection of two parallel lines on a plane is to be made by two convergent lines, because two rows of trees appear such, it would be forgetting that the proposition is as true for one that is blind as for himself.

But the preceding supposition of one born blind suggests two others: one of a man who has had his sight from his birth, but without ever having the sense of feeling; and the other of a man in whom the sight and touch were in perpetual contradiction. The former might be asked whether, if the sense he wants were given to him, and his sight be precluded by a fillet over his eyes, he should know bodies by the feeling? It is evident that geometry, provided he was acquainted with it, would furnish him with an infallible way for being certain whether the testimonies of the two senses be contradictory or not. It would be only taking the cube or the sphere into his hands, demonstrate its properties, and, if understood, pronounce that what he feels to be a cube is seen to be a cube, and that consequently what he holds is a cube. As to one who is a stranger to that science, I believe that he would not more easily discern the cube from the sphere by touch than M. Molineux's blind man distinguish them by the sight.

As to him in whom the sensations of sight and of feeling are in a perpetual contradiction, I know not what he would think of forms, order, symmetry, beauty, deformity, &c. He would, in all likelihood, be, with regard to those things, as we are with regard to the extension and real duration of beings. He would, in general, determine that a body has a form ; but he must be inclined to think that it is neither that which he sees nor that which he feels. Such a one might be displeased with his senses, but the senses would be neither pleased nor displeased with the objects. Were he disposed to charge one of them with deception, I fancy it would fall on the touch. A hundred circumstances would bias him to think that the figure of objects changes rather by the action of his hands on them, than by that of the objects on his eyes. But in consequence of these prejudices, the difference of hardness and softness, which he would find in bodies, would put him to no small perplexity. But from our senses not being in contradiction concerning figures, does it therefore follow that they are better known to us ? Who has told us that we have not to do with false witnesses ? Yet we pronounce sentence. Alas ! Madam, when human knowledge comes to be put in Montaigne's scale, we are ready to adopt his motto : " For what do we know ? What matter is ? No. What spirit and thought is ? Still less. What motion, space, and duration are ? Not in the least. What geometrical truths are? Ask any honest mathematicians, and they will own to you that their propositions are all identical, and that so many volumes, for instance, on the circle, amount to no more than repeating to us, in a hundred thousand different ways, that it is a figure in which all the lines drawn from the centre to the circumference are equal." * Thus we scarce know anything :

---

* A blind man, moving in the sphere of a mathematician, seems a phenomenon difficult to be accounted for. Tully mentions it as a thing scarce credible in his own master in philosophy, Diodorus, " That he exercised himself in philosophy with more assiduity after he became blind; and what he thought next to impossible, to be done without sight, that he professed geometry, describing his diagrams so expressly, that his scholars drew every line in its proper directions."

St. Jerom relates a more remarkable circumstance in Didymus of Alexandria, yet, what numbers of writings ! the authors of which have all pretended to knowledge. I cannot account for the world's not being tired of reading, and learning nothing, unless it be for the very same reasons as I have been talking to you for these two hours, without being tired, and without saying anything to you. I am, with great respect,

Madam,

Your most humble,

And most obedient Servant,

* * * *

---

who, "though blind from his infancy, and therefore ignorant of the very letters, not only learnt logic, but geometry also to perfection, which seems the most of anything to require the help of sight."

Trithemius, de Scriptoribus Eccles., mentions Nicaise de Voerde, at Mechlin, "who, though blind from the first year of his age, became so eminent in learning, that he taught the canon and civil law in the University of Cologne, and quoted books only from having heard them read to him." I have further heard of a Hollander, and some others, whom blindness did not hinder from excelling in mathematical learning. Indeed, if we consider that the ideas of extended quantity, which are the chief objects of mathematics, may as well be acquired from the senses of feeling, as that of sight; that a firm and steady attention is the principal qualification for this study; and that the blind are necessarily more abstracted than others; we shall perhaps find reason to think there is no other branch of science more adapted to their circumstances. *Life of Saunderson, prefixed to his Algebra.*

Professor Saunderson could spell very well; he knew the shapes of the letters, both small and capital, and would sometimes amuse himself, when opportunity offered, with reading inscriptions on tombstones with his fingers. He frequently regretted his not applying himself to learn to write in his younger years, which he made no question he could have easily accomplished. *Biographical Dictionary.*

REMARKABLE CASES OF BLINDNESS.

---

*An account of observations made by a young gentleman who was
born blind, or lost his sight so early that he had no remembrance of ever having seen, and was couched when between
thirteen and fourteen years of age. From Mr. Cheselden.*

THOUGH we say of this gentleman that he was blind, as we do of
all people that have ripe cataracts, yet they are never so blind
from that cause but they can discern day from night, and, for the
most part, in a strong light, distinguish black, white, and scarlet,
but they cannot perceive the shape of anything ; for the light,
by which these perceptions are made, being let in obliquely
through the aqueous humour, or the anterior surface of the
crystalline, that the rays cannot be brought into a focus upon the
retina ; they can discern in no other manner, than a sound eye
can see through a glass of broken jelly, where a great variety of
surfaces so differently refract the light, that the several distinct
pencils of rays cannot be collected by the eye into their proper
foci ; wherefore the shape of an object in such a case cannot be at
all discerned, though the colour may : and thus it was with this
young gentleman, who, though he knew these colours asunder in
a good light, yet, when he saw them after he was couched, the
faint ideas he had of them before were not sufficient for him to
know them by afterwards, and therefore he did not think them
the same, which he had before known by those names. Now
scarlet he thought the most beautiful of all colours, and of others

the most gay were the most pleasing ; whereas the first time he saw black, it gave him great uneasiness, yet after a little time he was reconciled to it ; but some months after, seeing by accident a negro woman, he was struck with great horror at the sight.

When he first saw, he was so far from making any judgment about distances, that he thought all objects whatever touched his eyes (as he expressed it), as what he felt did his skin, and thought no object so agreeable as those which were smooth and regular, though he could form no judgment of their shape, or guess what it was in any object that was pleasing to him. He knew not the shape of anything, nor any one thing from another, however different in shape or magnitude; but upon being told what things were, whose form he before knew from feeling, he would carefully observe that he might know them again ; but having too many objects to learn at once, he forgot many of them, and (as he said) at first he learned to know, and again forgot a thousand things in a day. One particular only, though it may appear trifling, I will relate : having often forgot which was the cat and which the dog, he was ashamed to ask, but catching the cat, which he knew by feeling, he was observed to look at her stedfastly, and then setting her down, said, "So, puss, I shall know you another time." He was very much surprised that those things, which he had liked best, did not appear most agreeable to his eyes, expecting those persons would appear most beautiful that he loved most, and such things to be most agreeable to his sight that were so to his taste. We thought he soon knew what pictures represented, which were shown to him, but we found afterwards we were mistaken ; for about two months after he was couched, he discovered at once they represented solid bodies, when to that time he considered them only as party-coloured planes, or surfaces diversified with variety of paint ; but even then he was no less surprised, expecting the pictures would feel like the things they represented, and was amazed when he found those parts, which by their light and shadow appeared now round and uneven, felt only flat like the rest, and asked, which was the lying sense, feeling or seeing ?

E

Being shown his father's picture in a locket at his mother's watch, and told what it was, he acknowledged a likeness, but was vastly surprised; asking, how it could be that a large face could be expressed in so little room? Saying, it should seem as impossible to him as to put a bushel of anything into a pint.

At first he could bear but very little sight, and the things he saw he thought extremely large ; but upon seeing things larger, those first seen he conceived less, never being able to imagine any line beyond the bounds he saw ; the room he was in, he said, he knew to be but part of the house, yet he could not conceive that the whole house could look bigger. Before he was couched, he expected little advantage from seeing, worth undergoing an operation for, except reading and writing ; for, he said, he thought he could have no more pleasure in walking abroad than he had in the garden, which he could do safely and readily. And even blindness, he observed, had this advantage, that he could go anywhere in the dark much better than those who can see ; and after he had seen, he did not soon lose this quality, nor desire a light to go about the house in the night. He said every new object was a new delight ; and the pleasure was so great that he wanted words to express it ; and his gratitude to his operator he could not conceal, never seeing him for some time without tears of joy in his eyes and other marks of affection : and if he did not happen to come at any time when he was expected, he would be so grieved that he could not forbear crying at his disappointment. A year after first seeing, being carried upon Epsom Downs, and observing a large prospect, he was exceedingly delighted with it, and called it a new kind of seeing. And now, being lately couched of his other eye, he says that objects at first appeared large to this eye, but not so large as they did at first to the other ; and, looking upon the same object with both eyes, he thought it looked about twice as large as with the first couched eye only, but not double, that we can any ways discover.

I have couched several others who were born blind, whose observations were of the same kind ; but they being younger, none of them gave so full an account as this gentleman.

Observations on Mr. Blacklock, who lost his sight in his infancy.

IT is indeed true that Homer, the most celebrated poet of antiquity, and Milton, who is without a rival among the moderns, were both blind. But Milton was not blind till he was fifty years old, and Homer, for aught we know, not till after he had written his Iliad and his Odyssey ; and it is not strange that their power of recollecting, combining, and expressing ideas, which had been perceived and treasured in their minds when they could see, should be increased when they became blind, as they were able to exert more intellectual force upon any certain object when every other was excluded. Blacklock's peculiarity as a poet is that he was blind almost from his birth, and how he, who can have no conception of any ideas that depend upon sight, should be able to express them, not only intelligibly, but with propriety ; how he should be able to heighten description, and decorate sentiment with figures and metaphors, which depend not only upon vision in general, but all the particular phenomena of visible objects, is most astonishing.

Mr. Spence observes, in a short account just published of Mr. Blacklock's life, writings, and character, that his notions of day may comprehend the ideas of warmth, variety of sounds, society, and cheerfulness ; and his notions of night the contrary ideas of chillness, silence, solitude, melancholy, and, occasionally, even of horror : that he substitutes the idea of glory for that of the sun ; and of glory, in a less degree, for those of the moon and stars. That his ideas of the beams of the sun may be composed of this idea of glory, and that of rapidity ; that something of solidity too may perhaps be admitted, both into his idea of light and darkness, but that what his idea of glory is cannot be determined. Mr. Spence also remarks, that Blacklock may attribute paleness to grief, brightness to the eyes, cheerfulness to green, and a glow to gems and roses, without any determinate ideas ; as boys at school, when in their distress for a word to lengthen out a verse, they find *purpureus olor* or *purpureum mare*, may afterwards use the epithet *purpureus* with propriety, though they know not what it means, and have never seen either a swan or the sea, or heard that a swan is of a light and the sea of a dark colour. But he supposes too that Blacklock may have been able to distinguish colours by his touch, and to have made a new vocabulary to himself by substituting tangible for visible differences, and giving them the same names ; so that green with him may mean something pleasing or soft to the touch, and red something displeasing or rough. In defence of this supposition it may be said with some plausibility, that the same disposition of parts in the surfaces of bodies which makes them reflect different rays of light, may make them feel as differently to the exquisite touch of a blind man. But there is so much difference in the tangible qualities of things of the same colour, so much roughness and smoothness, harshness and softness, arising from other causes, that it is more difficult to conceive how that minute degree, arising from colour, should be distinguished, than how a blind man should talk sensibly of the subject without having made such distinction. We cannot conceive how a piece of red velvet, woollen cloth, camblet, silk, and painted canvas should have something in common which can be distinguished by the touch, through the greatest difference in all qualities which the touch can discover, or in what mode green buckram should be more soft and pleasing to the touch than red velvet. If the softness peculiar to green be distinguished in the buckram, and the harshness peculiar to red in the velvet, it must be by some quality with which the rest of mankind are as little acquainted as the blind with colour. It may perhaps be said that a blind man is supposed to distinguish colours by his touch only when all other things are equal : but if this be admitted, it would as much violate the order of his ideas to call velvet red as to call softness harsh, or indeed to call green red ; velvet being somewhat soft and pleasing to the touch, and somewhat soft and pleasing to the touch being his idea of green.

But whatever be his mode of perception, he has used the names of mere visible qualities with the utmost propriety, through all their combinations and diversities of appearance.

An account of some astonishing particulars that happened to a lady, after her having had the confluent kind of the smallpox.

In the course of this disease, during which the lady was attended by the late Sir Hans Sloane, several threatening symptoms appeared, which, however, were at length overcome ; and the patient, being thought out of danger, took several doses of such purgative medicines as are usually administered in the decline of the disease, without any bad consequence.

But in the evening of the day on which she had taken the last dose that was intended to be given her on that occasion, she was suddenly seized with pains and convulsions in the bowels ; the pain and other symptoms became gradually less violent as the force of the medicine abated, and by such remedies as were thought best adapted to the case, they seemed at length to be entirely subdued.

They were, however, subdued only in appearance ; for at eleven o'clock in the forenoon of the next day they returned with great violence, and continued some hours. When they went off, they left the muscles of the lower jaw so much relaxed that it fell down, and the chin was supported on the breast. The strength of the patient was so much exhausted during this paroxysm, that she lay near two hours with no other sign of life than a very feeble respiration, which was often so difficult to be discerned, that those about her concluded she was dead.

From this time the fits returned periodically every day, at about the same hour. At first they seemed to affect her nearly in the same degree, but at length all the symptoms were aggravated, the convulsions became more general, and her arms were sometimes convulsed alternately : it also frequently happened that the arm which was last convulsed remained extended and inflexible some hours after the struggles were over. Her neck was often twisted with such violence that the face looked directly backwards, and the back part of the head was over the breast. The muscles of the countenance were also so contracted and writhed by the spasms that the features were totally changed, and it was impossible to find any resemblance of her natural aspect by which she could be known.   Her feet were not less distorted than her head, for they were twisted almost to dislocation at the instep, so that she could not walk but upon her ankles.

To remove or mitigate these deplorable symptoms many remedies were tried, and, among others, the cold bath ; but either by the natural effect of the bath, or by some mismanagement in the bathing, the unhappy patient first became blind, and soon after deaf and dumb.   It is not easy to conceive what could increase the misery of deafness, dumbness, blindness, and frequent paroxysms of excruciating pain ; yet a considerable aggravation was added, for the loss of her sight, her hearing, and her speech was followed by such a stricture of the muscles of the throat, that she could not swallow any kind of aliment, either solid or liquid.   It might reasonably be supposed that this circumstance, though it added to the degree of her misery, would have shortened its duration ; yet in this condition she continued near three-quarters of a year, and during that time was supported, in a very uncommon manner, by chewing her food only, which having turned often, and kept long in her mouth, she was obliged at last to spit out. Liquors were likewise gargled about in her mouth for some time, and then returned in the same manner, no part of them having passed the throat by an act of deglutition ; so that whatever was conveyed into the stomach, either of the juices of the solid food, or of liquors, was either gradually imbibed by the sponginess of the parts which they moistened, or trickled down in a very small quantity along the sides of the vessels.

But there were other peculiarities in the case of this lady, yet more extraordinary.   During the privation of her *sight* and *hearing*, her *touch* and her *smell* became so exquisite that she could distinguish the different colours of silk and flowers, and was sensible when any stranger was in the room with her.

After she became blind, and deaf, and dumb, it was not easy to contrive any method by which a question could be asked her and an answer received. This, however, was at last effected by talking with the fingers, at which she was uncommonly ready. But those who conversed with her in this manner were obliged to express themselves by touching her hand and fingers instead of their own.

A lady, who was nearly related to her, having an apron on that was embroidered with silk of different colours, asked her, in the manner which has been just described, if she could tell what colour it was ; and after applying her fingers attentively to the flowers of the embroidery, she replied that it was red, and blue, and green, which was true ; but whether there were any other colours in the apron, the writer of this account does not remember. The same lady having a pink-coloured ribbon on her head, and being willing still farther to satisfy her curiosity and her doubts, asked what colour that was. Her cousin, after feeling some time, answered that it was pink colour ; this answer was yet more astonishing, because it showed not only a power of distinguishing different colours, but different kinds of the same colour : the ribbon was discovered not only to be red, but the red was discovered to be of the pale kind, called a pink.

This unhappy lady, conscious of her own uncommon infirmities, was extremely unwilling to be seen by strangers, and therefore generally retired to her chamber, where none but those of the family were likely to come. The same relation, who had by the experiment of the apron and ribbon discovered the exquisite sensibility of her *touch*, was soon after convinced, by an accident, that her power of *smelling* was acute and refined in the same astonishing degree.

Being one day visiting the family, she went up into her cousin's chamber, and after making herself known, she entreated her to go down and sit with the rest of the family, assuring her that there was no other person present ; to this she at length consented, and went down to the parlour door ; but the moment the door was opened she turned back, and retired to her own chamber much displeased, alleging that there were strangers in the room, and that an attempt had been made to deceive her. It happened, indeed, that there were strangers in the room, but they had come in while the lady was above stairs, so that she did not know they were there. When she had satisfied her cousin of this particular, she was pacified ; and being afterwards asked how she knew there were strangers in the room, she replied, by the smell.

But though she could by this sense distinguish in general between persons with whom she was well acquainted and strangers, yet she could not so easily distinguish one of her acquaintance from another without other assistance. She generally distinguished her friends by feeling their hands, and when they came in they used to present their hands to her as a means of making themselves known : the make and warmth of the hand produced in general the differences that she distinguished, but sometimes she used to span the wrist and measure the fingers. A lady, with whom she was very well acquainted, coming in one very hot day, after having walked a mile, presented her hand as usual ; she felt it longer than ordinary, and seemed in doubt whose it was; but after spanning the wrist and measuring the finger, she said, "It is Mrs. M., but she is warmer to-day than ever I felt her before."

To amuse herself in the mournful and perpetual solitude and darkness, to which her disorder had reduced her, she used to work at her needle ; and it is remarkable that her needlework was uncommonly neat and exact. Among many other pieces of her work that are preserved in the family, is a pin-cushion, which can scarce be equalled. She used also sometimes to write, and her writing was yet more extraordinary than her needlework ; it was executed with the same regularity and exactness ; the character was very pretty, the lines were all even, and the letters placed at equal distances from each other ; but the most astonishing particular of all, with respect to her writing, is, that she could by some means discover when a letter had by mistake been omitted, and would place it over that part of the word where it should have been inserted, with a *caret* under it. It was her custom to sit up in bed at any hour of the night, either to write or to work, when her pain or any other cause kept her awake.

These circumstances were so very extraordinary, that it was long doubted whether she had not some faint remains both of hearing and sight, and many experiments were made to ascertain the matter ; some of these experiments she accidentally discovered, and the discovery always threw her into violent convulsions. The thought of being suspected of insincerity, or supposed capable of acting so wicked a part as to feign infirmities that were not inflicted, was an addition to her misery which she could not bear, and which never failed to produce an agony of mind not less visible than those of her body. A clergyman, who found her one evening at work by a table with a candle upon it, put his hat between her eyes and the candle, in such a manner that it was impossible she could receive any benefit from the light of it, if she had not been blind. She continued still at work, with great tranquillity, till putting up her hand suddenly to rub her forehead, she struck it against the hat, and discovered what was doing ; upon which she was thrown into violent convulsions, and was not without great difficulty recovered.

The family were, by these experiments, and by several accidental circumstances, fully convinced that she was totally deaf and blind, particularly by her sitting unconcerned at her work, during a dreadful storm of thunder and lightning, though she was then facing the window, and always used to be much terrified in such circumstances. But Sir Hans Sloane, her physician, being still doubtful of the truth of facts, which were scarce less than miraculous, he was permitted to satisfy himself by such experiments and observations as he thought proper ; the issue of which was, that he pronounced her to be absolutely deaf and blind.

She was at length sent to Bath, where she was in some measure relieved, her convulsions being less frequent, and her pains less acute ; but she never recovered her speech, her sight, or her hearing, in the least degree.

F

Many of the letters dated at Bath, in some of which there are instances of interlineations with a *caret*, the writer of this narrative hath seen, and they are now in the custody of the widow of one of her brothers, who, with many other persons, can support the facts here related, however wonderful, with such evidence as it would not only be injustice, but folly, to disbelieve.

FINIS.

LONDON: PRINTED BY WILLIAM CLOWES AND SONS, LIMITED, STAMFORD STREET
AND CHARING CROSS.

RE-PRINT, 1894

THE BLIND
1774

A LETTER

ON THE

EDUCATION OF THE BLIND

RE-PRINTED FROM

THE EDINBURGH MAGAZINE AND REVIEW

FOR NOVEMBER, 1774

LONDON

SAMPSON LOW, MARSTON & COMPANY

LIMITED,

St. Dunstan's House

FETTER LANE, FLEET STREET, E.C.

1894

RE-PRINT, 1894

THE BLIND

1774

A LETTER

ON THE

EDUCATION OF THE BLIND

RE-PRINTED FROM

THE EDINBURGH MAGAZINE AND REVIEW

FOR NOVEMBER, 1774

LONDON

SAMPSON LOW, MARSTON & COMPANY

LIMITED,

St. Dunstan's House

FETTER LANE, FLEET STREET, E.C.

1894

1894

Some Books and Papers about the Blind

REPRINTED BY

Messrs. SAMPSON LOW, MARSTON & COMPANY
LIMITED

St. Dunstan's House

FETTER LANE, FLEET STREET, LONDON

1774
THE EDUCATION OF THE BLIND. A LETTER IN THE EDINBURGH MAGAZINE AND REVIEW for NOVEMBER, 1774. Price **1s.**

1793
TRANSLATION OF AN ESSAY ON THE EDUCATION OF THE BLIND by M. HAÜY. Dedicated to the King of France in 1786. Price **1s.**

1801
HINTS TO PROMOTE BENEFICENCE, &c., by Dr. LETTSOM, with an account of the Blind Asylum at Liverpool. Price **1s.**

1819
TRANSLATION OF AN ESSAY ON THE INSTRUCTION AND AMUSEMENTS OF THE BLIND by Dr. GUILLIÉ. Published in Paris, 1817. Illustrated, **5s.**

1837
RECENT DISCOVERIES FOR FACILITATING THE EDUCATION OF THE BLIND. By JAMES GALL, of Edinburgh. Illustrated. Price **2s.**

1842
THE EDUCATION, EMPLOYMENTS, &c., **AT** THE ASYLUM FOR THE BLIND, GLASGOW. By JOHN ALSTON. Illustrated. Price **2s.**

1861
TRANSLATION BY REV. W. TAYLOR OF THE MANAGEMENT AND EDUCATION OF THE BLIND. By J. G. KNIE, of Breslau. Price **1s.**

A LETTER

ON THE

EDUCATION OF THE BLIND.

The following Letter, on the Education of the Blind, was written at the desire of a gentleman, whose curiosity was eagerly turned towards that subject. It was conceived to be satisfactory and valuable; and it is now laid before the public, from a strong persuasion that it may be of very general advantage.

To —— ————

SIR,—In the short interview which I had with you, no satisfactory solution could be given of the question which you proposed to me; I mean, What was the best method of educating a person deprived of sight? Much, I told you, depended on his fortune; much upon his temper and genius; for unless these particulars were known, every answer which could be given to your question must be extremely general, and of consequence extremely superficial. Besides, the task is so much more arduous, because, whoever attempts it can expect to derive no assistance from those who have written upon education before him. And though the blind have excelled in more than one science, yet except in the case of Saunderson, Professor of Mathematics in the University of Cambridge, concerning whom we shall afterwards have occasion to speak, it does not appear that any of them have been conducted to that degree of eminence, at which they arrived, upon a premeditated plan. One should rather imagine that they have been led through the general course and ordinary forms of discipline, and that, if any circumstances were favourable to their genius, they rather proceeded from accident than design.

This fact, if not supported by irrefragable evidence, should, for the honour of human nature, have been suppressed. When contemplated by a man of benevolence and understanding, it is not easy to guess whether his mortification or astonishment would be most sensibly felt. If a heart that glows with real philanthropy must feel for the whole vital creation, and become, in some measure, the *sensorium* of every suffering insect or reptile, how must our sympathy increase in tenderness and force, when the distressed individuals of our own species become its objects ? Nor do the blind bear so small a proportion to the whole community, as even, in a political view, to be neglected. But in this, as in every other political crime, the punishment returns upon the society in which it is committed. For those abandoned and unimproved beings, who, under the influence of proper culture and discipline, might have successfully concurred in producing and augmenting the general welfare, become the nuisances and burdens of those very societies who have neglected them.

There is perhaps no rank of beings in the sensible universe who have suffered from nature or accident, more meritorious of public compassion, or better qualified to repay its generous exertions, than the blind. They are meritorious of compassion ; for their sphere of action and observation is infinitely more limited than that of the deaf, the lame, or of those who labour under any other corporeal infirmity consistent with health. They are better qualified to repay any friendly interposition for their happiness ; because, free from the distraction which attends that multiplicity of objects and pursuits that are continually obvious to the sight, they are more attentive to their own internal economy ; to the particular notices of good and evil impressed on their hearts ; and to that peculiar province in which they are circumscribed by the nature and cultivation of their powers.

It was formerly hinted in conversation, that if the pupil should not be placed in easy circumstances, music is his readiest and most probable resource. Civil and ecclesiastical employments have either something in their own nature, or in the invincible prejudices of mankind, which render them almost entirely inaccessible to those who have lost the use of sight. No liberal and cultivated mind can entertain the least hesitation in concluding that there is nothing, either in the nature of things, or even in the positive institutions of genuine religion, repugnant to the idea of a blind clergyman. But the novelty of the phenomenon, while it astonishes vulgar and contracted understandings, inflames their zeal to rage and madness. Besides, the adventitious trappings and ceremonies assumed by some churches as the drapery of religion, would, according to these systems, render the sacerdotal office painful, if not impracticable, to the blind.

I have, some years ago, read of a blind gentleman, descended of the celebrated Lord Verulam, who, in the city of Brussels, was with high approbation, created doctor of laws ; but from that period he seems to have been lost in impenetrable obscurity ; nor do we hear that he ever exerted those distinguished talents in courts of judicature. There can, however, be no doubt that a blind man may discharge the office of a chamber-council with success ; but, as a barrister, his difficulties become more formidable, if not absolutely insuperable. For he should remember all the sources, whether in natural equity or positive institutions, whether in common or statutory law, from whence his arguments ought to be drawn. He must be able to specify, and to arrange, in their proper order, all the material objections of his antagonists : These he must likewise answer as they were proposed, *extempore.*

When, therefore, you consider how difficult it is to temper the natural associations of memory with the artificial arrangements of judgment, the desultory flights of imagination with the calm and regular deductions of reason, the energy and perturbation of passion with the coolness and tranquillity of deliberation, you will form some idea of the arduous task which every blind man must achieve, who undertakes to pursue the law as a profession. Perhaps assistances might be drawn from Cicero's treatise on Topics and on Invention, which, if happily applied and improved, might lessen the disparity of a blind man to others, but could never place him on an equal footing with his brethren. And it ought to be fixed as an inviolable maxim, that no blind man ought ever to engage in any province in which it is not in his power to excel. This may at first sight appear paradoxical ; but it is easily explained. For the consciousness of the obvious advantages possessed by others, habitually predisposes a blind man to despondency ; and if he ever gives way to despair (which he will be too apt to do when pursuing any acquisition where others have a better chance of success than himself), adieu, for ever adieu, to all proficiency. His soul sinks into irretrievable depression ; his abortive attempts incessantly prey upon his spirit ; and he not only loses that vigour and elasticity of mind which are necessary to carry him through life, but that patience and serenity which alone can qualify him to enjoy it.

In this detail of the learned professions, I have intentionally omitted physic ; because the obstacles which a blind man must encounter, whether in the theory or practice of that art, are better known to you than myself. From this, therefore, let us pass to more general subjects.

I have formerly hinted that the blind were objects of compassion, because their spheres of action and observation were limited ; and this is certainly true. For what is human existence, in its present state, if you deprive it of action and contemplation ? Nothing then remains, but the distinction which we derive from form, or from sensitive and locomotive powers. But for these, unless directed to happier ends by superior faculties, few rational beings would, in my opinion, be grateful. The most important view, therefore, which we can entertain in the education of a person deprived of sight, is to redress, as effectually as possible, the natural disadvantages with which he his encumbered ; or, in other words, to enlarge, as far as possible, the sphere of his knowledge and activity. This can only be done by the improvement of his intellectual, imaginative, or mechanical powers ; and which of these ought to be most assiduously cultivated, the genius of every individual alone can determine. Were men to judge of things by their intrinsic natures, less would be expected from the blind than others. But, by some pernicious and unaccountable prejudice, people generally hope to find them either possessed of preternatural talents, or more attentive to those which they have, than others. For it was not Rochester's opinion alone,

"That if one sense should be suppress'd,
It but retires into the rest."

Hence it unluckily happens, that blind men, who, in common life, are too often regarded as raree-shews, when they do not gratify the extravagant expectations of their spectators, too frequently sink in the general opinion, and appear much less considerable and meritorious than they really are. This general diffidence at once deprives them both of opportunity and spirit to exert themselves, and they descend, at last, to that degree of insignificance in which the public estimate has fixed them. From the original dawnings, therefore, of reason and spirit, the parents and tutors of the blind ought to inculcate this maxim, that it is their indispensable duty to excel ; and that it is absolutely in their power to attain a high degree of eminence. To impress this notion on their minds, the first objects presented to their observation, and the first methods of improvement applied to their understanding, ought, with no great difficulty, to be comprehensible by those internal powers and external senses which they possess. Not that I would render improvement quite easy to them, if such a plan were possible. For all difficulties which are not really or apparently insuperable heighten the charms, or enhance the value of those acquisitions which they seem to retard. But, care should be taken that these difficulties be not magnified or exaggerated by imagination ; for it has before been mentioned, that the blind have a painful sense of their own incapacity, and consequently a strong propensity to despair continually awake in their minds. For this reason, as well as to render them more independent, parents and relations ought never to be too ready in offering their assistance to the blind in any office which they can perform, or in any acquisition which they can procure for themselves, whether they are prompted by amusement or necessity. Let a blind boy be permitted to walk through the neighbourhood without a guide, not only though he should run some hazard, but even though he should suffer some pain.

If he has a mechanical turn, let him not be denied the use of edge-tools ; for it is better that he should lose a little blood, or even break a bone, than be perpetually confined to the same place, debilitated in his frame and depressed in his mind. Such a being can have no employment but to feel his own weakness and become his own tormentor, or to transfer to others all the malignity and peevishness arising from the natural, adventitious, or imaginary evils which he feels. Scars, fractures, and dislocations in his body are trivial misfortunes compared with imbecility, timidity, or fretfulness of mind. Besides the sensible and dreadful effects which inactivity must have in relaxing the nerves, and consequently in depressing the spirits, nothing can be more productive of jealousy, envy, peevishness, and every passion that corrodes the soul to agony, than a painful impression of dependence on others, and of insufficiency for our own happiness. This impression, which, even in his most improved state, will be too deeply felt by every blind man, is redoubled by that utter incapacity of action which must result from the officious humanity of those who would anticipate or supply all his wants, who would prevent all his motions, who would do or procure everything for him without his own interposition. It is the course of nature that blind people should survive their parents ; or, it may happen that they should survive those who, by the ties of blood or nature, are more immediately interested in their happiness. When, therefore, they fall into the hands of the world in general, such exigencies as they themselves cannot redress, will be coldly and languidly supplied by others. Their expectations will be high and frequent, their disappointments many and sensible. Their petitions will often be refused, seldom fully gratified, and even when granted, the concession will often be so ungraceful as to render its want infinitely more tolerable than its fruition. For all these reasons, I repeat it once more (it can never be too frequently reiterated), that, in the formation of a blind man, it is infinitely better to direct than supersede his own exertions. From the time that he can move and feel let him be taught to supply his own exigencies, to dress and feed himself, to run from place to place, either for exercise or in pursuit of his own toys or necessaries.

In these excursions, however, it will be highly proper for his parent or tutor to superintend his motions at a distance, without seeming to watch over him. A vigilance too apparent may impress him with a notion that malignity, or some other selfish motive, may have produced it. When dangers are obvious and great, such as we incur by rivers, precipices, &c., those who are entrusted with the blind will find it neither necessary nor expedient to make their vigilance a secret. They ought then to acquaint their pupil that they are present with him, and to interpose for his preservation whenever his temerity renders it necessary. But objects of a nature less noxious, which may give him some pain, without any permanent injury or mutilation, may, with design, be thrown in his way ; providing, however, that this design be always industriously concealed. For, his own experience of their bad effects will be an infinitely more eloquent and sensible monitor than the abstract and frigid councils of any adviser whatever.

For the encouragement of such parents as choose to take these advices let me inform them that though, till the age of 20, some blind persons were on most occasions permitted to walk, to run, to play at large, they have yet escaped, without any corporeal injury, from these excursions. Parents of middle, or of higher rank, who are so unfortunate as to have blind children, ought, by all possible means, to keep them out of vulgar company. The herd of mankind have a wanton malignity, which eternally impels them to impose upon the blind, and to enjoy the painful situations in which these impositions place them. This is a stricture upon the humanity of my species, which nothing but the love of truth and the dictates of benevolence could have extorted from me. But I have suffered so much from this diabolical mirth in my own person, that it is natural for me, by all the means in my power, to prevent others from becoming its victims.

Blind people have infinitely more to fear from the levity and ignorance, than from the selfishness and ill-nature of mankind. In serious and important negotiations, pride and compassion suspend the efforts of knavery or spleen ; and that very infirmity, which so frequently renders the blind defenceless to the arts of the insidious, or to the attempts of malice, is a powerful incentive to pity, which is capable of disarming fury itself. Villainy, which often piques itself more upon the arts by which it prevails, than upon the advantages which it obtains, may often with contempt reject the blind, as subjects beneath the dignity of its operation ; but the ill-natured buffoon considers the most malicious effects of his merriment as a mere jest, without reflecting on the shame or indignation which they inspire when inflicted on a sensible temper.

But vulgar credulity and ignorance are no less dangerous to those who want sight, than the false and mechanical wit so universally practised in common life. We know, we sympathetically feel the strong propensity of every illiterate mind to relate or to believe whatever is marvellous and dreadful. These impressions, when early imbibed, can scarcely be eradicated by all the conspiring efforts of mature reason and confirmed experience. Those philosophers who have attempted to break the alliance between darkness and spectres, were certainly inspired by laudable motives. But they must give us leave to assert that there is a natural and essential connection betwixt night and *orcus*. Were we endowed with senses to advertise us of every noxious object before its contiguity could render it formidable, our panics would probably be less frequent and sensible than we really feel them. Darkness and silence, therefore, have something dreadful in them, because they supersede the vigilance of those senses which give us the earliest notices of things. If you talk to a blind boy of invisible beings, let benevolence be an inseparable ingredient in their character. You may, if you please, tell him of departed spirits, anxious for the welfare of their surviving friends ; of ministering angels, who descend with pleasure from heaven to execute the purposes of their Maker's benignity ; you may even regale his imagination with the sportive gambols and innocent frolics of fairies ; but let him hear as seldom as possible, even in stories which he knows to be fabulous, of plaintive ghosts, vindictive fiends, or avenging furies. They seize and pre-occupy every avenue of terror which is open in the soul ; nor are they easily dispossessed. Sooner should I hope to exorcise a ghost, or appease a fury, than to obliterate their images in a warm and susceptible imagination, where they have been habitually impressed. If horrors of this kind should agitate the heart of a blind boy (which may happen, notwithstanding the most strenuous endeavours to prevent it), the stories which he has heard will be most effectually discredited by ridicule. This, however, must be cautiously applied, by gentle and delicate gradations. If he is inspired with terror by effects upon his senses, the causes of which he cannot investigate, indefatigable pains must be taken to explain these phenomena, and to confirm that explication, whenever it can be done, by the testimony of his own senses and his own experience. The exertion of his locomotive and mechanical powers (the rights of which I have formerly endeavoured to assert) will sensibly contribute to dispel these fears.

His inventive faculties ought likewise to be indulged with the same freedom. The *data* which they explore may be presented in such a manner as to render discoveries easy; but still let invention be allowed to co-operate. The internal triumph and exultation which the mind feels from the attainment and conviction of new truths, heightens their charms, impresses them deep on the memory, and gives them an influence in practice, which they could not otherwise have boasted.

There are a sort of people in the world whose views and education have been strictly confined to one province, and whose conversation is, of consequence, limited and technical. These, in literary intercourse, or fashionable life, are treated with universal contempt, and branded with the odious name of mere men of business. Nor is it any wonder that the conversation of such should prove nauseous and disgusting. It would be arrogance in them to expect that indifferent persons should either enter into their private interests or the peculiarities of their craft, with a warmth equal to their own. I have known the intrusion of such a person involve a numerous company in gloom, and terminate the freedom and vivacity of agreeable discourse in lazy yawning and discontented silence. Of all innocent characters this ought to be avoided by the blind; because, of all others, it is the character which they run the greatest hazard of adopting. The limitation of their powers naturally contracts their views and pursuits, and, as it were, concenters their whole intellectual faculties in one, or, at best, in few objects. Care should, therefore, be taken to afford the mind a theatre for its exertions as extensive as possible, without diverting it from one great end, which, in order to excel, it ought for ever to have in prospect.

There are few sciences in which the blind have not distinguished themselves. Even those whose acquisitions seem essentially to depend upon vision, have at last yielded to genius and industry, though deprived of that advantage. Mr. Saunderson, whom I formerly named, has left behind him the most striking evidences of astonishing proficiency in those retired and abstract branches of mathematics which appeared least accessible to persons of his infirmity. Sculpture and painting are not, perhaps, the most practicable arts for a blind man ; yet he is not excluded from the pleasing creation and extensive regions of fancy. However unaccountable it may appear to the abstract philosopher, yet nothing is more certain in fact, than that a blind man may, by the inspiration of the muses, or, to strip the figure of its mythological dress, may, by the efforts of a cultivated genius, exhibit in poetry the most natural images and animated descriptions, even of visible objects, without either incurring or deserving the imputation of plagiarism.

In the sister art of music, there are at present living, and noble instances, how far the blind may proceed. For Saunderson's method of calculation, both in arithmetic and algebra, see the account prefixed to the quarto edition of his own treatise on that subject : See also *Lettres sur les aveugles, à l'usage de ceux qui voient, par M. Diderot.* I am informed that these letters are lately translated into English. By the board and pins there mentioned, Saunderson is not only said to have performed all his numerical operations, but even to have constructed all his rectilineal figures. In the higher parts of mathematics, such as conic sections, the same solid figures which are mediums of perception to those who see, may perform the same useful office to the blind. But, for the structure of superficial figures, I should imagine that a kind of matter might be found soft enough to be easily susceptible of impressions, yet hard enough to retain them till effaced by an equal pressure. Suppose, for instance, a table were formed, four feet broad and eight in length ; for the figures, that they may be the more sensible to the touch, ought to be larger than ordinary. Suppose this table had brims, or a moulding round it, rising half an inch above the surface : Let the whole expanse then be filled with wax, and the surface above pressed extremely even with a polished board, formed exactly to fit the space within the mouldings. This board will always be necessary to efface the figures employed in former propositions, and prepare the surface for new ones. I think I have pondered the minutest inconveniences that can arise from this method of delineating and conceiving geometrical truths ; and, after all, the table appears to me the best and the least troublesome apparatus that a blind man can use. I can see no reason why general ideas of geography or topography might not be conveyed to him in the same manner, by spheres, composed of, or covered with the same impressible matter. The knowledge of astronomy might likewise be of infinite use, both by enlarging his ideas of the universe, and by giving him higher and more confirmed impressions of that energy by which the stars are moved, and of that design by which their motions are regulated. But these objects are too vast ; their distances, their magnitudes, their periods of revolution, are too complex to be comprehended in the mind, or impressed in the memory, without sensible mediums. For this purpose an orrery or some machine of a similar construction, will be indispensably requisite.

The science of causes and effects might likewise yield him the most sublime and rational entertainment of which an intelligent being, in its present state, is susceptible. By this he might enter into the laws, the vicissitudes, the economy of nature. Nor is it absolutely necessary that he should be an ocular witness of the experiments by which these laws are detected and explained. He may safely take them for granted ; and if, at any time, a particular experiment should prove faithless, he may, from general principles, be able to discover its fallacy, whether in the nature of the subject, the inaptitude of the instruments, or the process of the execution. The laws of motion, the various ratios or proportions of forces, whether simple or compound, he may calculate and ascertain by the same means, and in the same method, so happily used by Saunderson.

Moral and theological knowledge he may easily obtain, either from books, or instructions delivered *viva voce*. The last, if communicated by one who understands and feels the subject, with a proper degree of perspicuity and sensibility, are infinitely the most eligible. By morals, I would not merely be understood to mean a regular and inculpable series of action, but the proper exertion and habitual arrangement of the whole internal economy, of which external actions are no more than mere expressions, and from which the highest and most permanent happiness alone can proceed. By theology, I do not mean that systematic or scholastic jargon, which too frequently usurps its venerable name ; but those sublime and liberal ideas of the nature and government of a Supreme Being, whether discoverable by nature or revealed in Scripture, which inforce every moral obligation, which teach us what is the ultimate good of our nature, which determine our efforts, and animate our hopes in pursuing this most important of all objects. What Cicero says of the arts and sciences may, with great propriety, be applied to religion : " Nam caetera, neque temporum sunt, neque aetatum omnium, neque locorum ; at haec studia adolescentiam alunt, senectutem oblectant, secundas res ornant, adversis perfugium ac solatium praebent : Delectant domi, non impediunt foris ; pernoctant nobiscum, peregrinantur, rusticantur." To this may be added, that the joys of religion are for ever adequate to the largest capacity of a finite and progressive intelligence ; and as they are boundless in extent, so they are endless in duration. I have already, more than once, observed that the soul of a blind man is extremely obnoxious to melancholy and dejection. Where, therefore, can he find a more copious, intimate, permanent, and efficacious source of comfort than in religion ? Let this, therefore, be inculcated with the utmost care and assiduity. Let the whole force of the soul be exerted in showing him that it is reasonable. Let all the noblest affections of the heart be employed in recommending it as amiable ; for I will venture to assert, that the votary of religion alone is the man,

Quem, si fractus illabatur orbis,
Impavidum ferient ruinae.

When the situation of the blind, and its natural effects upon their character are considered ; when we reflect how exquisite their distresses, how pungent their disappointments, how sensible their regrets, how tedious and gloomy their periods of solitude, we must be wretches indeed if we can grudge either labour or expense in procuring them every source of entertainment which, when procured, remains in their own power, and yields what may be in some measure termed *self-derived enjoyment.* These amusements are prolific of numberless advantages : They afford us at once entertainment and exertion : They teach us to explore a thousand resources for preservation and improvement, which would otherwise have escaped our attention : They render us awake and sensible to a thousand notices, both of external and intellectual objects, which would otherwise have passed unobserved.

Thus far I have proceeded without mentioning philological learning, though I know it to be attainable, by the blind, in a high degree, and though I am conscious of its importance both to their use and ornament. But as it is not indispensable, and as its acquisition is tedious and operose, I thought it less necessary to be early and minutely specified. We cannot doubt that learning different languages adds to the treasure of our ideas, and renders those which we possess more clear and definite. It must be acknowledged that the possession of other languages elucidates our own. The technical terms of almost every science are exotic ; and without clearly understanding those, we cannot properly possess the ideas of which they are the vehicles. But these motives are common to every candidate for philological improvement with the blind.

The art of reasoning, the knowledge of history, and a taste for the *belles lettres*, are easily attainable by the blind ; and as they are copious funds of entertainment they should be inculcated, though at the expense of considerable care and labour.

The relations of persons subjected to this misfortune, if in easy circumstances, will find it highly conducive to the improvement of their charge to select some one among his coevals, of a sound understanding, a sweet and patient temper, a docile mind, a warm heart, and a communicative disposition. These two should be taught to find their interest and happiness in their connection one with another. Their bed, their board, their walks, their entertainments, their lessons, should be common. These are the best eyes with which art can endue a blind man, and, if properly selected, they will yield very little in utility and perfection to those of nature ; nay, at some junctures, they may be preferable.

If the blind must depend upon the exercise of their own powers for bread, I have already pointed out music as their easiest and most obvious province ; but let it at the same time be remembered that mediocrity, in this art, may prove the bitterest and most effectual curse which a parent can inflict upon his offspring, as it subjects them to every vicious impression or habit, which may be imbibed or contracted from the lowest and most abandoned of mankind. If your pupil, therefore, be not endowed with natural talents, exquisitely proper, both for the theory and practice of this art, suffer him by no means to be initiated in it. If his natural genius favours your attempts, the spinet or organ are the most proper instruments for him to begin ; because, by these instruments, he may be made more easily acquainted with the extent of the musical scales, with the powers of harmony, with the relations of which it is constituted, and, of course, with the theory of this art. It would be not only unnecessary, but impracticable to carry him deep into the theory before he has attained some facility in the practice. Let, therefore, his head and his hands (if I may use the expression) be taught to go *pari passu*. Let the one be instructed in the simplest elements, and the others conducted in the easiest operations first. Contemplation and exercise will produce light in the one and promptitude in the other. But as his capacity of speculation and powers of action become more and more mature, discoveries more abstract and retired, tasks more arduous and difficult may be assigned him. He should be taught the names and gradations of the diatonic scale, the nature and use of time, the diversity of its modes, whether simple or mixed. He should be taught the quantity or value of notes, not only with respect to their pitch but to their duration. Yet let him be instructed not to consider these durations as absolutely fixed, but variable according to the velocity of the movements in which they are placed. Thus, we often reckon a semi-breve equal to four vibrations of a pendulum, a minim to two, a crotchet to one. But if the number of aliquot parts, into which a semi-breve is divided, be great, and consequently the value of each particular part small, the minim, crotchet, quaver, &c., will diminish in their intrinsic durations, though they must always preserve the same proportions relatively one to another. He should never be habituated to take a piece of music either from the sound of a voice or an instrument. His companion ought to read the music by the names and values of its characters with the same exactness as the words in any other language. When he becomes a considerable adept in the art, tangible signs may be invented by which he may not only be enabled to read but even to set music for himself. Such exercises will render him infinitely more accurate, both in his principles and practice, than he would otherwise be.

There is a hint of such tangible signs given in Tansure's musical grammar, p. 93, and which, though like the rest of the book, obscure and undigested, may be improved and applied with advantage. When he becomes a more profound theorist, if he has adopted the notion that music and geometry are congenial and inseparable (which, however, in my judgment is frivolous), he may peruse Malcolm's essay on music, and another treatise on the same subject, lately published by an Irish clergyman, whose name I have forgot. But if he chooses to hear the same principles delivered without that unnecessary parade and ostentation of profundity, let him be instructed by d'Alembert, Rameau, and Rousseau's musical dictionary. It is true that the forms and proportions of instruments, the thickness, length, and tension of musical strings may be mathematically adjusted : Their relations one to another may be determined by the coincidence of their vibrations, or by the number and velocity of these vibrations, when dissonant : but experience and a good ear are amply sufficient for these purposes. Yet, if the necessity of geometry in music should still remain an indelible article in his creed, he may peruse Dr. Smith's philosophical principles of harmony. There has also lately been published an explication of Tartini's theory, entitled *The Principles and Power of Harmony*, which, after he has made considerable progress, may be read to him with sensible improvement.

It gives me pain that this epistle, with all the looseness and inaccuracy of a letter, should have all the length and tediousness of an essay. Leisure and premeditation might have enabled me to dispose my thoughts more methodically, and to express them more successfully. If, however, they should contain any hints useful for the improvement of the blind, my intention is fully accomplished, and my pains amply rewarded.

I am, Sir, with great esteem and respect,

Your most obedient, humble Servant,

DEMODOCUS.

Edinburgh,
Sept. 10, 1774.

LONDON: PRINTED BY WM. CLOWES AND SONS, LTD., STAMFORD STREET AND CHARING CROSS.

RE-PRINT, 1894

AN ESSAY

ON

THE EDUCATION

OF

THE BLIND

BY

M. HAÜY

(DEDICATED TO THE KING OF FRANCE)

PARIS, 1786

LONDON

SAMPSON LOW, MARSTON & COMPANY

LIMITED

St. Dunstan's House

FETTER LANE, FLEET STREET, E.C.

1894

RE-PRINT, 1894

AN ESSAY

ON

THE EDUCATION

OF

THE BLIND

BY

M. HAÜY

(DEDICATED TO THE KING OF FRANCE)

PARIS, 1786

LONDON

SAMPSON LOW, MARSTON & COMPANY

LIMITED

St. Dunstan's House

FETTER LANE, FLEET STREET, E.C.

1894

POEMS

BY THE LATE REVEREND

DR. THOMAS BLACKLOCK;

TOGETHER WITH

AN ESSAY ON THE EDUCATION OF THE BLIND

BY M. HAÜY.

TO WHICH IS PREFIXED

A New Account of the Life and Writings of the Author,

By Mr. MACKENZIE, Author of the MAN OF FEELING, &c.

———————————

EDINBURGH:

Printed by ALEXANDER CHAPMAN and COMPANY;

Sold by W. CREECH, Edinburgh, and T. CADELL, London.

MDCCXCIII.

1894

Some Books and Papers about the Blind

REPRINTED BY

Messrs. SAMPSON LOW, MARSTON & COMPANY

LIMITED

St. Dunstan's House

FETTER LANE, FLEET STREET, LONDON

1774

THE EDUCATION OF THE BLIND. A LETTER IN THE EDINBURGH MAGAZINE AND REVIEW for NOVEMBER, 1774. Price 1s.

1793

TRANSLATION OF AN ESSAY ON THE EDUCATION OF THE BLIND by M. HAÜY. Dedicated to the King of France in 1786. Price 1s.

1801

HINTS TO PROMOTE BENEFICENCE, &c., by Dr. LETTSOM, with an account of the Blind Asylum at Liverpool. Price 1s.

1819

TRANSLATION OF AN ESSAY ON THE INSTRUCTION AND AMUSEMENTS OF THE BLIND by Dr. GUILLIÉ. Published in Paris, 1817. Illustrated, 5s.

1837

RECENT DISCOVERIES FOR FACILITATING THE EDUCATION OF THE BLIND. By JAMES GALL, of Edinburgh. Illustrated. Price 2s.

1842

THE EDUCATION, EMPLOYMENTS, &c., AT THE ASYLUM FOR THE BLIND, GLASGOW. By JOHN ALSTON. Illustrated. Price 2s.

1861

TRANSLATION BY REV. W. TAYLOR OF THE MANAGEMENT AND EDUCATION OF THE BLIND. By J. G. KNIE, of Breslau. Price 1s.

AN ESSAY

ON THE

EDUCATION OF THE BLIND

OR,

An Explication of the different Means, confirmed by successful
Experiments, to render them capable of Reading by the Assistance of Touch, and of printing Books, in which they may
obtain the Knowledge of Languages, of History, of Geography,
of Music, &c., of performing the different Offices necessary in
mechanical Employments, &c.

DEDICATED TO THE KING,

BY

M. HAÜY,

Interpreter to his Majesty, the Admiralty of France, and the
Hôtel de Ville, of the City of Paris ; Member and Professor
of the Academical Office for Writing, in which Ancient and
Foreign Characters are taught to be read and ascertained.

PARIS:

Printed in the Original by BLIND CHILDREN, under the Superintendence of M. Clousier, Printer to the King, and sold for their
Benefit at the House where they are educated, in the Street
called *Rue Notre Dame des Victoires.*

MDCCLXXXVI.

Under the Patronage of the Academy of Sciences.

To the KING OF FRANCE.

SIRE,

THE Protection with which your Majesty honours distinguished Talents ascertains your Claim to their Reverence and Respect. But when their Productions have a Tendency to console the Miseries of suffering Humanity, they have still a more powerful Title to attract the attention of Louis the Beneficent. It was under the influence of Sentiments inspired by a Title so amiable, which is deeply engraven on all the Hearts of France, that I conceived the desire of presenting to your Majesty the Fruits of my Labours; if they have any Value, they will owe it to the double Advantage of appearing under a Patronage so august, and of becoming Vehicles to the Bounty expected from their Sovereign by the Young and unhappy, who have been early deprived of the Benefit of Light with all its numerous and important Resources.

I am,

With the profoundest respect,

Sire,

Your Majesty's most humble,

most obedient

and most faithful subject and Servant,

HAÙY.

PREFACE.

AMONGST the unfortunate, who have been deprived, whether from the instant of their birth, or by some early accident in the course of their lives, of that organ which most sensibly contributes to our enjoyment of the delights and advantages arising from society, there have been found some who, by the pregnancy of their genius, and the force and perseverance of its exertions, have found out for themselves certain employments, which they were able to execute, and by these pursuits have proved successful in alleviating the miseries of a situation, in itself so afflicting. Some of them, full of penetration, have enriched their memories with productions of genius, and have imbibed from the charms of conversation or from reading, at which they were happily present, knowledge of a nature and extent which it was impossible for them either to acquire or collect from their own internal resources alone, or from the precious repositories in which it was confined. Others, endued with a dexterity, which might do honour to the most enlightened artist, have performed mechanical tasks with an exactness, neatness, and symmetry, which could only have been expected from hands informed and regulated by the advantage of sight. But in spite of these happy dispositions in the blind, these marvellous exhibitions, which ought rather to be called prodigies, than natural events, could only be, in the persons by whom they were displayed, the slow results of indefatigable industry and obstinate application, and seemed alone to have been reserved for a small number amongst them, who were peculiarly prerogatived by nature, whilst the rest of their brethren appeared consigned by destiny to idleness, languor and dependence, without a possibility of escaping from a durance so horrible in its nature, and so permanent in its continuance. Thus with respect to all social utility and importance, people in these unhappy circumstances were to be accounted dead members, even in those societies where their existence was protracted, and its exigencies supplied ; and the most part of them victims at once to the double calamity of blindness and indigence, had no other portion assigned them but the miserable and sterile resource of begging, for protracting, if we may so speak, in the horrors of a dungeon the moments of a painful and burdensome existence. It is to be essentially serviceable to this class of suffering mortals that I have invented a General Plan of Institution, which, by principles and utensils proper for their use, might facilitate to some of these what they could not otherwise accomplish, without almost insuperable difficulty, and render practicable to others, what it appeared impossible for them to execute. I felt the difficulty of this enterprise in its full extent, that it was too arduous to be performed by myself alone ; I have therefore been assiduous in my researches for support and assistance. Beneficent characters have, on all hands, exerted themselves with ardour, that they might co-operate in promoting this labour of love. They have laid the foundation of a fabric whose structure will at once reflect honour on their own hearts and on the age which their lives adorn. Each of them indeed, with a laudable emulation, seems to have disputed with me for the cordial pleasure of perfecting and finishing a monument so congenial and so grateful to humanity ; and I confess it with delight, if it was permitted to any to claim an honour from such an undertaking, it is they more than any one else, who have a just claim to that honour. I shall therefore avoid, in the sequel of this work, every expression which may seem to imply any design of appropriating that merit to myself ; and I shall there speak only in the person of those who have insured their unalienable right to my gratitude, whether they have contributed to the maturity of this plan by the exertions of their understanding, or by any other means.

ADVERTISEMENT TO THE FRENCH EDITION.

THE Frontispiece of the Original Work, the Dedication, the Preface, this Advertisement, the Notes, the Opinion of the Academy of Sciences, and that of the Printers, the Examples of the forms of the several operations in printing, which may be executed by the blind, and the Table of Contents, have been printed by blind children in the typographical characters generally used. For what remains of the work, they have employed the characters invented for their peculiar use*, the impression of which they trace in reading, when the creases, made in the paper by the types, are not effaced.

---

* A specimen has been sent for from Paris, and will be annexed if it can be procured.

AN ESSAY

ON THE

EDUCATION OF BLIND CHILDREN.

―――――

CHAP. I.

The Intention of this Plan.

BEFORE we give an account of the motives of our institution, let
us be permitted to say a few words on that readiness which we
declare ourselves to possess, not only to answer all the objections
which may be urged against us, but even to enter into a minute
detail of all the circumstances, whose solution the public have a
right to expect from us. Though there is scarcely any invention
which has not, by its novelty, excited the clamour of envy and of
ignorance, we are bold enough to flatter ourselves that our plan
has nothing to fear from the malignity of their attacks. The
nature of our design, the wisdom of the age in which we live, the
humanity of our countrymen—all these circumstances conspire to
assure us that we shall only have to resolve, in the sequel of this
work, such difficulties as may be proposed by a wise and well-
intended criticism ; a criticism rather designed to favour our
attempts than to discourage us in their prosecution. It is with
this hope that we are determined to answer every objection which
shall appear to us, either as lying against the motives or plan of
cultivation, which we have proposed for the blind. We will do
more ; we will endeavour to dissipate in the imagination of our
readers every prepossession, even in our favour, which may deceive
those who have not been present at our probationary exhibitions,
and to whom the too zealous partisans of our plan may have

A 3

represented as marvellous and unaccountable, such circumstances
as are its natural and proper effects. In offering thus a faithful
delineation of our method, considered in its proper point of view,
it is our intention to leave no impressions on the minds of the
public with respect to our establishment, but such real and just
ideas as they ought to entertain : to teach the blind reading, by
the assistance of books, where the letters are rendered palpable by
their elevation above the surface of the paper, and by means of
this reading to instruct them in the art of printing, of writing,
of arithmetic, the languages, history, geography, mathematics,
music, &c., to put in the hands of these unfortunate people such
arts and occupations as are merely mechanical ; spinning, for
instance, knitting, bookbinding, &c. From such an institution
two objects are in view, both of which benevolent men will own
to be of importance.

First, to employ those among them who are in easy circumstances in an agreeable manner. *Secondly*, to rescue from the
miseries of beggary those to whom fortune has been parsimonious
of her favours, by putting the means of subsistence in their
power ; and, in short, to render useful to society their hands, as
well as those of their guides.

Such is the end pursued by our institutions.

<h2 style="text-align:center">CHAP. II.</h2>

Answer to the Objection against the Utility of this Plan.

THE public has done us the justice unanimously to agree that we
have accomplished the first object of our institution in presenting
an amusement to the blind who share the bounties of fortune,
and if any doubt have arisen it can only be concerning the possibility of realising the hopes which we have given of blending in
our establishment the useful with the agreeable. "In teaching
your blind," say the objectors, "all the parts of education which
" you propose, can you have conceived the project of peopling the
" republic of letters and arts with men of learning, professors, and

" artists, each of whom, though blind, shall be capable of making
" a distinguished figure in these conspicuous departments, or can
" they even be certain of deriving the means of subsistence each
" from the labours of his own vocation ?" No, we never pretend
that those of the blind who even discover the most shining parts
shall enter into competition, either in the liberal sciences or
mechanical arts, with scholars or artisans who are blessed with
the use of sight, even when their talents rise not above mediocrity ; but when any or all of these provinces are not properly
supplied with persons who to the advantage of sight add pro-
fessional abilities, the blind may then exert their powers, whether
natural or acquired, as well in promoting private as public utility;
and in this view it requires no mighty effort of courage to recommend them to the public benevolence and attention ; and though
their talents should not be sufficient to pre-engage the general
taste in their favour, or the necessity of employing them, so
considerable as to open a resource for their exigencies, yet the
force of humanity alone may be adequate to produce an effect so
desirable. How often have we already seen beneficence ingenious
in prescribing tasks to these unhappy labourers, that it might
have an opportunity of supplying their indigence without
wounding their delicacy. This is what at first occurs as an
answer to the objection urged against the general utility of our
plan, till our readers be convinced by a detail of this work, and
still more effectually by experience, to what degree our scheme of
education may be carried, and how essentially it may contribute
to the subsistence of those among the blind who are born in the
depth of want and obscurity.

CHAP. III.

Of Reading, as adapted to the Practice of the Blind.

READING is the only method of adorning the memory, so that it
may command the stores which it has imbibed with facility,
promptitude, and method. It is, as it were, the channel through
which every different kind of knowledge is communicated to us.

Without this medium literary productions could form nothing in the human mind but a confused heap of disarranged and fluctuating ideas. To teach the blind, therefore, to read, and to form a library proper for their use, must constitute the object of our first care. Before our time various but ineffectual experiments had been tried ; sometimes by the assistance of characters moving upon a board and raised above its surface (*a*) ; at other times by the use of letters formed upon paper with the puncture of a pin (*b*), the principles or elementary characters of reading had been rendered obvious to the perception of the blind. Already had the wonders of the art of writing, which before had appeared chimerical, been realised. Already, under their touch, which was now found a substitute for vision, had the conceptions of the blind assumed a body. But these gross and imperfect utensils only presented to the blind the possibility of attaining and enjoying the pleasures and advantages of reading without affording them the proper means for acquiring them. We had no difficulty in exploring them ; their principles had existed for a long time, and were daily exhibited to our eyes. We had observed that a printed leaf issuing from the press presented to the eye, on the contrary side, the letters higher than its surface, but reversed both in their position and in their order.

We ordered typographical characters to be cast of the form in which their impression strikes our eyes, and by applying to these a paper wet, as the printers do, we produced the first exemplar which had till then appeared of letters whose elevation renders them obvious to the touch without the intervention of sight. Such was the origin of a library for the use of the blind.

After having successively employed characters of different sizes, according as we found the touch of our pupils more or less delicate and susceptible, it appeared proper to us, at least during the first

---

(*a*) It is without doubt, by these means that the blind man of Puiseaux, of whom M. Diderot speaks in his letter on the blind, p. 8, taught his son to read.

(*b*) We have seen some words thus marked by punctures upon cards in the hands of Mlle. Paradis. This virtuosa is 20 years of age; she was born in Vienna in Austria, the place of her ordinary residence. A kind of apoplexy deprived her suddenly of her sight, at the age of two years. She has principally applied herself to music, and constituted in 1784, at Paris, the chief pleasures of the spiritual concert.

periods of our progress, to confine ourselves to that type which has been used in printing the greatest part of this work. This character appears to us as a proper medium amongst those which can be felt and distinguished by different individuals who are deprived of sight, according to the various degrees of tactile nicety with which nature has endued them ; or at least according to the degrees of sensibility which diversities of age or occupation may have left them. It will be easily conceived, that when these means are found, there is no more difficulty in teaching a blind person the principles of reading, than in teaching one, whose visual powers are in their highest perfection, and that the blind may pass by an easy transition from the perception of typographical to that of written characters. We do not here speak of characters written in the manner of those who see ; for all our endeavours to form characters rising to the touch by the assistance of ink have proved abortive. We have therefore substituted in their place impressions made upon strong paper, with an iron pen, whose point is not slit. It is unnecessary to mention, that in writing to the blind we do not make use of ink, that the character is deeply impressed, distinctly separated, a little larger than common, and nearly of the same kind with those now in the hands of our reader ; that, in short, we never write but on the side of the paper contrary to that which is read, and in such a manner that the position and order of the letters may appear proper when the page is turned. These precautions being scrupulously observed, the blind may read tolerably letters from their correspondents who see, those formed by their own hands, or by the hands of others in similar circumstances (c). They will do more, they will equally distinguish, on the same paper, musical characters and others rendered sensible by our method of procedure, as we shall immediately shew in the sequel.

(c) M. Weissenbourg, a boy dwelling at Manheim, having become blind between the seventh and eighth year of his age, celebrated for the knowledge which he has acquired, has preserved the faculty of writing; but this advantage, which is only an object of curiosity, will become of real utility, if, as we hope, he adopts our method.

CHAP. IV.

*Answer to various Objections against the Method of Reading
proposed for the Blind.*

1. "THE elevation of your charaters will doubtless be very soon
"depressed," says an objector, "and of consequence no longer per-
"ceptible to the blind by touch." No person is ignorant of the
acuteness of that sense in several individuals, who from their
infancy have been obliged to use it, in order to supply the want of
that which nature has denied them. A surface which appears the
smoothest to our eye, presents to the fingers of the blind in-
equalities which escape the notice of that organ, though by its
assistance those who see exult in being able to perceive the
remotest stars that adorn the spacious concave of heaven ; and
when our pupils distinguish a typographical character by feeling,
which may elude even a microscopic eye, when between the thickness of two given objects, if the one differs from the other only
by the fourth part of a French line, they can clearly perceive that
difference ; when, in short, they read a series of words, after the
elevation of the letters is depressed, what have we to fear from
the frequent use of their books, except the absolute destruction of
the volumes themselves, a misfortune to which those who see are
equally liable ?

2. "Your books," it is objected, "are too voluminous. You
"swell a 12mo to the enormous and unwieldy size of a folio ; and
"by thus altering its convenient form, you render it less portable
"and useful." We might satisfy ourselves with answering to this
objection that our art of printing is yet in its infancy, but progressive, and may perhaps one day become perfect, as that which
is obvious to the sight has already done ; that it may likewise have
its Elzevirs, its Barbous, its Peters, its Didot, &c. And since its
commencement, how many and how important are the obligations
which it already owes to M. Clousier, printer to the King, who
assists us by his advice with as much zeal as disinterestedness.

We add that during the interval between its present and its more perfect state we are employed in adapting a method of epitomising, which will considerably diminish the size of our volumes. Of this we hope to give the first specimen in a work which will be immediately printed after this is finished (d). Besides, we will make a selection of authors, nor shall any one enter into our press but such works as by their reputation have merited that distinction ; so that on one hand, if by the magnitude of our characters we enlarge our volumes, on the other we shall lessen them by a judicious abridgement ; and perhaps one day the library of the blind may become the library of taste and learning.

3. " But confess, then, that your blind scholars read slowly, and " that the spirit of the most animated composition will evaporate " beneath their fingers, while the words are languidly pronounced " without energy and without emotion." Our pupils, it is true, read in slow succession ; besides the little practice, which an institution so lately begun allows them in reading, they have the disadvantage of only perceiving one letter at once, as readers who see themselves must do, were their eyes obliged to traverse an opening between each letter equal to the space occupied by one typographical character in this work.

But we hope that after frequent practice in reading and in making use of the abbreviations we have mentioned above, our blind pupils will proceed with greater quickness. Besides, we have never entertained the ambition of qualifying them to be readers for princes, or to declaim in public with all the graces of oratory. Let them only, by means of reading, learn the elements of science ; let them find in this exercise an effectual remedy against that intolerable melancholy which corporeal darkness and mental inactivity united in the same person are too apt to produce ; these ends attained, will fully accomplish our wishes.

4. " But what good purpose will it serve to teach the blind the " letters ? Why instruct them in the art of printing books for

---

(d) Examples of these abbreviations, within the capacity and reach of all readers, are in the Treatises of Philosophy, in the Dictionaries, the new Methods and other Elementary Books of Education.

" their peculiar use ? They never will be able to read ours. And,
" from the knowledge which they will acquire by reading, will
" any considerable advantage result to society ? " Permit us, in
our turn, to ask you, To what purpose is it that books are
printed amongst all the people who surround us, and exclusively
intended for the peculiar use of each ? Do you read the
language of the Chinese, that of Malabar, or of Turkey ? Can
you interpret the Peruvian Quipos, and so many other tongues
indispensably necessary to those who understand them ? Should
you then be transported to China, to the Banks of the Ganges, to
the Ottoman Empire, or to Peru, you will there be precisely in
the same predicament with one of our blind pupils. With regard
to the utility which the knowledge of a blind man in reading
may produce to society, without deviating from the sentiment
expressed near the end of the following page of this work, we
may with pleasure appeal for its reality to the experiment so
often repeated under our own eyes, and of which the public itself
has been a witness in our exhibitions ; we mean the experiment
of a blind child teaching one who saw to read (*e*). We appeal
for its reality to the example of the blind person at Puiseaux (*f*).
We appeal to you, in short, ye tender and respectable parents,
born to a liberal share of fortune's favours, whose son is just
entered into the world, but shall never see the light of heaven ;
what a sensible satisfaction it is to us to find ourselves in a
capacity to alleviate the transports of your grief ! Yes, our plan
of education bids fair on one hand to restore to your son, already
tenderly loved, the dearest prerogative of intellectual existence ;
on the other to furnish you with the means of gratifying those
desires with which your taste for learning and genius inspires
you, to procure him an education worthy of a child born in a
distinguished rank. And you men of learning, who enlighten

(*e*) According to the proposal made in advertisements, annunciations and various
intimations on the 3rd of December, 1786, page 3204, in the first article of demands, on the
5th of the same month we caused one of our blind to begin teaching a child who saw, to
read. During the lessons, the master had beneath his fingers a white book printed in
relievo for the blind, whilst the other had under his eyes the same edition in black. This
child gave, for the first time, proofs of his advancement in the exercises performed by the
blind at Versailles, during the Christmas holidays in the same year.

(*f*) This blind person, as we have said before, Note (*a*), p. 12, gave to his son lessons
in reading.

us by your exertion of corporeal sight, if the fatigues of unre-
mitted labour for our instruction should one day extinguish that
organ, permit us at that unhappy crisis to offer you the means at
once of continuing the benefit of your lessons to us, and to you
the enjoyment of an advantage of which they are in some
measure the agreeable fruits. Homer, Belisarius, and Milton,
afflicted with blindness, would with pleasure have consecrated to
the service of their country those years of their lives which
followed that catastrophe.

CHAP. V.

Of the Art of Printing, as practised by the Blind for their
peculiar Use.

THE analogy which the manner of reading adapted to the blind
has with their method of printing, having reduced us to the
necessity of giving by anticipation, in detail, some circumstances
which relate to the origin of their art of printing, it remains for
us to explain the principal operations of that art, as adapted to
their practice. It will be much the same case with respect to
the mechanical operations of printing among the blind as with
those who see, It is doubtless impossible for every individual to
have an exclusive possession of it (*g*). The necessity of habitually
knowing and practising the different branches of that art, the
multiplicity and high price of the utensils requisite for its execution, the civil privileges with which its professors must be
endued, all these conspiring obstacles limit its pursuit to a society
of the blind, solely formed and intended for its practice. It is in
our academy for their education where we hope to constitute the
chief place (if we may use the expression), from whence will issue
such typographical productions, for instance, as are proper for
the use of all the blind who, in their misfortune, shall have the

---

(*g*) One knows how easy it is to abuse printing in all respects; and not satisfied with
the rectitude of our intentions, and the indulgence with which people have honoured our
infant printing, the productions of which bear a character of originality easily distinguish-
able, we have formed to ourselves an inviolable rule not to suffer anything printed to issue
from us without the sanction of M. Clousier, printer to the King, and which has not been
executed under his eyes, or those of some person commissioned by him.

sweet consolation of being born within the dominions of our
Monarch (*h*). Let us proceed to the manner in which our blind
pupils perform their typographical labours. We have given to
their cases the order of the alphabet, so as to preserve, immediately under their hands, the characters which they shall have
most frequent occasion to use. We preferred that distribution
under the apprehension that the blind would be less clever than
we have really found them. It is upon the same principle that
we make them set their types in a case lined with a copper
bottom, and pierced with several lines of small holes, from
whence, by the assistance of a pointed instrument, they bring out
the types which are to be changed. It is upon the same principle that we cause to be adjusted, in the inside of these cases,
iron rulers (moveable by means of their screws), one at the side
and the other at the bottom of the page, to keep the lines in it
regular. It is, in short, upon the same principle that we raise
these cases horizontally in longitude upon four feet, of which the
two that support the upper end of the page are one-half lower
than those upon which the under end rests ; so that without
making use of a composing stick the blind compositor may place
the words at proper distances, and that they may not be inverted
whilst he is composing the remainder of the page.

The way in which the typographical characters of the blind
present themselves naturally indicates that the arrangement ought
to be made from left to right, as we have observed chap. 3d. And
in order to make reading easy to the blind, at least in the first
periods of their education, it may prove a happy expedient to
leave spaces between the words, and even sometimes between the
letters. It is easy to see that when one prints in relievo he
cannot print on the other side without being in danger of
destroying the former impression, by tracing which with their
finger only the blind can read. Likewise, for preserving the pages
in the same order that they have in books for the use of those
who see, the blind are obliged to paste together, back to back, by

---

(*h*) Till establishments similar to ours be formed in other nations, it will be a pleasure
to us to cause to be printed in relievo, and in other languages, by our blind pupils, books
destined for the use of strangers who are deprived of sight.

their extremities, the four pages of a sheet coming from the press ; and then the arrangement of the cases is made in an order different from that of persons who see. Thus the leaves being pasted, they form them into books, by simply stitching and covering them with pasteboard without beating them.

The office of the ordinary printing-press is easily done, by help of a cylindrical press, which is moved by a lever from one extremity to the other, along two bars of iron, between which are placed the forms, or pages that are set, after the manner of printers (i).

We may employ with success the same process for printing in relievo for the use of the blind, musical characters, geographical maps, the principal strokes of designing, and, in general, of all the figures of which the knowledge may be obtained by means of touch. It is upon account of these last objects, above all, that we hope the admirable discovery of M. M. Hoffman will be precious to the blind ; we share by anticipation their sentiments of gratitude towards those estimable artists (k).

To the press of which we have spoken a little above we have thought it proper to add a kind of tympanum, by the assistance of which the blind may, at their pleasure, tinge with black, copies of an edition perfectly similar to those which they print on white paper for their own private use.

This procedure, which is equally applicable to music, to geographical maps, or to designs, &c., puts the blind artist in a capacity not only of giving an account to himself of all the productions which he wishes to convey to those who see, but likewise easily to direct their studies by the similarity of copies, on the supposition of his being employed to give them lessons.

(i) This press is the invention of Sieur Beaucher, chief lock-smith. It has amply and successfully accomplished our wishes, as to the facility with which it is managed without any great effort by a blind child, and by which it admits the mechanism which we have adapted to it. We believe, however, that a perpendicular pressure given to the whole leaf at the same instant, will leave behind it a more solid impression ; we hope to find this in a press of another kind, which the Sieur Beaucher has described to us.

(k) Although in pages 8 and 14 of this work we have not repeated the names of some of the distinguished printers whom we have heard celebrated, we cannot forbear to confess that according to our manner of thinking, there are many others who appear to us to exercise their employment with éclat. We even perceive, in those who compose the body of this society, a general emulation. And obliged, by the nature of our institution, to serve a kind of apprenticeship to this art, we would quote with pleasure a considerable number

CHAP. VI.

On the Art of Printing, as practised by the Blind for the Use of those who See.

IF we have been happy enough to discover the means of rendering printing useful to the blind for their own use ; if it is to us that they owe the advantage of henceforth possessing libraries, and of taking from books formed on purpose for themselves, notions of letters, of languages, of history, of geography, of mathematics, of music, &c. ; we are not the first who dared to try to make them impress their ideas upon paper by help of typographical characters. We have seen in the hands of Mademoiselle Paradis (*l*) a letter printed by her in the character called *Pica*, and in the German language, full of sentiments the most delicate, as well as the best expressed. This attempt gave birth in my mind to the idea of applying the blind to the art of printing for the use of those who see ; it has succeeded with us in every kind of work, whether with large or common types, as one may judge by the different specimens which they have exhibited, and which are to be found at the end of this work, if they can possibly be procured.

After our manner of proceeding, the blind, formed according to our institution, compose a typographical plate in imitation of these models, with so much more ease as they are almost continually of the same form ; it suffices to write for them the subject with a pen of iron, of which the top is not split, or with the handle of a penknife as we have shewn above in the 3d Chapter.

After having exercised the blind upon the different branches of the art of printing in the manner of those who see, there are

---

of well-known productions from different presses which leave no further improvement to be wished ; as well for the neatness of the characters, as for the choice of paper, and which have served us as models in the study of printing which we had to go through. Besides, far from erecting ourselves as judges in opposition to persons who cultivate the arts and sciences, whether from situation or taste, we praise even attempts that have not been crowned with success.—*See Translation published with " Blacklock's Poems."*

(*l*) This production was executed by the assistance of a little press, which M. de Kempelan, the inventor of the automatic chess-player, had formed for her.

found few kinds in which they have not succeeded. We have seen them successively compose, adjust, impress, moisten the paper, touch it, print, &c., &c. (m). We appeal, besides, to competent judges in that affair, and we refer our reader to the report of M. M., the printers, which agrees with that of the Academy of Sciences.

CHAP. VII.

Of Writing.

THE example of Bernouilli, who had taught a young blind girl to write, and that of M. Weissenbourg, who, deprived of sight from seven years of age, has procured for himself the advantages of fixing also his ideas upon paper by writing, have encouraged us to try the means of putting the pen into the hands of our pupils. But always occupied in our real point of view, that is to say, in rendering our institution in every respect useful to those individuals who were its objects, we have thought that it could not but be curious to cause the blind to write, if they could arrive at reading their own hand ; this is what engaged us in causing to be made for their use a pen of iron, the top of which was not split, and with which writing without ink, and supported with a strong paper, they produce upon it a character in relievo which they can afterwards read, in passing their fingers along the elevated lines on the back of the page. This elevation, however slight it may appear, is always sufficient, especially if care is taken to place below the paper upon which the blind write a soft and yielding surface, such as several leaves of waste paper, of pasteboard, or of leather. With respect to the proper mechanism of teaching the art of writing to those who are born blind, it is by no means difficult to be executed ; you have only to teach your

---

(m) If there is any operation among the blind which requires to be directed by those who see, it is printing for the use of these last we acknowledge. This speculation has been often repeated to us upon other different branches of our institution. But have not clear-sighted persons who labour at the press themselves need of a guide to whose skill they are obliged to pay deference? And in the other states of life do we not see persons more enlightened, directing those who are less, whilst those are in a situation to conduct people less experienced than they? 'Tis thus that, in the day of battle, the general of an army gives orders, the intention of which his subaltern officers are ignorant. It is thus that the pilot conducts to the end of their voyage the learned academicians, who are unskilled in the art of navigation.

pupil to trace, with a pointed instrument, the characters ranged in form of lines. But instead of directing the process of this pointed instrument by means of characters in relievo, as M. Weissenbourg has done, it is better to conduct it by letters graven hollow on some plate of metal. We have besides this precaution taken that of giving our printed letters the form of written, in order early to accustom the blind pupil to catch the resemblance. At last, when he has acquired the habit of distinguishing their forms, there remains nothing more for him to write straight but to place upon his paper a frame internally furnished with small rising lines, parallel to the direction of the writing, and distant from one another about nine-tenths of an inch. These parallel lines serve to direct his hand, whilst he transports it from left to right, in order to trace the characters.

CHAP. VIII.

Of Arithmetic.

WE have admired the ingenious tables of Saunderson (*n*) and those of M. Weissenbourg (*o*) ; the reason why we have adopted neither of these methods was from another view, viz., that we might preserve, without interruption, the strictest analogy possible between the means of educating the blind and those who see, we have thought that the manner of these last ought to be preferred. Likewise, when our pupils calculate, one may follow their operations step by step.

We have caused to be made for them to this end, a board pierced with different lines of square holes, proper for receiving moveable figures and bars for separating the different parts of an operation.

(*n*) The arithmetical table of Saunderson was formed of a board divided into small squares placed horizontally and separated one from the other at equal distances; each little square was pierced with nine holes, viz., one on the midst of each side. It was by the different positions of the pegs uniformly placed in different holes that Saunderson could express any kind of number.

(*o*) We have seen, in the hands of Mlle. Paradis, arithmetical tables which we believe to have been those of M. Weissenbourg. But without a particular study, one cannot follow the operations which are performed by the help of these tables. We do not know if our pupil could operate with equal swiftness and certainty by these means as he could by those of persons who see, and we have no other merit but that of rendering them palpable to him.

We have added, to render this board more useful, a case composed of four rows of little boxes, containing all the figures proper for calculation, and which are placed at the right hand of the blind person while he operates. The only difficulty which occurred was to represent all the possible fractions without multiplying the characters which express them. We have thought of causing to be cast 10 simple denominators in the order of the figures 0, 1, 2, &c., even to 9 inclusively ; and likewise 10 simple numerators in the same order, moveable in order to be adapted at the head of the denominators. By means of this combination, there is not a fraction which our pupils cannot express.

One may see from what has been said, that our method has a double advantage.

1. A father of a family, or a tutor, can easily direct a blind child in the study of arithmetic.

2. This blind child, when once instructed, may also conduct, in his turn, the arithmetical operations performed by a child who sees.

The blind have, besides, so great a propensity for calculation that we have often seen them following an arithmetical process and correcting its errors by memory alone.

CHAP. IX.

Of Geography.

WE owe to Madame Paradis the knowledge of geographical maps for the use of the blind. She herself had it from M. Weissenbourg ; but we are astonished that neither the one nor the other has carried to a higher degree of perfection, the utensils which contribute to the study of that science.

They mark the circumference of countries by a tenacious and viscid matter, covering the different parts of their maps with a kind of sand mixed with glass, in various manners, and distinguish the order of towns by grains of glass of a greater or lesser size.

We are satisfied with marking the limits in our maps for the use of the blind, by small iron wire rounded ; and it is always a difference either in the form or size of every part of a map, which assists our pupils in distinguishing the one from the other.

These means we have chosen in preference, on account of the ease which they afford us of multiplying, by the assistance of the press, the copies of our original maps for the use of the blind. It will, besides, be more apt than any other to offer itself to the execution of details the most delicate which can affect the touch of these individuals; and the first of our pupils have brought themselves to such admirable perfection in the use of geographical maps, that people see them with surprise, at our exhibitions, distinguish a kingdom, a province, an island, the impression of which is presented to them, independent of other parts of a map, upon a square piece of paper.

CHAP. X.

Of Music.

In tracing the plan of the education of the blind, we have at first looked upon music only as an appendage fit for relaxing them after their labour. But the natural propensity in the greatest number of the blind for this art; the resources which it can furnish to several among them for their sustenance; the interest with which it inspires those who deign to be present at our exhibitions, have all forced us to sacrifice our own opinion to the general utility.

The blind have natural propensities for this art. A considerable number of them, deprived of the means of living, seize with eagerness, through necessity, an employment towards which their inclination had already so powerfully attracted them. It is only the want of instruction, without doubt, which reduces some of them to the necessity of wandering in the streets, from door to door, grating the ear by the aid of an ill-tuned instrument, or a hoarse voice, that they may extort an inconsiderable piece of money, which is frequently given them with an injunction to be silent (*p*).

(*p*) If the taste and inclination which certain blind persons have shown for the violin, or for such instruments as can easily be joined with it, were directed by art, perhaps they might make use of it for gaining more decently their livelihood. An estimable citizen,* who approves of all the parts of our institution, without discovering for any of them a particular predilection, suggested to us in the course of one of our exhibitions, that one might usefully employ in the train blind musicians at festivals.

* Mr. Thierry, Author of the Traveller's Almanack.

Others less unfortunate, and giving themselves up by choice to an instrument which affords them more resource, follow the career of Couperin, of Balbatre, of Sejan, of Miroir, of Carpentiers (q).

Our institution will furnish all of them with assistance, whether in the study or practice of their art. Before our time, teachers of the blind were obliged to make them comprehend, by playing them over and over, the small pieces of music which they wished to execute. We have caused to be cast musical characters proper to represent upon paper all its possible varieties, by elevations on its surface in the manner of those which we have devised to represent words (r).

By the assistance of our printed music, then the blind pupil may learn at present the principles of that art, and impress on his memory the different pieces of music with which he wishes to enrich it (s).

He may likewise form to himself a library of taste, composed of the most enchanting musical productions ; and in short he himself may transmit to us the fruits of his own genius (t).

With respect to the music introduced into our particular exhibitions, we beg of our readers only to consider it as a decent recreation, which we have seen ourselves obliged to grant to our pupils. Our institution is, in its origin, a kind of workhouse, the different artists and labourers of which amuse their toils from

(q) All the world knows the merit of Mr. Chauvet, blind organist of Notre Dame de Bonne-Nouvelle. They quote in France several other blind people whose talents ascertain the utility of this study for our pupils. How comfortable for us will it be one day to have extracted from this art of harmony the means of subsistence for a part of these unfortunate people, and to have seen them become, by a happy choice, the instruments of beneficence.

(r) It has been objected to us with propriety, that our blind pupils cannot execute and feel the musical characters at the same time, which people who see call performing at sight, but this never was the end which we proposed. What matters it though they perform a piece of music by heart, provided they perform it correctly and faithfully.

(s) No person is ignorant how faithful and sure are the memories of the blind, and with what readiness they furnish them. It is likewise known what a clear conception the greatest number of them discover in difficult operations of mind ; talents so astonishing, that one would almost doubt whether nature was more parsimonious in her gifts with respect to them, or anxious to recompense them for those which she has refused.

(t) Mlle. Paradis, who was employed in the study of composition during her continuance in Paris, and who then sought the means of figuring the chords, learned with pleasure that we were making trials on the same subject. We regret that her abrupt departure to go and reap, under another climate, the fruits of her talents, did not leave us time to offer her the result of our procedures, to assist her in fixing upon paper the matter of her study.

time to time with harmony. And we have, with less reluctance, permitted them to execute some little pieces, even in their public exercises, that the most part of the beneficent people, who have deigned to be present at them, have shown the most lively and sensible compassion on hearing their performances.

CHAP. XI.

Of the Occupations relative to Manual Employments, or Handicrafts.

BEFORE the birth of our institution, some of the blind, doubtless fatigued with that wretched inactivity to which their deplorable situation seemed to condemn them, made efforts to shake it off. (*u*) Convinced of their fitness for several manual employments, we had no other anxiety but that of selecting such tasks as were proper for them. We applied them with success to spinning. (*x*) Of the thread which they spun we succeeded in making them twist pack-thread, and of this pack-thread we made them weave girths. Their labours at the Boisseau (*y*) in making small walking staves of cords, in the working of nets, in sewing, in binding books, all were tried to our satisfaction ; and we wanted labourers rather than work ; so many are the kinds of manual employment, which one may trust to the unfortunate persons who are deprived of the pleasure of sight.

(*u*) Amongst the blind who, not having the advantage of enjoying the pension of Quinze-Vingts, are obliged to ask their livelihood in the capital, we have seen several who occupied themselves in employments relative to handicrafts. The number of these which we can make the blind exercise in our workhouses is very considerable; and we are not afraid to assert, that, if we continue to be favoured, we shall arrive one day at placing all the blind under shelter from indigence by employing them advantageously.

(*z*) Blind children, who are under instruction in the house of our institution, spin by the assistance of the ingenious machine invented by the Sr. Hildebrand, a mechanic. One among them turns a principal wheel which gives to several smaller wheels a motion which each spinner can stop, quicken or retard, at his pleasure, without disturbing the general order.

(*y*) The translator takes here the liberty of retaining the original French word, not being able to find an English name for the same utensil. Boisseau properly signifies a bushel, but likewise means an instrument of timber, of a semiglobular form, and about one foot and a half in length, very light, which is placed upon the knee for working. They make use of it in plaiting small round cord, or working girdles of silk, or other works which they call done with the boisseau, to distinguish them from those which are made upon frames.

After these first trials, we will neglect nothing to put early into the hands of a blind child, born of indigent parents, an occupation from which he may one day draw his sustenance. We will thus extirpate the inclination to beggary ; and we will finish (if the expression may be allowed us) by grouping our picture, as well as by giving animation to the individual figures it contains.

CHAP. XII.

Of the Manner of Instructing the Blind, and a Parallel of their Education with that of the Deaf and Dumb.

As we have principally attached ourselves to simplify the means and the utensils proper for the instruction of the Blind, we flatter ourselves we have placed their education within the reach and compass of all the world. This operation, besides that it is easy in itself, requires more courage than knowledge in a master. We believe then, that upon this subject we have no particular advice to give.

By the aid of our books in relievo, every one can teach them to read. Upon the musical works formed in our press every professor of that art may give them lessons. With an iron pen, with plates and moveable characters, executed according to our models, the first masters in writing may teach them that art and arithmetic. In short, there wants nothing but maps in relievo to direct their studies in Geography ; and so of other things (*y*).

We cannot conclude this reflection on the degrees of facility with which the blind may be educated, without drawing a parallel between it and the method of educating the deaf and dumb. However surprising to the eyes of the public the result of our procedure may appear, we are very far from implicitly joining in that rash admiration of some persons who are very willing to give

---

(*y*) We will take pleasure in directing the construction of utensils useful for the instruction of the blind who are strangers. The books and works of music shall be furnished by our blind pupils, and sold for their benefit alone. When we shall have put the last hand to the objects which demand our chief care, we hope to employ ourselves in their amusements, and in everything which can form a decent and innocent recreation for the blind. We believe that it ought equally to enter into our views to teach blind children to walk alone, and without a guide.

this result a preference to the art of instructing the deaf and
dumb : an art, we dare say, incredible to those who have never
been witnesses of the success to which it has been conducted by
the virtuous ecclesiastic, who is its original author ; and with
regard to which, several, even of those who have seen the proofs
of this art, neither know how to estimate its merit or to feel its
difficulties.   Let any person in reality follow them step by step ;
let him take the Abbé in the first instant of time, when he
begins to wish to make his first signs understood by his pupil.
Let such a one explain to us by what enchanting and magical
talents he teaches the deaf to distinguish the moods of a verb ; its
tenses, and the inflections of its persons.   How will one tell us in
what manner he insinuates into their minds metaphysical ideas ?
By what marvellous secret he makes himself understood by the
motion of his lips alone, and maintains a kind of conversation with
them, extremely expressive, quite silent as it is ; and it will be
agreed, that the talent of impressing the soul with new ideas, in
speaking to the eyes alone, by gesticulations infinitely more eloquent than those of all our orators, is much superior to the talent
of awaking in the soul ideas which are already engraven on it, by
causing to concur with the impression of the voice, upon the organ
of hearing, the delicacy of a touch exercised in seizing the nicest
elevations on the surface of a paper.   It is a long time since we
have been anxious to pay this tribute to M. l'Abbé de l'Epée ; we
congratulate ourselves on having this task to perform in such
favourable circumstances, and we flatter ourselves that our readers
will feel all the justice of the deference we pay him (z).

___

(z) We speak with so much more knowledge of the cause of instructing the deaf and
dumb ; and our opinion is so much more agreeable to truth. that obliged, by circumstances
from which we could not extricate ourselves, to consecrate the leisure which the instruction
of the blind left us to that *of a young man found upon the coast of Normandy*, who is deaf
and almost dumb, we have felt in every step how difficult the enterprise was, beyond the
reach of our powers, and a task alone for M. l'Abbé de l'Epée. We propose to ourselves
to give the history of this unfortunate young man. The composition of it shall be done
by him, and the print by blind children. The whole shall be introduced by proposals for
subscription ; the benefits arising from which shall be divided into two equal parts, and
given one half to the blind children, and the other to that unfortunate young man.

CHAP. XIII.

Of Languages, History, Mathematics, &c.

It is chiefly for the study of all these objects, that the books which we have invented for the use of the blind, will be to them of immense utility. Elementary works of languages, of mathematics, of history, &c., will be in reality the first foundation of their library. Those which they can produce themselves, and which shall merit the public approbation, will be justly entitled to a place there (a).

We will take particular care to join in their library works equally fitted to form the heart and cultivate the mind of our blind pupil, in fixing, as the basis of these studies, the most essential of all studies—that of religion. By the assistance of such principles, we will inculate the love of his duty, and in particular, gratitude towards his benefactors. In enlivening his days by the interesting details of history, we will cause him to know the French, among whom he will congratulate himself on having received his existence. We will engrave upon his memory the principal facts of their history, and the marks of beneficence and humanity which are mixt with the relation of their achievements. We will cause him, above all, to remark that, in every period of time, the French have distinguished themselves by an inviolable attachment to their Kings ; and from the faithful picture which we will draw to him of a Monarch, who, formed by himself to inspire that attachment, includes in his equity and beneficence all the particular motives which can add to the energy of this hereditary sentiment, he will feel, as we do, that the most desirable state to which a nation can arrive, is that where the submission of several millions of people towards a common master, presents itself under the image of the respectful tenderness of a large family towards a father who constitutes its happiness.

(a) It was certainly a desirable and happy thing for Saunderson, author of various productions, to commit them himself to paper, and without being obliged to depend on the fidelity of a Secretary, to be able at every instant to render himself an exact account.

One of our pupils shewing a disposition to poetry, we beg of our readers to permit us to encourage it in subjoining a specimen of his rising talent, after the models of different works in printing, which can be executed by the blind, and which are at the end of this volume.

AN

HISTORICAL SUMMARY

OF THE

Rise, the Progress, and the Actual State of the Institution of the Blind Children.

MANY respectable persons have carried the concern which they felt for our institution, even to demand how such an idea could possibly enter into our mind; by what means we attempted the execution of it ; and by what degrees it advanced to the point in which it is at present. Anxious to satisfy a curiosity so laudable, we are eager to subjoin here a concise narrative of the rise, progress, and actual state of our establishment.

A novelty of a kind so singular has attracted for several years the united attention of a number of persons at the entry of one of those places of refreshment situated in the public walks whither respectable citizens go to relax themselves about the decline of day.

Eight or ten poor blind persons, with spectacles on their noses, placed along a desk which sustained instruments of music, where they executed a discordant symphony, seemed to give delight to the audience. A very different sentiment possessed our soul, and we conceived, at that very instant, the possibility of realizing, to the advantage of those unfortunate people, the means of which they had only an apparent and ridiculous enjoyment : the blind, said we to ourselves, do they not know objects by the diversity of their forms? Are they mistaken in the value of a piece of money ? Why can they not distinguish a C from G in music, or an *a* from an *f* in orthography, if their characters were rendered plain ?

We reflected sometimes on the utility of this undertaking ; there another observation came to strike us. A young child, full of understanding, but deprived of sight, listened, with advantage, to correct the errors of his brother in reading. He even frequently besought him to read his elementary books to him. He, more employed in objects of amusement, shut his ears to the solicitations of his unhappy brother, whom a cruel disease carried off very soon.

These different examples soon convinced us how precious it would be to the blind to possess the means of extending their knowledge, without their being obliged to wait for, or sometimes even in vain to demand, the assistance of those who saw.

If the execution of these means appeared to us possible, it did not fail at first to present us with some difficulties. We had need of encouragement, we confess. Mademoiselle Paradis arrived in this metropolis. She shewed us her attempts, and those of M. Weissenbourg. We collected those of the blind who lived before our time; we put into execution several of their proceedings; to these we joined the results of our own, and we formed a general plan of the Institution. There was only wanting a person upon whom we might try our first experiments. Providence deigned, without doubt, to direct our choice upon him.

François le Sueur, struck with blindness in consequence of convulsions at the age of six weeks, had not, at the age of seventeen years and a half, any notion relative to literature. Descended from a respectable family, but entirely deprived of the advantages of fortune, and constrained to seek the means of subsistence in the place frequented by people least easy in their circumstances, although perhaps the most laborious, the blind youth scarcely enjoyed the use of reason, when he was afraid of being burdensome to his parents; he soon found himself under the necessity of going and presenting himself at the gates of our temples, there to crave that kind of unsubstantial and momentary assistance which is given by those who enter, which the indigent often obtain with difficulty from the rich, who industriously avoid their importunities. Full of joy at the least acquisition, he flies with eagerness to the bosom of his unhappy family, to divide the fruit of his solicitations, with the authors of his being, and with three sisters and two brothers, whereof the last is still upon the breast. It was in the midst of this hard life, as little calculated to inspire as to favour a taste for the sciences, that our first pupil began his education. Soon did a noble enthusiasm wholly take possession of him ; he snatched from the necessity of labouring for his existence, those moments which he consecrated to study. His efforts were not slow in being followed with success. They demanded of us to see the result of our proceedings ; we seized the favourable circumstance of an Academical Assembly, where we were appointed to read a memorial. We took for its subject certain reflections on the education of the blind. M. le Noir, then the magistrate, charged with the administration of the police, was president of this assembly. He saw our first attempts, received them with that concern with which he presently inspired Ministers, protectors of arts and indigence. M. le Compte de Vergennes, M. le Baron de Breteuil, Mr. Comptroller General, and Mr. Keeper of the Seals, were kindly willing to permit that the young Sueur should perform his exercises in their presence, and all these respectable witnesses encouraged our first pupil by their beneficence.

But whilst we were employed in delineating our plan of education for blind children, already had a company of beneficent gentlemen, composed of members of the first distinction, for their birth, their employments, their fortune or their talents ; depositaries of the public benefits of which every one inclines to increase the mass according to his wealth ; who snatching an interval from their business or their leisure hours go twice every month to employ themselves at the bottom of a cloister, far from the public observation, about the means of diminishing the number of the unfortunate ; already, I say, had the Philanthropic Society laid the foundation of this institution. Twelve poor blind children received from this company each one the assistance of twelve livres per month. Satisfied with our first trials, they designed to intrust us with the care of these unfortunate people. We were not slow in conceiving the hope of adding, to the assistance which they had given them, the product of their labours. What obligations have we not to acknowledge to the whole of this respectable society ? And why is it not permitted to us to name those of its members, who having neither reputation nor fortune to acquire, have shared with us, modestly and in silence, the numerous details into which the education of this establishment leads us ?

Very soon did our institution acquire a new degree of importance in the eyes of the public. Then they ceased to believe that the power of receiving by touch the education which we proposed was restricted to an individual alone favoured with the propensities inspired by nature. Of the fourteen blind children instructed in the first rudiments, there were then found only three whose progress had been slow ; because enjoying still a weak ray of light, they obtained at least from touch what remained to them almost entirely lost from the weakness of their sight.

There remained no more to put the last hand to this establishment but the testimony of the learned upon these means. The Academy of Sciences has designed to employ itself in examining them, and drew up the report which we have inserted at the end of this work.

Led by the suffrages of people instructed, by their own experience, by the emotions of a heart disposed to favour the good, the public have been eager from all quarters to contribute to the expense of rearing a house which we have built for suffering nature.

The Royal Academy of Music performed on the 19th of February, 1786, for the benefit of blind children, a concert, in which the audience were divided on one hand between the noble disinterestedness of the members, and on the other between the talents which they displayed on that occasion.

In short, the Lyceum, the Museum, and the Hall of Correspondence disputed among themselves with emulation the agreeable satisfaction of seeing, in the midst of their academical meetings, young blind children lisp out the first elements of reading, of calculation, &c., and in the scenes of learned emulation, where Genius alone had till then found encouragement, beneficence has, for the first time, been seen decreeing a crown.

Enthusiasm gained over particular societies ; and the exercises of blind children were always terminated by some acquisition in their favour, sent to the house of the Philanthropic Society, who joining their assistance to what was produced by the funds of the Institution, distributed the sums to them with the tenderness which a good mother equally feels for every one of her children.

Thirty of these unfortunate children, with these assistances, partake the advantages of our institution. Several others, too young to be set to work, receive no less that relief to which their sad situation seems to secure them a right. But in the actual state in which our establishment is, we beg our readers not to regard it but as a beginning. We hope that their sagacity will show them, in these first fruits, a pledge of that success which they promise in the sequel. It is thus that an attentive observer of the productions of nature sees, that the buds which the spring causes to shoot forth from all parts of the trees, announces the fruits which autumn will produce.

SWEET Harmony, from heav'n descend,
    Inspire and tune my languid strain ;
To me thy kind assistance lend,
    My genius in its flight sustain.
O deign, delightful God of day,
To guide and animate my way ;
    I seek the sacred vale alone,
My muse, alas ! too apt to fear,
When no bright beams her journey cheer,
    Trembling, approaches Helicon.

To barren idleness our days,
    By cruel fate were once confined ;
Our woes kind Industry allays,
    Once more to social life consign'd :
The various useful tasks and arts,
Which she to us with ease imparts,
    Shall soon our ling'ring hours console ;
To cheerful hope once more we rise ;
Our being, erst consum'd in sighs,
    Grows less oppressive to the soul.

Typographies, by which imprest,
  The learned's thoughts embodied shine,
Their immortality attest :
  Treasures, O France, which now are thine.
Eyeless, thank heav'n's supreme decree,
We can to late posterity
  Transmit the light of every sage ;
Though blind, we can in open day
Truth's venerable form display,
  And shew the glories of our age.

Greece, fruitful source of arts refin'd,
  To mortals raptur'd and surpris'd,
Gave perfect masters of each kind,
  At once beheld and idolis'd.
Yet though their times we justly praise,
Illum'd by such effulgent rays,
  Did then the dumb articulate ?
Or had the hopeless blind been taught,
From tactile signs to construe thought,
  To read, to write, and calculate ?

Though Nature from our darken'd eyes,
  For ever veils her charms sublime,
The form of earth and ev'n of skies,
  By Fancy's aid we figuring climb ;
We trace the rivers to their source,
Of stars we calculate the course ;
  From Europe to th' Atlantic shore,
Successive journeys we pursue,
Thanks to the hand whose prudence due
  Guides us in Geographic lore.

Dear brethren of affliction, aid
  My songs, th' auspicious days to bless,
Which wrap our fate in softer shade,
  And tend to make its horrors less.
And while my Muse, with grateful lays,
To sing the virtues all essays,
  Which in our zealous patrons glow ;
The gratitude their worth inspires,
Shall burn with unextinguish'd fires,
  And in our bosoms ever grow.

By HUARD,

Blind, and Pensioner to the Philanthropic
Society of Paris.

FINIS.

LONDON: PRINTED BY WM. CLOWES AND SONS, LIMITED, STAMFORD STREET AND CHARING CROSS.

4

RE-PRINT. 1894

THE BLIND

HINTS

DESIGNED TO PROMOTE

BENEFICENCE, TEMPERANCE

AND

MEDICAL SCIENCE

VOL. 2

[PAGES 117 TO 136]

BY

JOHN COAKLEY LETTSOM, M. & LL.D., &c.

LONDON

J. MAWMAN

1801

Printed by J. Nichols, Red Lion Passage, Fleet Street

LONDON

SAMPSON LOW, MARSTON & COMPANY

LIMITED

St. Dunstan's House

FETTER LANE, FLEET STREET, E.C.

1894

1894

Some Books and Papers about the Blind

REPRINTED BY

Messrs. SAMPSON LOW, MARSTON & COMPANY

LIMITED

St. Dunstan's House

FETTER LANE, FLEET STREET, LONDON

1774
THE EDUCATION OF THE BLIND. A LETTER IN THE EDINBURGH MAGAZINE AND REVIEW for NOVEMBER, 1774. Price 1s.

1793
TRANSLATION OF AN ESSAY ON THE EDUCATION OF THE BLIND by M. HAÜY. Dedicated to the King of France in 1786. Price 1s.

1801
HINTS TO PROMOTE BENEFICENCE, &c., by Dr. LETTSOM, with an account of the Blind Asylum at Liverpool. Price 1s.

1819
TRANSLATION OF AN ESSAY ON THE INSTRUCTION AND AMUSEMENTS OF THE BLIND by Dr. GUILLIÉ. Published in Paris, 1817. Illustrated, 5s.

1837
RECENT DISCOVERIES FOR FACILITATING THE EDUCATION OF THE BLIND. By JAMES GALL, of Edinburgh. Illustrated. Price 2s.

1842
THE EDUCATION, EMPLOYMENTS, &c., AT THE ASYLUM FOR THE BLIND, GLASGOW. By JOHN ALSTON. Illustrated. Price 2s.

1861
TRANSLATION BY REV. W. TAYLOR OF THE MANAGEMENT AND EDUCATION OF THE BLIND. By J. G. KNIE, of Breslau. Price 1s.

SECTION VII.

HINTS

RESPECTING THE

EMPLOYMENT OF THE BLIND.

On the subject of the Deaf and Dumb previously introduced, we lamented that the extinction of one sense
necessarily induced the loss of speech, and almost of mental
perception. The BLIND, indeed, are debarred of one sense,
the creative one of vision; but so far from annihilating any
others, it seems to render some of them more acute, as the
wonderful histories of blind persons testify, from the æra
of Homer, to the recent periods of Milton, Handel, and
Sanderson. Many, however, born in poverty, have become
by neglect a lasting burthen to their friends and to the
community in general, and who might have been rendered
useful by an early introduction to pursuits most practicable
under their confined powers; and by acquiring the means
of a livelihood, become productive members of the state.

An institution, therefore, upon such a basis of private
and public interests, has a claim upon public support, and
which it has in a considerable degree happily received.

In this liberal nation, Liverpool stands foremost in
instituting an asylum or school of instruction for the Blind;

which has been communicated to the public in the second volume of " Reports of the Society for bettering the Condition, and increasing the Comforts of the Poor," by THOMAS BERNARD, Esq., the author of numerous other essays for promoting general beneficence. The degraded chimney-sweeper,* as well as that outcast of society, the common beggar,† have interested his solicitude, and engaged his protection ; and thus whilst indigence and misery are succoured, he promotes science ‡ on the grand scale of national improvement and public good ; and his excellent charge to the overseers of the hundred of Stoke,§ breathes so much genuine humanity, and sound instruction, as to entitle it to the most general dissemination ; for no person can peruse it without reaping information, and experiencing an expansion of sympathy towards his suffering fellow-creatures.

The example so laudable in the inhabitants of Liverpool could not long escape the attention and imitation of the benevolent citizens of London, and a Society for the Benefit of the BLIND is now instituted by them, upon the plan annexed. Among the active members of it, I am happy in placing that distinguished oculist JAMES WARE, Esq., who first communicated the plan to me, and whose example with pleasure I adopted.

---

* Extract of an account of a chimney-sweeper's boy, with observations and proposal for the relief of Chimney-sweepers, by Thomas Bernard, Esq. Reports, Vol. I., p. 108, No. XIX.

† Extract from an account of an attempt to ascertain the circumstances of the beggars of London, and the best mode of relieving them, by the same. Vol. I., p. 122, No. XXII.

‡ Extract from an account of the institution for applying science to the common purposes of life, so far as it may be expected to affect the poor, by the same. Vol. II., p. 145, No. LV.

§ Charge to overseers of the poor, by the same. Vol. I., Appendix, p. 251, No. IV.

*Extract from an Account of the Asylum (or School of
Instruction) for the Blind at* Liverpool. *By* THOMAS
BERNARD, *Esq.*

IN December, 1790, an asylum was established at Liverpool,
for the benefit of the indigent Blind. It was set on foot
by the Rev. Henry Dannet, the Rev. John Smyth, and
others; not for the town merely, but open to every part of
the world.—To render the Blind happy in themselves, and
useful to society, is the benevolent and excellent plan of
this institution; which may be more correctly termed, a
SCHOOL OF INSTRUCTION FOR THE BLIND: where they who
have been taught a trade, withdraw after two, three, or
four years, to make way for others; and thus, by a continual succession, the benefit is very extensively diffused.

This charity does not separate the poor from their
families, and destroy the dearest and most tender connexions; but (leaving those ties undissolved, which to
persons deprived of sight are most essential, and without
which, indeed, life is hardly worth retaining) affords the
indigent Blind the means of instruction, the materials for
industry, and the wages of labour. They have comfortable
working-rooms provided for them, where they are instructed
and employed about eight hours a day, and receive a
pecuniary compensation according to their ability and industry. They continue to lodge and board with their
friends, or at lodgings provided for them, and attend only
as *day scholars* in the house. The number of Blind persons
instructed and employed in the asylum during the two
first years, ending in January, 1793, was from twenty-five
to forty-five: of these, some had already learnt their trades,
and had returned home to enjoy the benefit of what they
had been taught; a very few, already too much habituated

to idleness, had returned to their former way of life; but the greater number still remained on the establishment, in a course of improvement and occupation.

In January, 1794, the committee gave notice, that twenty more Blind persons would be admitted; the circumstances of each case being first ascertained by answers to printed queries, which were to be had at the asylum. As queries similar to these would be very useful in almost all charities, I have inserted them in a note.* During their continuance

---

* QUERIES, to be answered by a Medical Gentleman.

What is the nature and supposed cause of the applicant's blindness?
Is it total?
Is it deemed incurable?

QUERIES, to be answered by a Clergyman.

What is the name of the blind person?
What the age?
How long has he or she been blind?
What is the place or parish where the party was born?
To what place or parish does the party now belong?
What is the party's present place of residence?
How long has he or she resided there?
Has the person ever followed any trade, occupation, or employment, and what?
How is the person at present supported?
Is the party married?
If married, what is his or her family?
Hath the party any estate, annuity, salary, pension, or income, for life, or otherwise; and what is the amount thereof?
If any, how doth it arise?
Did the party ever receive alms or relief from any parish as a pauper; and if any, from what place or parish?
Are the blind person's parents living or dead?
If living, what are their names, residence, and condition, or circumstances, and also, what family have they?
Has the blind person been a common beggar, wandering minstrel, or played upon any instrument at alehouses within two years before application for admission?—Such persons being entirely excluded.
Does the party bear a character of regularity, decency, and sobriety?

in the school, each person is allowed, towards his or her support, a sum not less than eighteen pence, nor more than five shillings weekly; except in some extraordinary cases, or in those of married persons, who receive an additional allowance of sixpence a week.

Of the Blind in the Asylum, six are instructed in music, to qualify them as organists of parish churches. When any of the female musical pupils are also employed in the other trades of the asylum, they have an extra weekly allowance on that account. Blind persons, who have already made some progress on the harpsichord, are admissible, and allowed to continue to perfect themselves; and, in case of any one of the musical pupils having behaved well in the asylum, and appearing to be properly qualified on quitting it, the committee has the power to purchase and present such pupil with a musical instrument.* The

---

* Though only a few are *regularly* instructed in music, yet all of them are taught to join in the hymns and songs for the blind at the asylum; and several are engaged to sing at different churches in the town. One of their hymns, by the Rev. Mr. John Smyth, of Liverpool, is beautiful and interesting :—

HARK! sisters, hark! that bursting sigh!
    It issued from some feeling heart;—
Some pitying stranger sure is nigh;—
    Tell us, oh! tell us who thou art.

Sad is the lot the sightless know;
    We feel, indeed, but ne'er complain;
Here gentle toils relieve our woe—
    Hark! hark! that piteous sigh again.

If breath'd for us, those heaving sighs,
    May heaven, kind stranger, pity thee!
If starting tears suffuse thine eyes,
    Those tears, alas! we cannot see.

But ev'ry sigh, and ev'ry tear,
    And ev'ry boon thy hand has giv'n,
All in full lustre shall appear,
    Recorded in the Book of Heav'n.

age of admission for males is from fourteen years to forty-five, and for females from twelve to forty-five years; except in the case of the musical pupils, who, if of promising genius, are admitted at as early an age as eight years; or, if already partly instructed, may be received after the age of forty-five.

This charity, though established for the indigent, does not exclude those in better circumstances from receiving instruction on terms extremely advantageous to them.—It must not be expected, that in any institution of this nature, the profits arising from the labours of the Blind, can greatly contribute towards the expense of the establishment. Allowance must be made for the unavoidable waste of materials at first, in every kind of article which the Blind are taught to manufacture, as well as for the wages of teachers and attendants, and for the unproductive employment of the musical pupils. Besides this, it is to be considered, that as soon as their labour comes into profit, they are, and very properly, desirous of returning to their homes, to enjoy the benefit of the instruction which they have received. The great and proper object of such a charity is not the magnitude of the profit by work, but the number of helpless persons rendered capable of maintaining themselves, and of filling up their time with utility and satisfaction.

The women are employed in spinning yarn for window-cords, for sail-cloth and for linen cloth. The men, in making baskets, lobby-cloths (a coarse kind of carpeting for passages), bears (a species of door-mat), whips, and clock and window-cords. Of those manufactures, whips* appear to have been the most productive article. The making of baskets, though perhaps less profitable, is more useful for

---

* The manufacture of whips is since discontinued. January 5, 1799.

the Blind; as they are easily taught, in the course of a short time, to make good baskets and hampers; and may then return to their friends, and nearly, if not entirely, maintain themselves by following their employment at home. Their average receipt from the sale of the different articles manfactured in the house, has been, for the four preceding years, rather more than £500 a year. As a knowledge of the particulars of the different articles may assist persons engaged in forming similar establishments, I have prepared a statement of them for four years last past, from the annual accounts of the asylum. It is as follows:—

	1794.			1795.			1796.			1797.		
	£	s.	d.	£	s.	d.	£	s.	d.	£	s.	d.
Whips	128	12	0	182	1	10	63	10	4	92	16	10
White rope bears	14	18	11½	16	17	10	12	19	7	2	5	0
Tarred bears	61	1	7	58	4	1	62	6	1	62	18	11½
Baskets, Hampers, &c. ...	24	6	5½	11	11	0	53	9	8	79	13	11½
Points, Gaskets, &c.	6	14	8½	12	7	5½	32	17	0	64	13	9
Sheeting	36	4	7	37	19	8½	49	14	0	77	15	2½
Huckabac	17	10	5	10	1	5½	11	15	11½	27	18	8½
Untarred lobby-cloths ...	42	16	4	47	0	5½	55	5	8	29	10	10
Tarred ditto	15	16	1	23	19	11	49	2	3	79	14	2
Oakum	8	1	8½	9	15	1	4	8	1	7	15	5
Yarn	38	9	6	41	7	11½	51	9	3	0	0	0
Window-sash and curtain line	19	12	2	28	1	2½	38	14	10	38	12	6
Worsted mats	0	0	0	5	17	0	1	14	6	1	1	0
£	414	4	6	584	5	0	487	7	2½	564	16	4

Under so deplorable a calamity as the loss of sight, especially with the habitual idleness that attends youth and middle age without instruction, and without the means or power of occupation, a great degree of successful industry and exertion can hardly be expected. The benefits of the institution have been received with eagerness and gratitude. Of those admitted into the asylum, there are very few who have not fully answered the benevolent wishes of the conductors. Only three have proved incapable of learning; two have been dismissed for misconduct, and

one has returned to his trade of begging. There are ten,
who had been strolling fiddlers, and have since learnt a
trade in the school; but who have nevertheless resumed
their former occupation : and who can wonder at their
recurring to an art, which habit and want of sight must
have made pleasant, and almost necessary to them; when
he considers how great is the blank in the mind of blind
persons, and how much of that may be filled up by their
own music; though sometimes with less delight to their
hearers, than to themselves? They have, however, the
benefit of having learnt a trade, whereby in future they
may add to their other means of support. Of the rest
there were, at the commencement of this year, forty-nine
persons doing well in the house. There is one who is gone
out organist of the church of Halsall, near Ormskirk, who
is also a good basket-maker, and weaver of lobby cloths;
three, who have qualified themselves in music; one of
whom is now an organist, the other two* teachers. There
is one blind woman now maintaining herself by spinning,
and five men (one at Bury, one at Bristol, and three at
Liverpool), who are at present supporting themselves comfortably, at home, by making baskets and hampers.

The average fund of this charity arises from subscriptions and donations. The great disbursement consists in
wages paid the blind and their teachers; to which are to
be added some trivial expenses. The difference between
these and the nett produce of the goods manufactured by
the Blind, constitutes the expense of the charity; and
is supplied by voluntary subscriptions and donations,

---

* One of these is employed as a teacher at the asylum, and is capable of
quilling, stringing, and tuning instruments; those at the asylum being
wholly under his care. He is now providing very comfortably for himself
and his family, by tuning instruments, and teaching music, in the town of
Liverpool. 5 January, 1799.

amounting to about 650*l.* a year, and by the contributions of the friends, or parishes, of the blind persons employed. Upon my visiting the asylum to-day (3d of August, 1788), I found forty-three blind persons at work; sixteen of whom were females, and twenty-seven males. The allowance to them, for their support,* does not exceed five shillings a week; of which their parish is expected (or their friends, if able) to contribute a part. This has the effect of affording a bounty on work, and encourages very potently the acquisition and practice of habits of industry. If any persons refuse to apply, or are incapable of learning, they are dismissed the school, and their places supplied with more proper objects.

OBSERVATIONS.

THE loss of sight is in itself a very severe calamity; but it is a great aggravation of it, that the Blind are impressed with the humiliating idea, that they are useless in themselves, and in many cases a burthen to others; that their

---

* The Blind employed in the asylum continue to live with their friends, or (if strangers) are lodged and boarded in the town. A building is now erecting for the accommodation of such as have no domestic connexions at Liverpool. I take the liberty of recommending to the governors, the establishing for such persons on the establishment, *as wish to attend it,* a cheap dinner; such as those mentioned in the Society's Reports, No. 4 and No. 33, and inserted at the end of this Section, p. 137.

condition is considered as hopeless and irremediable ; as if the loss of one faculty were a sufficient reason for neglecting the cultivation of all the rest. To remove this prejudice, to call into action such other powers of body and mind as they may yet be enabled to exercise,—to alleviate, as far as may be, one of the greatest afflictions incident to our nature, and to afford active employment for those hours, which would be otherwise spent in gloom and despondency ; to render the Blind happy in themselves, and useful to society, is the noble and exemplary object of the asylum at Liverpool.

Instead of offering gratuitous relief, which does not appear well calculated eventually to diminish their misfortune ; instead of feeding and clothing them in a state of restraint and confinement, separated from their friends and connexions, and without occupation or exertion on their part ; the school for the Blind instructs them *to maintain themselves;* and while it leaves them an option of conduct and situation, affords them the power of benefiting by the charity as far as they think proper ; it preserves the ties of families, restores them to their friends, improved and advantaged in the means of life ; and combining the best parts of the best charities, it obtains all these great and importants objects with the utmost economy, and at a very trifling expense.

Schools of instruction for the Blind would be very useful as county charities ; to which any parishes or individuals, who contributed to the fund, should have a power of recommending objects upon certain terms. He who enables a blind person, without any painful excess of labour, to earn his own livelihood, does him more real service than if he had pensioned him to a greater amount ; and if the sums, which benevolence applies to support Blind persons *without* *their own labour*, were employed in instructing them * to *labour for themselves*, there cannot be much doubt, but that they would be sufficient to the object of maintaining all the well disposed Blind, who want relief in this country.

Of all their trades, basket-making has answered best for the poor persons themselves. In many other instances, the instruction of the Blind requires a different process, and a peculiar mode of education; but this art is soon learnt, and the business set up on a very small capital. In parishes, the teaching the necessitous Blind that, or some similar occupation, would be a blessing to them, and a great relief to the parish, on whom they must otherwise be pensioners for life.

I cannot avoid adding a wish that the Blind, after they have learnt a trade, might *all* be gratified with a little instruction in music, as a relief to their vacant hours. The loss of sight is generally supplied by the increased acuteness of the other senses. There has been no instance of a blind person at the Foundling-Hospital, who has not been instructed in music, and to whom that instruction has not proved a support and a blessing.

3rd August, 1798.

---

* An establishment has been formed at Edinburgh, for the indigent Blind, on the model, and from information derived from the committee of the asylum at Liverpool. There were twenty-two blind persons receiving the benefit of it in May, 1796. Another is now forming at Bristol. It is hoped that other places will follow the example. I may be allowed to add, that there would be both economy and kindness in giving the same kind of assistance to poor persons, who have had the misfortune to lose a limb, and thereby to be deprived of the common advantages of labour. In such cases, a little attention, and a *very little parochial assistance applied in time*, would prevent the sufferer from continuing to be a burthen to himself and the public.

LONDON:
PRINTED BY WILLIAM CLOWES AND SONS, Limited,
STAMFORD STREET AND CHARING CROSS.

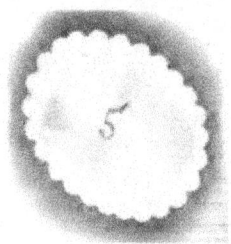

Plate IV.—Frontispiece.

LEARNING TO WRITE.

REPRINT 1894

AN

ESSAY

ON THE

Instruction and Amusements

OF THE

BLIND.

By DOCTOR GUILLIÉ,

DIRECTOR-GENERAL, AND PRINCIPAL PHYSICIAN TO
THE ROYAL INSTITUTION FOR THE BLIND AT
PARIS, KNIGHT OF THE LEGION OF HONOUR,
MEMBER OF THE ROYAL ACADEMY OF
SCIENCES, AND OF MANY OTHER
LEARNED SOCIETIES.

WITH ENGRAVINGS.

London:

PRINTED FOR RICHARD PHILLIPS;

SOLD BY JOHN SOUTER, ST. PAUL'S CHURCH-YARD;
L. J. HIGHAM, CHISWELL-STREET; AND BY ALL
BOOKSELLERS.

(*Price 8s. in boards.*)

1819.

REPRINTED AND PUBLISHED BY
SAMPSON LOW, MARSTON AND COMPANY, LTD.,
ST. DUNSTAN'S HOUSE, FETTER LANE, LONDON
1894

Edinburgh: T. and A. Constable, Printers to Her Majesty

TO

DR. JENNER,

OF BERKELEY,

THE EVER ILLUSTRIOUS DISCOVERER

AND

INTRODUCER OF THE PRACTICE OF

Vaccination,

WHICH HAS CONFERRED SUCH INCALCULABLE

BENEFITS ON THE WHOLE HUMAN RACE,

THIS WORK,

OF A DISTINGUISHED FRENCH PHILANTHROPIST,

IS DEDICATED

WITH PROFOUND RESPECT,

AND SINCERE ATTACHMENT,

BY

THE TRANSLATOR.

London, March 26*th,* 1819.

The Publishers issue this reprint, by the desire, and at the cost, of a gentleman who for many years has taken a deep interest in the welfare of the Blind, and believes that, owing to the recent legislation on the subject, the book will be found useful as well as interesting.

PREFACE OF THE TRANSLATOR

In Paris, the original of this interesting Work, which is calculated to rescue from the misery of idleness the most helpless of human beings, was printed at the Institution for the Blind, BY THE BLIND THEMSELVES; thereby serving as a practical illustration of the efficacy and value of the labours of the benevolent Author.

It is to be hoped that its translation into English, and its re-publication in this Empire of philanthropy, will lead to the establishment of similar Institutions among ourselves, and, consequently, that some future English edition may enjoy the same pleasing recommendation to public notice as the original French.

That the Work will produce such a gratifying result the Translator entertains no doubt; and he is persuaded that the characteristic ingenuity of Englishmen will lead even to many improvements of the French System, though the world

will ever have cause to acknowledge its obligations
to the amiable and persevering Guillié.

Nor is it in a public sense only that the Work
recommends itself ; it will serve to solace thousands of firesides, where no comfort has hitherto
appeared ; and while it amuses listless hours,
will enable those to earn their own subsistence,
who may hitherto have been a hopeless burden
to their sympathising families.

London, March 31*st,* 1819.

CONTENTS

PART III
Of the Instruction of the Blind.

Section I.

LIST OF ILLUSTRATIONS.

INTRODUCTION

As we commonly make use of the rapid, but not always sure, organ of sight, in order to discern the objects around us, we think that the blind can know nothing that exists, and can never escape from the narrow circle which surrounds them : they are considered as degraded beings, condemned to vegetate on the earth ; and it is thought that enough is done for them, when they have been taught to remember the names and forms of objects in common use ;—we are not sufficiently penetrated with this truth, that the blind who are not instructed are all their lives like new-born infants, who cannot provide for themselves : that they would die if not taken care of.

The education of those who have sight begins, we may say, from their birth : they easily imitate the sports of the companions of their childhood, and repeat their slightest motions ; they read the physiognomy of their nurse ; and the looks of a mother are their best lesson. All this is lost to the blind, entombed for ever in darkness. They are obliged to create everything, having seen nothing ; an action apparently the most simple to other children is a novelty to them. This is, undoubtedly, the cause of that silent and

A

timid attitude in the blind, during the first years
of their life, and of that habit of concentration
which never leaves them.

As it is ascertained that they are deprived of
the faculty of learning by imitation in their childhood, we should endeavour to supply this defici-
ency by method ; and all that is done afterwards
will be only with the view of putting them on an
equal footing with other men.

It would be a great mistake, therefore, to confound the blind with common children, and to
think they may be instructed in the same manner.
The teacher will never succeed, unless he is
thoroughly persuaded that the blind perceive
things quite differently from us ; that they do not
attach the same ideas to words ; in short, unless
he becomes the pupil of his disciple, and studies
with him.   Always obliged to examine what is
presented, or what is said to them, the blind contract very early, and almost *instinctively*, a great
habit of analysis : and we must, consequently,
expect from them the most original, most extraordinary, and sometimes also the most embar-
rassing questions.   The moral world does not
exist for this child of nature ; most of our ideas
are to him without reality ; he acts as if he were
alone ; he refers all to himself.   It is from this
deplorable state that we must endeavour to draw
him, by teaching him that there are relations and
ties of communication between him and other men.

But this instruction of the blind must advance

with an almost insensible progress; we must
not be in too great a hurry to gather the fruit;
it cannot be begun too early; for the first impressions they receive are never effaced, and it
is of great importance that these impressions
should be conformable to the direction we wish
to give to the blind.

It is evident that speech cannot imitate the
form of objects, and that there is no resemblance
between sounds and colours: teaching alone,
properly exercised, is understood everywhere,
without convention and without commentary; it
is the natural language of the blind. This, therefore, is the sense which it is necessary to choose
to be the intermediary between the man who
has only four senses and him who has them all;
and, in fact, it is on this principle that the whole
theory of their instruction is founded.

The blind, thus instructed, will not be a
calamity to their families, and the insurmountable barrier that was supposed to exist between
the man who sees and the man who does not
see, will be removed, if the ingenious process
invented for their instruction be put in practice.
Restored to society and to themselves, they will
one day bless the memory of those who erected
this monument of beneficence.

It cannot be said that those who formed a
system of instruction for the blind had neither
guides nor models; on the contrary, they had
the great advantage of walking in the footsteps

of those who had previously instructed them : they too could take advantage of the mistakes of their predecessors. The fruitless essays which many persons, all animated by the same spirit of charity, had already made, sufficiently showed what remained to be done ; but it required all the zeal and devotion of an ardent and enthusiastic man to undertake to write and arrange these scattered elements, in order to make a whole of them, with the addition of the results of his own experience.

The man who devoted himself to this work, and who founded the first school that existed in Europe for the instruction of the blind, was Valentine Haüy. The reader, I imagine, will be pleased to be informed by what chance he conceived the idea of his plan of instruction.

To the relation which he gives of it himself, 1 shall add the history of the establishment from its foundation down to the present time, together with the considerable meliorations that have been successively made.

'A novelty of a singular kind,' says M. Haüy,[1] 'attracted, several years ago, a concourse of people at the entrance of one of those places of refreshment, in the public walks, where the better sort of people go to divert themselves, now and then, in an evening.

'Eight or ten poor blind men, with spectacles

[1] Préa's *Historique*, p. 119.

on, placed by the side of a desk with music
on it, used to perform a discordant symphony,
which seemed to give great amusement to the
spectators. I, however, felt myself affected in
a very different manner, and immediately conceived the possibility of realising, for the benefit
of these unfortunate creatures, those means
which they were thus employing in such an
imperfect and ridiculous manner. "Does not
the blind man," said I to myself, " know objects
by the difference of their forms? Does he mistake the value of a piece of money? Why
should he not distinguish an *ut* from a *sol*, an *a*
from an *f*, if these characters were rendered
palpable, etc."'

The first asylum which beneficence opened for
young blind persons, was instituted in 1784, at
the expense of the philanthrophic society, which
intrusted M. Haüy with their instruction. This
society, so justly celebrated for its charitable
works, was at the whole expense of the establishment, which was settled in the street Notre-
Dame-des-Victoires. In 1785, the number of
pupils maintained gratuitously was twenty-five.
Their instruction was so far advanced by the
following year, that they were admitted to the
honour of performing an exercise at Versailles,
before the king.

On the 16th of February 1785, M. Haüy
submitted to the judgment of the Royal Academy of Sciences, a memorial, in which he ex-

plained the means he proposed to employ for the
instruction of the blind.

A report was drawn up by MM. Desmarets,
Demours, Vecq. d'Azir, and de la Rochefoucault,
commissaries chosen for this purpose, in which
they said, ' That the method of M. Haüy re-
sembled that of the blind man Payscaux,[1] and
of Mlle. Salignac ; that the process for the
study of geography was nearly the same as
that of M. Weissembourg, of Mannheim ;[2] that
M. Lamouroux had formerly got moveable characters cast for music, etc. etc.'[3]

Nevertheless, they admitted the printing of
books in relief was his own invention ; and after
having given an account of the operations performed in their presence, by the young Lesueur,
who was born blind, they concluded their report
as follows :—' We propose to the Academy to give
its approbation to the method which M. Haüy
has presented to it, and to exhort him to make it
public, and to assure him that it will willingly
receive any new account that he may give of his
efforts to carry it to the degree of perfection of
which it is susceptible.'[4]

The Institution thus subsisted, against a thousand obstacles, till 1791. At that period Louis
XVI. ordered that it should be maintained at the
expense of the state, and placed, with that of the

---

[1] Report of the Academy, p. 7.   [2] Id. p. 9.
[3] Id. p. 3.   [4] Id. p. 13.

deaf and dumb, in the old convent of the Celestines, near the Arsenal; and a law of the 21st of
July, confirming the degree of the directory of
the department of Paris, regulated the dispositions of its administration.

Another law of the 10th Thermidor, year 3,
separated the institution of the working blind
from that of the deaf and dumb, and placed the
first of these establishments in the house of the
Filles Sante-Catherine, street des Lombardes.
The number of the pupils was raised to 86, one
for each department, and the pension to 500
livres. There was then no administration nor
committee of superintendence to control the
operations; the steward settled the accounts with
his clerk.

The 26th Pluviose, year 9, a decree of the
consuls, which was executed rather suddenly,
ordered the working blind to be transferred
directly to the establishment of the Quinze-Vingts,
and the administration of them to be confided to
that hospital. In consequence of this measure,
the young blind, under the denomination of
blind of the second class, were confounded, for
the space of fourteen years, with the poor blind
people lodged in the hospital of the Quinze-
Vingts, though there was no other connection
between them than the similarity of infirmity.
The first of these establishments is one to which
persons may be admitted at all periods of life,
without having been born blind, and where each

individual lives by himself; while the other is a
college devoted to the instruction of persons born
blind, who are maintained there for a limited
time, living in common, subject to general rules,
and taught to gain a livelihood by work, and
who, after having been eight years in the institution, are restored to society.

We cannot but applaud the zeal of the administration of the Quinze-Vingts, and the efforts
it made to meliorate the situation of the young
blind, during the whole time it was charged with
the interests of the institution. But an invincible
obstacle constantly sprang up, and thwarted all
improvement, which obstacle was the incoherence
of the two establishments united together. The
degeneration became more sensible every day;
the regulations fell into disuse; the young blind
remained idle a great part of the day; the study
of music was almost their only occupation, as
they were no longer employed in manual labour,
and only went to two classes in the day. Everything, in short, announced the approaching ruin
of an establishment which, some years before, had
excited general interest.

The administration, convinced of the necessity
of early habituating to labour children who, for
the most part, belonged to poor parents, attempted
to employ them with advantage in the two manufactures of cloth and tobacco, which it established
in 1806, within the hospital, for the blind of the
first class, and the individuals of their families

who had their sight; but considerable losses soon obliged them to renounce both these enterprises, which, moreover, did not at all meet the charitable intentions of the administration : besides the great inconvenience of the old and young blind being brought together, their labour was useless, as it never could be profitable to them, since they only concurred in it as assistants, without learning, in all its parts, a business which they might afterwards follow elsewhere for a livelihood.

On the 8th of February 1815, the king, at the same time that he ordered the hospital to be replaced under the direction of the Grand-Almoner of France, also ordered that the institution should be separated from this hospital, that it should belong to the administration of the Minister of the Interior, and should be henceforward managed and governed by a special administration.

This transfer, retarded by the events of the year 1815, was effected on Tuesday the 20th of February 1816, and the institution is now placed in the ancient seminary of St. Firmin, rue St. Victor, No. 68.

Everything was to be done over again after this transfer, both as to arrangement and instruction ; but the most urgent point was the moral re-organisation of the institution : to change the spot without changing manners, to admit new scholars without having previously dismissed those whose presence was prejudicial would have been more dangerous than useful. It was necessary, therefore, to decide on this painful sacrifice ; it was necessary to return to their families a great number of pupils, the unfortunate depositaries of a spirit of insubordination and licentiousness which they had imbibed in their former habitation, and of which the tradition would have been preserved by them.

Forty-three pupils went out of the Quinze-Vingts, and were not admitted at St. Firmin. This ablation disorganised the different parts of the course of instruction ; but the zeal of the teachers overcame all obstacles : they laboured eagerly to form new pupils, and success crowned their efforts. At the present moment all is repaired. The classes are filled with pupils distinguished by their aptitude ; there are even several who already at the public exercises excite the astonishment and admiration of the visitors. We are happy, therefore, to seize this opportunity of doing the justice they deserve to our colleague Mr. Dufau, second teacher of the boys, and to Miss Cardeilhac, mistress of the girls, by publicly declaring the obligations which the administration owes them for the assiduous pains they have taken to obtain so rapidly such results.

This digression will, I hope, be pardoned ; I thought it necessary, in order to give a complete idea of the origin and progress of an establishment which, from its utility, seems so worthy of the interest it excites.

This treatise will be divided into three parts :

the first, comprising five chapters, will contain general considerations on the genius and character of the blind ; the second, which will contain two, will be allotted to memorials of the celebrated blind, who have distinguished themselves in the. sciences and arts ; the third, composed of twenty-two chapters, divided into two sections, will be especially devoted to an account of the proceedings employed in the Institution, and of the different modifications they have undergone down to this time.

I shall think myself happy if I have been able to attain the end I proposed to myself in this Essay. I did not wish to compose a merely speculative treatise, or a romance on the instruction of the blind ; I wished to offer to those who have not had the happiness of being instructed in this house the means of being so in the bosom of their family. I wished to prove, by the results of long experience, that the blind may be instructed in some sciences and some arts, as well as other men ; that they have dispositions which may be unfolded by methods peculiar to them ; and that, by the aid of divers mechanical professions, to which they are brought up, they may easily make a livelihood for themselves.

Far, therefore, from making a secret of the means that we employ, we should wish them to be known wherever there are any blind persons, and by so doing we only second the beneficent views of Government.

Our wishes are now realised in part, as several institutions, founded on the same principles as ours, and according to instructions requested of us, have been established in different countries.[1] How glorious it is for France, so fruitful in useful establishments, to have been the first to give the impulse to this new species of beneficence, and to see other nations eager to admit among them, and naturalise our institutions!

Happy children! may we now say with assurance to the blind, you will be comforted! no longer, as formerly, will you be repulsed by your fellow-creatures, and considered as a degraded species : the cruel exception which separated you from the rest of men will no longer exist ; the wrongs of nature are repaired ; your

---

[1] The mother of the Emperor Alexander founded in 1806, at Petersburg, an institution for the blind of that vast empire. The Archduke John of Austria, in the journey which he made to Paris, in 1815, took notes himself for a similar establishment at Vienna. M. Kalina de Jatenstein, a philanthropist, no less charitable than disinterested, has instituted, at his own expense, a school for the blind at Prague. He was acquainted with none of our processes before he visited the establishment at Paris ; and we considered it a duty to furnish him with the necessary materials for completing what he had so well begun. It is affirmed that the King of the Low Countries is going to found in his kingdom, where there are so many blind, an institution similar to ours, and for this purpose a very minute detail of our management and mode of teaching has been already transmitted to the Dutch Ambassador. The friends of humanity would learn with pleasure that the two fine asylums at London and Liverpool, where the blind receive no instruction, were converted into schools similar to that of Paris, which all the English of distinction, who come to the Continent, are eager to visit.

infirmity and the misfortune of your birth will be no longer a reproach. It is to make honest men and sincere Christians of you that generous persons hold out their helping hand, and strive to create means for your instruction : they felt how desperate your situation would be if you were not supported and encouraged by the consolations which religion showers especially on the unhappy. Ah ! how guilty would you be were you ungrateful ! Never forget this noble intention of your benefactors, and consider that an opposite conduct would be the greatest outrage you could commit against their memory.

As for me, the depositary of this precious tradition, I congratulate myself every day on having been called to co-operate in so good a work, and I flatter myself, that when nothing of me remains but some inanimate clay, you will still preserve among you, my dear children, the remembrance of him who consecrated his life to your happiness and prosperity.

INSTRUCTION OF THE BLIND

PART I

GENERAL CONSIDERATIONS ON THE GENIUS AND CHARACTER OF THE BLIND

CHAPTER I

Whether the loss of one Sense turns to the advantage of the others

A QUESTION has long been agitated, whether the loss of one sense increases the intensity of the others ; whether those who are born deaf and dumb, or blind, have any real advantages over other men, resulting from a peculiar development of the senses they have remaining. The solution of this important question might throw a great light on the explanation of several phenomena of the human mind, and in this respect it deserves the thorough attention of philosophers and metaphysicians.

Struck with the error into which many persons have fallen in this respect, I joined my researches on the blind to those which my illustrious colleague, the Abbé Sicard, had made on the deaf and dumb, in order to learn what was the cause of it, and I became convinced that neither the deaf nor the blind are superior to other individuals enjoying the use of all their senses : the address which is observed in the blind, with respect to the touch, and the aptitude of the deaf and dumb to seize all the characters of the physiognomy, result from the necessity they are in, at first, of almost continually making use of the sense of touch to supply the want of sight ; and the others, of employing their sight to supply hearing and speech ; the organ is in every respect similar to that of those who enjoy their sight, and though the person born blind, that was operated upon by Cheselden, after the extraction of the cataract no longer perceived objects by the touch as he did before, it was not that, by recovering his sight, he lost the faculty of touching, but only that he then employed it merely as an auxiliary sense, and to correct the sight. The opposite effect happens to persons who become blind after having seen during some part of their life : both require to form the education of the new sense they gain ; the senses which replace those that are lost are more exercised ; they sometimes acquire, I allow, an exquisite fineness, which greatly augments their susceptibility ; but the eye of the deaf can never hear, and the fingers of the blind will never see. It would result from the false principle we are endeavouring to destroy, that an individual who had lost two, and even three senses, would find a compensation in the superior faculties of those which remained ; thus, the young girl, who was a few years since at the Institution of the deaf and dumb, and who was at once deaf, dumb, and blind, and thus reduced to two senses, should have found, according to this strange supposition, in touch and smell alone, the means of acquiring ideas, more or less perfect respecting light, sound, and speech. Nothing is more contrary to evidence ; she had only a vegetative existence ; she was deprived of the impression or vibration, which external objects make on our senses, which for that reason are called *organic sensations*, and cannot exist when the organ destined to perceive and transmit them does not exist ; her soul, as if imprisoned, must have been condemned to absolute inaction.[1] Nevertheless, this young girl, to whom it was impossible to com-

---

[1] Le Roy, a physician, who published in 1812 a very interesting dissertation on laughter, made many experiments on this young person, in order to excite her to laughter, which, as we know, is the immediate effect of a peculiar mode of intellectual perception (that I shall call *mental perception*) produced in us by a ridiculous or droll idea, the idea of derision. We may easily suppose he did not succeed ; he only excited a convulsive laugh, which is the result of a factitious sensation, occasioned by the mechanical excitation of the skin, known by the name of titillation or tickling.

B

municate anything, was perhaps susceptible of
those interior emotions, foreign to the organic
sensations, which seem to depend more on the
mind than the senses ; and have more relation to
insensible and moral, than to physical and sensible objects. I sometimes saw her face colour,
and appear in the state we are in ourselves, when
shame or fear surprises us. She then perhaps
experienced joy or sorrow, pleasure or displeasure,
inclination or aversion ; and as our pleasures and
pains evidently belong to our soul, of which they
are the direct perceptions, without belonging to
the body to which it is united, she might very
likely feel those emotions which we have called
sentiments of the soul, and do not even require
the necessity of reflection.

Let us conclude, that if, as has been well
proved, there is nothing in our mind which has
not come by the senses,[1] when deprived of these
intermediaries, we must necessarily want the
ideas they give us, because no compensation can
physically re-establish the equilibrium when it
has been once destroyed. The art of the instructor
of the blind, and of the deaf and dumb, consists
therefore in conducting artificially to the mind,
by new methods, the ideas it would otherwise
have been ignorant of. The trouble of such an
education, with the obstacles to be overcome, if

---

[1] Nihil est in intellectu quod non prius fuerit in sensu.—
ARISTOTLE.

known, would afford a convincing proof that the
privation of one, or of several senses, is the
greatest and most irreparable of evils, and can
only exist at the expense of our happiness, and
of the improvement of our faculties.

CHAPTER II

Of the Memory of the Blind

THE memory of the blind is prodigious. Can this phenomenon, certain as to its existence, and unknown as to its nature, depend, as is supposed, on their not being distracted by sight? or may there be any cause in their organisation to unfold this faculty in a particular manner?

Though the occasional cause on which memory depends in its exercise and functions will probably always remain a mystery, let us cast a rapid glance over this precious prerogative of man, and examine on what the increase of that of the blind can depend.

The memory has been compared to a magazine in the form of archives, in which is deposited the impression, more or less exact, of an infinity of things of which we have had the image or sensation; an impression which our mind renews and revives at pleasure, and which, when excited, gives, in some sort, a new existence to the ideas and images of the things which it knew a length of time before. Locke compared it to a brazen

tablet filled with characters, which time insensibly
effaces, if the graver be not sometimes passed
over it. Malebranche says that it consists in the
traces which the animal spirits have imprinted on
the brain, which are the cause of the facility that
we have to remember things; and he adds that
the reason why old people lose the memory of
past things is, that their fibres are mixed with
many humours, which they cannot dissipate,
because they want heat. I have mentioned this
last definition of memory, by a celebrated man,
only to prove how much we are indebted to the
physiological sciences, for the precision and
exactness which the moderns employ in their
definitions; for if the name of Malebranche did
not impress a certain degree of respect, one could
not help calling this ridiculous definition of
memory a downright raving, void of sense and
reason.

There is in man a memory of sensation, and a
memory of intelligence. The first recalls his
perceptions of physical feelings; the second
recalls his reflections, judgments, reasonings,
speculations, and the pleasures and pains of the
moral order of things. He differs in this from
the brute, which has only a memory of sensation,
and never of intelligence, because knowledge
purely sensitive does not imply a substance
properly spiritual.

It is principally with this second memory of
intelligence that the blind are eminently pro-

vided. They are deprived, it is true, of the means
which those that see have of forming an artificial
memory ; but they have perhaps an internal
method, resulting from the very great facility
they have of analysing, as I shall demonstrate
later.

According to Charlevoix,[1] in Japan the records
of the most important events are confided to the
memory of the blind. The annals of the empire,
the histories of great men, or the ancient deeds
of families, are not more certain documents than
the memory of these illustrious blind men, who,
communicating their knowledge to each other,
form an historical tradition which nobody pretends to contradict. They have academies where
they take degrees, and exercise themselves not
only in cultivating their memory, but also in
putting what they know into verse, and decor-
ating the finest passages of history with the
charms of poetry and music. They have their
general, their officers, and magistrates, and enjoy
great consideration.

In order to find a physical reason for the
inconceivable phenomenon of the memory, some
philosophers have supposed, ingeniously enough,
a sort of *natural harpsichord* in the brain, composed of an infinite number of strings, of which
an innumerable quantity are in unison, so that,
as in the artificial harpsichord, the string that is

---

[1] *History of Japan*, chap. ii. p. 203.

touched shakes the one in unison with it, and makes it vibrate, without shaking the others.

In this hypothesis our memory would have its effect in the following manner : the name of Alexander being pronounced, makes an impression on our ear, and agitates in the *sensorium* the fibre to the vibration of which is attached, in our mind, the idea of Alexander.

This fibre being shaken, shakes successively all those in unison with it, and which were moved simultaneously at the time we read the life of that great captain.

It consequently shakes, round the seat of the soul, the different fibres, the vibration of which renews and revives all the successive ideas that have anteriorly existed in us, on the subject of Alexander, who, we thus recollect, was the son of Philip, enslaved Greece, dethroned Darius, invaded Asia, vanquished Porus, ravaged Egypt, and finally died at the siege of Babylon.

The effort we make to learn by heart, and to retain anything, shakes successively and repeatedly a series of fibres that are in unison in the brain, or which, if we may say so, the effort maintains so harmonised and arranged, that the vibration of one of them must put all the others successively in action, and give rise in our mind to so many renewals of ideas or sensations.

In perfect memories, the shaking of one of these fibres communicates the vibration to all the others, because the unison is in them. In faulty

memories there are vacant spaces, because some
of the fibres previous to the unison relax, and
lose the harmony, and in losing it remain mute
and motionless.   (L. Para.)

This interior memory is that which we suppose the blind make use of instinctively.   Penetrated with this idea, we carefully avoid, either
in teaching them, or even in conversing with
them, to make them pass too abruptly from one
idea to another, especially when the ideas are
dissimilar, and would leave too great a number
of degrees among them unoccupied.   We endeavour, on the contrary, by proceeding analytically,
to connect what we wish to teach them with
what they already know, and, to use the theory
explained above, always to touch a string that
vibrates with another.   In this manner, the impressions are profound and permanent.   The
blind, who, moreover, take their time to do well
what they do, always act successively.   Nothing
shocks them so much as incoherence.   Helvetius
pretends that a great memory is a phenomenon
of order ; [1] that it is almost entirely factitious,
and that, between men well organised, a great
inequality of memory is less the effect of an unequal perfection in the organ which produces it
than of an unequal attention in cultivating it.
According to him, it is to order that the sagacity
of the mind is often owing, and the extent of

---

[1] *De l'Esprit*, chap. iii., discourse 3.

the memory always. It is also the want of order, an effect of indifference for certain sorts of study, which in some respects absolutely deprives persons of their memory, who, in other respects, seem endowed with a most extensive one. The immortal Bishop of Hippo said, in this same sense, *Ordo ducit ad virtutem*.

The memory of the blind may possibly then be connected with the spirit of order which they generally possess, and to the habit of classing their ideas in their head, in such a manner that they can easily awaken a whole series. We see very few blind who, when insane, are in that state of mental alienation which necessarily implies an incoherence in the ideas, and a total divergency in the functions of the brain. Their concentrated attention is the cause why objects, which would only leave an insensible impression on us, are very strongly engraved on their mind. This faculty, which is conditional, is troubled or weakened in them, as in those who see, by disease, delirium, imbecility, etc., but in a much less degree, and this naturally follows from the principles we have established above. I have had occasion several times to verify this fact in the different acute maladies in which I have treated them.

It has been said that a great memory is seldom allied with a sound judgment. This assertion, though long since repeated, is far from being demonstrated : Lesueur, the Massieu of the blind, the first pupil who was instructed by the methods we follow at present, had a prodigious memory, and an exquisite judgment; and almost all the blind I have known united these valuable qualities to a high degree. I conceive that there may be individuals endowed with a mechanical memory, and without judgment ; but I cannot understand how one can have a perfect judgment without memory. *Memory is a tool of marvellous service,* said Montaigne, *and without which judgment can hardly perform its office.*[1] Some persons have carried the faculty of retaining to an almost incredible degree. Seneca informs us of himself, that by a great effort of memory he could repeat two thousand detached words in the same order that they had been pronounced. Muretus relates that a young Corsican had found the art of forming his memory in a surprising manner : he could retain three thousand words, Greek, Latin, barbarous, without any connection between them, and most of which had no meaning. He recited them in the same order in which they had been dictated to him, descending from the first to the last, and afterwards ascending from the last to the first. He asserted that he could even learn thirty-six thousand with the same rapidity. He taught his method to a Venetian nobleman, whom he put in a way of doing the same as himself, in a very short time.[2] We have seen how Feinagle

---

[1] Montaigne, book ii. chap. 17.
[2] Muretus, *De quorundam admirabili memoriâ.*

formed artificial memories in our days. But it is not for this species of memory that the blind are remarkable ; they are principally distinguished by that which connects itself with facts or ramifications susceptible of being unfolded by judgment and reflection.

CHAPTER III

On the Faculties that are developed in the Blind, and of the Pre-eminence of some of these Faculties over those of Persons who have their Sight

I SHALL have very little to say in order to develop this question, which, in many respects, falls into those we have already treated. I think I have sufficiently proved that the loss of one sense does not turn to the profit of the others, and that nothing can be a compensation to the blind for the loss of the organ of which they are deprived; but if there be no *physical* compensation, Providence has not left them entirely without consolation, and has endowed them with a great fertility of imagination, and much rectitude of judgment.

I shall not speak of Homer, who composed his admirable poems when blind; nor of Milton, who has spoken of light in such a delightful manner at the beginning of the third book of *Paradise Lost*; nor of our immortal Delille, and so many other illustrious blind; this would be going out of the range I have prescribed to myself: by such proofs as these I feel I should weaken my arguments. I have known persons born blind, who were excellent poets, or learned musical composers ; I have seen others very clever in business, and who managed their affairs so well that it would have been very difficult to have deceived them.

To prove that the blind have certain qualities which display themselves in a much higher degree of perfection than in those who have sight, is, in other words, to show into what errors the latter are drawn by the sense of sight.

The blind have a great facility of decomposing their ideas, either analytically or synthetically. Two blind persons, both pupils of this Institution, may be cited as striking examples of this fact : the first is Paingeon, who, by the spirit of order with which he is endowed, has acquired transcendent knowledge in mathematics, and after having gained, in 1806, all the first prizes in the general competition of the four lyceums of Paris, was named, by the Grand Master of the University, professor of mathematics in the Lyceum of Angers, where he teaches with the greatest success ; the other is J. Delille (now in the house of the Quinze-Vingts), who has carried very far the philosophy of the French language ; a perfect steadiness, and an admirable precision in his definitions, are the particular characteristics of this person, whom we are proud of having formed.

This great facility of analysis and decomposition that is observed in those who are born blind is much more intense while they are in a state of nature ; we perceive that it grows weaker, when, from ideas that have been communicated to them, they adopt our processes and formulas of reasoning, undoubtedly because acting then like us, with an instrument less than we have, they are badly served. In the first state, on the contrary, they are men with four senses, performing operations like us, and not supposing it to be necessary to have five, any more than we could see how a man would act that had six.

Malebranche, and Berkeley after him, were, therefore, very absurd to maintain, without any proof, the striking idea of a world merely fantastic, and that our senses deceive us in everything, while it is well proved, on the contrary, that there is no testimony more certain than that which they give us ; since, whenever any of these natural conductors is wanting, we are obliged (as in teaching the blind, and deaf and dumb) to create artificial means in order to convey to the mind the ideas which, in the natural state, they are destined to convey to it.[1]

---

[1] A company of five persons, each with only one sense, would be very amusing ; there is no doubt but they would all look on each other as madmen. The more peculiar notions any one sense possessed, the more extravagant would it appear to the others : the result would be, that the most extravagant among them would infallibly think himself the wisest ; that each sense would scarcely be contradicted but in what it knew best, and that they would be almost always four against one. (Diderot, *Letters on the Blind.*)

With respect to their physical perfection, nobody disputes their pre-eminence over us in the
exactness of the perception of their ideas by
feeling, that sense so eminently exact, which
rarely deceives, and which Buffon, therefore,
called *a geometrical sense.* We know to how
many mistakes our sight exposes us ; and how
often we are obliged to join feeling with it not to
be deceived ; this, however, is not always practicable, and we are often deluded by the information of our eyes.

CHAPTER IV

Moral State of the Blind;—Nature of their
Ideas

Touched with that compassion which the misfortunes of others excite in all men of feeling,
every one is eager, from a very laudable curiosity,
to be informed of the moral state of the blind.
We are desirous to know if, on many things, they
have the same ideas as ourselves; what are the
natural sentiments which affect their minds, and if
they are feeling and grateful. We inquire if they
are active and curious; if they are susceptible of
ennui; what are the ideas they form of ugliness
and beauty; if they have the same opinions as
we on good and evil, and on our acquired ideas;
if the disposition to atheism with which they are
reproached is founded or not; in short, what are
their tastes, habits, and defects?

However wide may be the circle of these questions, I shall endeavour to answer them succinctly,
without entering into a crowd of details foreign
to my subject, and which moreover belong to
metaphysics; I shall confine myself to what
experience and observation have taught me;

happy if I can excite towards those unfortunate
beings, whose history I write, that tender interest
which they inspire in me, and which so strongly
attaches me to them !

The want of sight not only deprives the blind
of the sensations which that organ gives to those
who have sight, but also extends its influence
over all their thoughts, which it modifies and
distorts ; all their ideas, therefore, are false or
contrary to the notions we have, because, as
Condillac has well observed, coloured nature has
no existence for them ; it is blindness which
plunges them in the ignorance in which they are
of decorum, and which deprives them of the
sentiment of social decencies. Modesty, which
is one of the graces of youth, is to them almost
an imaginary being, though they have a sort of
timidity, which, it is true, belongs perhaps rather
to fear than shame, but which greatly augments
their embarrassment in certain circumstances.

Unfortunate in all their relations with other
men, they are very imperfectly acquainted with
those emotions which draw us towards each
other, and decide our affections and attachments.
Sensibility has not, for them, those charms
which make us place it in the rank of the
sweetest as well as the most amiable virtues.
Unhappy creatures ! their situation, which forces
them to be on their guard against all the world,
makes them often place in the same class their
benefactors and their enemies ; and without

c

meaning it, perhaps, they appear ungrateful. It is these motives which make them form connections with the blind rather than with those who have sight, whom they consider as a different class of beings. Is it that they apprehend our inconstancy, or distrust our superiority, or else find more points of association among each other ?

They will easily be excused, when we reflect on the number of signs that are lost to him who is deprived of sight. Those external motions, which are painted so expressively on the countenance, that faithful mirror of the soul, do not exist for them. They are continually, in their relations with other men, as one is with an individual whom one knows only by correspondence : we know perfectly well that he exists, but we cannot conceive how.[1]

If not very open-hearted, on the other hand, nature gives them an ample compensation by endowing them with a prodigious activity of imagination and an insatiable desire of knowledge, which, in them, is a substitute for many

---

[1] As of all the external demonstrations which excite in us commiseration and ideas of suffering, the blind are only affected by complaint. I suspect them, in general, of inhumanity. What difference is there, to a blind man, between a man who makes water, and a man who without complaining is bleeding ? We ourselves, do we not cease to feel compassion, when the distance, or the smallness of objects, produces in us the same effect as the privation of sight does in the blind ? (Diderot, *Letters on the Blind.*)

affections that they want, or at least for the expansion which such sentiments might have. This state of their imagination banishes *ennui*, which is one of the least inconveniences of blindness ; for we meet with very few blind persons who have not formed some sort of occupation for themselves, and with complete success.

Obliged to judge of men and things intrinsically, they must necessarily obtain truer results than we : moreover, as I have repeatedly said, they see things in a more abstract manner than we, and in questions of pure speculation are less subject to be deceived ; for abstraction consists in separating in thought the sensible qualities of bodies from each other, and error commonly springs from a defective separation. They have no need, like us, to guard themselves against the illusions of the senses, since they cannot be seduced by appearances : the charms of the countenance, the richness of clothes, the sumptuousness of apartments, the dignity of office, and the prejudices attached to birth, are nothing to them : it is the moral man whom they appreciate. How much more certain must their judgments be, in this respect, than ours !

A soft and sonorous voice is to them the symbol of beauty. They know pretty exactly, by the compass of the voice, what is the stature and size of the person who speaks, the largeness of the room they happen to be in, etc. But with what nicety of discernment must these attentive observers judge, by this means, of the temper and of certain shades of character which escape us, because we have not the same interest in remarking them ? By a sort of anticipated intuition they see the soul through its covering.[1]

There are, in fact, more relations than has hitherto been supposed between the divers degrees of the vocal organ and the disposition. In this point of view, one might form a curious comparison between animals and man, by forming the first link of the chain by those savage beasts, the terror of the forest, and continuing it down to those peaceable animals who are born in our enclosures to feed and clothe us. This study, very worthy of a philosopher, would lead, I am persuaded, to some useful results.

The blind have been accused, in general, of atheism very unjustly. Those who have advanced this strange assertion, were either not sincere, or had some interest in propagating an error which might prop up some others. Why give such an idea of those who have the greatest want of the consolations which religion showers on the unfortunate and unhappy ? Do they not know in part the works of the Creator ? The

---

[1] Sir John Fielding, a relation of the author of *Tom Jones*, who lived in our time, was blind ; but this did not prevent him from filling, with great distinction, the place of *chief magistrate of the police office*, in London. He kept in his mind the description of many hundred thieves, and was never mistaken when they were brought before him.

taste of fruits, the sweetness of flowers, the song of birds, and the vicissitude of the seasons: must they not make them sensible of the existence of the admirable Architect of the universe?

Nevertheless, I will not justify them entirely from the reproach of impiety, which has been made against them with some foundation. I am more convinced than anybody that that law, anterior to all sensible impressions, which God gave to man on drawing him out of nothing, is engraved in their hearts; but I am obliged to confess also, that they do not always follow the impulse of that interior voice, which approves and consoles when we do good, and torments and gnaws when we do evil: conscience, in short, has not that influence over their actions which it has over ours. It is easy to deduce the consequences that flow from a similar state, and what may be their ideas on good and evil, and on the notions we have acquired.

I have never known a blind atheist; but if we happened to meet with one so unfortunate as not to acknowledge the Creator in his works, we might repeat to him what Dr. Holmes formerly said to the celebrated Saunderson, who had expressed some doubts on this point: *Put your hand on yourself, the structure of your body will dissipate so gross an error.*

Like us they wish for what is the most difficult to obtain. All blind people have a decided taste for independence and liberty. Nothing, how-

ever, is more contrary to their real interests than
the use of a thing which they could only abuse.
The art of those, therefore, who are with them,
consists less in satisfying them than in making
them believe they are satisfied. By this means
we avoid exasperating the natural defects they
may have, all of which appertain more or less
to their infirmity, which cannot be imputed to
them as a crime.

Their self-love, which is the most prominent
of all their defects, and, perhaps, the origin of
all the others, is compensated by some valuable
qualities; their invincible patience and extreme
tenacity in their enterprises, render them capable
of surmounting the greatest obstacles without
ever being disheartened.

CHAPTER V

*Parallel between the State of the Blind and that
of the Deaf and Dumb*

PEOPLE are constantly asking us, which are the
most unhappy, the deaf and dumb, or the blind ?
To what is the gaiety of the one and the profound melancholy of the other owing ? We
shall resolve this question to the advantage of
the blind, because we really think them less unhappy.

Strangers to all that passes around them, the
deaf and dumb, who see everything, enjoy nothing. Like Tantalus, whom fiction represents
as devoured by an inextinguishable thirst in the
midst of water, they are continually subjected
to cruel privations. An insurmountable barrier
separates them from the rest of mankind; they
are solitary in the midst of us, unless we know
that artificial language which the talent and
charity of their ingenious teacher has created
for them ; and the habit which they have of
reading the countenance is even very often a
subject of anxiety to them. They do not always
guess right ; doubt and uncertainty increase their
impatience and suspicions : a serious cast, like

melancholy, then invades their countenance, and proves that with us they are in a real state of privation. Obliged to concentrate their thoughts in themselves, the activity of their imagination is thus greatly increased ; and as attention and judgment necessarily follow the perception of ideas, they fatigue themselves prodigiously. Few deaf and dumb persons, therefore, are to be found in the lists of longevity, because the frictions are too lively, and to use a common, but exact expression, the sword wears the scabbard.

The blind, more favoured than these children of silence, enjoy all the means of communication with other men. No obstacle hinders them from hearing or being heard, since the ear, which has been so philosophically defined the vestibule of the soul, is always open to them. The exchange is rapidly made, because they speak the vulgar language. Though condemned to live in profound darkness, their infirmity, in a manner, turns to their advantage, because being secure from the illusions of the sight, they are not, like us, assailed with fright : all the phantoms created by the exaltation of our imagination are unknown to them.

They walk with equal security both by day and night ; while we, constantly exposed to form false judgments of the objects that present themselves to our eyes in the different situations in which they are placed, cannot deliver ourselves entirely from the sort of internal fear which the darkness of the night makes almost every man feel, and on which is founded the apparition of spectres and frightful figures which so many people say they have seen.

It would be easy to prove that the blind have several other advantages over the deaf and dumb; but it would be exposing myself to repeat, without much advantage, what I have already said; besides, would it not be idle to insist too long on a parallel between dumbness and blindness, when we can have no choice between these afflicting mutilations, which we can only lessen by attention when they exist?

PART II

BIOGRAPHY OF BLIND MEN WHO HAVE BEEN
ILLUSTRIOUS IN THE SCIENCES AND ARTS.

CHAPTER I

Of Blind Men illustrious in the Sciences

HISTORY has preserved the remembrance of
blind persons who acquired great knowledge
by themselves before there existed any method
of instruction for them. Their number is considerable ; but I shall confine myself in this
chapter to point out the most remarkable, and to
indicate the authors I have consulted ; for the
more extraordinary things are, the more authen-
ticity should be given to them. I have thought
that this short biography of celebrated blind persons would be agreeable to the reader, and
would serve at the same time to prove the utility
of the present mode of instruction, in which the
various methods invented, down to the present

time, have been collected together and methodically arranged. We shall see in the third part
of this work the improvements they have undergone, and with what ease the blind are now instructed.

The number of the blind was very considerable in Asia and Italy in the time of the Romans.
The great number who wrote at that epoch on
the diseases of the eyes might serve as a proof
of this ;[1] but the mode of instruction employed
in those times has not reached us.

Diogenes Laertius and Thrasyllus relate,[2] that
several philosophers deprived themselves voluntarily of their sight, in order to meditate more
freely. Among others, they quote Democritus
of Abdera. But is it probable that this philosopher, who laughed at everything, blinded himself in order to philosophise, which can be done
just as well with the possession of one's sight?
The testimony of a great man may sometimes give credit to the most absurd fables ;
and it was probably Cicero who gave some con-

---

[1] I endeavoured to demonstrate the truth of this assertion at
the opening of my Lectures on the Diseases of the Eyes, delivered
at the Institution in 1816. A very interesting dissertation on
the antique stones which the oculists used for seals, by M.
Tochon d'Annéry, Member of the Institute, proves also that
there were many apothecaries or empirics in Italy, who sold
remedies against the complaints of the eyes (Κολλούριον) contained in earthen vases, of which that learned academician has
given a description.

[2] Diog. Laert. lib. ix. ; Vossius, De Philosoph., chap. 11.

sistency to this :[1] for I think it would have been unworthy of a philosopher to treat himself as a criminal ; and crucifixion, and privation of sight were, in those times, punishments reserved for criminals.

The Roman orator says that Diodotus, his master of philosophy, applied with more assiduity to the study of that science after having lost his sight ; and, what appeared to him a prodigy, he taught geometry with so much precision that his disciples had not the least difficulty to understand how they were to trace the most complicated figures.[2]

Historians relate things of Diodotus, the Stoic, calculated to excite the greatest admiration. He was at once a philosopher, a musician, and geometrician ; but what they say will appear incredible, though he never saw, he taught geometry so well, that he left nothing unexplained to his numerous disciples.[3]

Aufidius, a Roman citizen, who lost his sight in his youth, was not the less distinguished in the pursuits of literature, and even wrote a Greek history.[4]

Eusebius, the Asiatic, having become blind at

---

[1] Democritus impediri etiam animi aciem aspectu oculorum arbitrabatur. (Cicero, *Tusc. Disp.*, v. 39.)

[2] Cicero, *Tusc. Disp.*, v. 39.

[3] J. Zahn, *Speculae Physico-mathem. Hist.*, tom. iii. cap. 6.

[4] *Id., Sens. extern. Mirab.*, Sect. 2.

the age of five years, acquired great knowledge and profound erudition, and lectured with great facility.[1]

St. Jerome has left us the history of Didymus of Alexandria, his master, of whom he speaks with the greatest respect. This illustrious blind man, who lost his sight at the age of five years, flourished in the fourth century. Rufinus Paladius, Isidore, and several other celebrated men, were his disciples. He acquired vast knowledge by having the sacred and profane authors read to him ; was one of the most able mathematicians of his time ; and applied himself especially to theology, for which he had a particular taste. The professorship of the famous school of Alexandria was confided to him. He composed several excellent works, the chief of which is his *Treatise on the Holy Ghost*, translated into Latin by St. Jerome. Didymus was as pious as learned ; nevertheless, his attachment to the opinions of Origen, whose books he had commented, caused him to be condemned, after his death, at the council of Lateran. St. Athanasius and St. Anthony had the greatest esteem for him. He acknowledged one day to the latter the affliction he felt at being deprived of his sight ; when the holy hermit made him the following answer :—
' I am astonished that so judicious a man as you should regret a thing which is common to the

[1] Cassiodorus, *De Inst. Div. Litter.*, cap. 5.

most contemptible animals as well as to man, and that you are not delighted to possess one which is only to be found in saints and angels, by which we see God himself, and which lights in us the flame of such a luminous science.' Didymus died in 398, aged eighty-five years.[1]

Nicaise, of Malines, was in great reputation in the fifteenth century, from the extent of hi knowledge. It was considered as a prodigy, that being blind from the age of three years, he could perfect himself so much in the study of the most sublime sciences. He taught the canon and civil law publicly in the university of Cologne, and quoted from memory long passages which he had never seen. Having been chosen a doctor of Louvain, the Pope allowed him to be consecrated a priest. He employed the rest of his life in preaching, and died at Cologne in 1492. Urithème and Valère have made mention of him in the *Bibliothèque des écrivains de Pays-Bas.*

Schegkius (James), born at Schorndorf, in the Duchy of Würtemberg, taught philosophy and medicine at Tübingen, for thirteen years, with great success. When he lost his sight he was so little affected by it that he refused the assistance of an oculist who offered his services. He

---

[1] Hyeron, *De Vir. Illustr.*, cap. 109 ; Socrates, lib. iv. cap. 25 ; Rufinus, lib. ii. *Eccles. Hist.*, cap. 7, et *Platina.*

said *he had seen many things in life he would rather not have seen, and would even have wished on some occasions that he had been deaf.* He published several treatises on divers points of philosophy, medicine, and controversy. He died at Tübingen, in 1587.

Fernando (John), born in Belgium, whose father was a Spaniard, and very poor, was blind from his birth ; he surmounted these two great obstacles to literary advancement, and became a poet, logician, and philosopher, and even so excellent a musician, that he would compose pieces out of his head equal to those of the first musical composers.[1]

Asconius (Pedianus), an historian, who lived several years without sight, wrote, notwithstanding, with great elegance, treatises on grammars, in which there is no trace of his infirmity.[2]

We read in the annals of the town of Prague, that a blind Scythian, whom Charles IV., Emperor and King of Bohemia, met near Nuremberg, before he was elected, recognised him, though he was disguised, and answered with great propriety all the questions he put to him on the succession of the kings of Bohemia, and on the state in which the kingdom would be in future. What has been said of that prince, who ruined his house to gain the empire, and then ruined the empire to re-establish his house, is

---

[1] Zahn, p. 114.   [2] Fulgosus, lib. viii. cap. 7.

only a paraphrase of the last answer of the blind Scythian.

Schomberg (Uldaric), born in Germany about the beginning of the seventeenth century, who became blind at three years old with the small-pox, devoted himself, notwithstanding, to the pursuits of literature, which he taught with honour at Altorf, Leipzig, Hamburgh, etc.[1]

Bourchenu de Valbonnais, born at Grenoble in 1651, became blind very young, a short time after the naval fight of Solebay, where he was present. This accident did not prevent him from publishing a *History of Dauphiné*, in two volumes folio. He had made profound researches concerning his country, and also published a *List of the Nobility of Dauphiné*.[2]

Saunderson (Nicholas), was born in 1682, in the province of York. To name this illustrious blind man is almost to have told his history, his extraordinary talents having been so famed for near a century.

He went through his classical studies very well, and was drawn by inclination to the study of mathematics, of which, from the smallness of his fortune, he was obliged to give lectures that were well attended. He spoke to his pupils as if they had been blind, which must have given him a great advantage over them. He explained

---

[1] Harknock's *Alt und neu Preussen*, 1684.
[2] Feller.

the works of Newton on light and colours. I shall mention later what is the nature of such demonstrations which appear miraculous.

Whiston having abdicated the Professorship of Mathematics at Cambridge, Saunderson was named his successor, in 1711. It was at this period that he published his *Elements of Algebra*, an extraordinary work, and full of singular demonstrations, which a man with sight would not, perhaps, have imagined.

He invented a palpable arithmetic, and a board pierced with holes, in which placing pegs or pins of different sizes, that had a different value according to the place they occupied, he performed with facility the most complicated operations. The reader will be gratified, I imagine, to find here the figures of these boards, and the description of them by Hinchliff, the pupil, friend, and successor of Saunderson, in the work which he published at Dublin, in 1747.

His board for calculating was thin and smooth, and rather more than a foot square; it was fixed in a little frame, the edges of which were raised a very little above the board, which contained a great number of parallel lines of the same number, forming right angles with the first. The edges of the board had grooves, at the distance of about two inches from each other, and to each groove belong five of the parallels we have mentioned, each square inch being divided into one hundred small squares. At

D

each point of intersection, the board is pierced with a little hole destined to receive a peg: for it was by means of these pegs that he expressed the numbers. He employed two sorts of pegs, or pins, of different sizes; at least their heads were different, and were easily distinguished by the touch. He had a great quantity of these pegs, in two boxes, that were always before him, the points of them being taken off. Let us now see what use he made of the pegs and the board.

For this purpose we shall first observe, that each numerical character has, in the board, its particular square, composed of four other small contiguous squares, described above, and which, by that alone, left a small interval between each character; and this character was different, according to the difference of size or situation of one or two pegs, of which it was always composed. He had formed the following system: a great peg in the centre of the square (and this was its only place), signifies a zero; I shall, therefore, designate it by that name; its principal function consists in preserving the order and the distance between the characters and the lines. This zero is always present, excepting in the only case where the unity is to be unmarked, which is expressed by the substitution of a small peg, in place of the large one in the centre. If two is to be expressed, the zero must be put back in its place, and the little peg placed precisely

PLATE I.

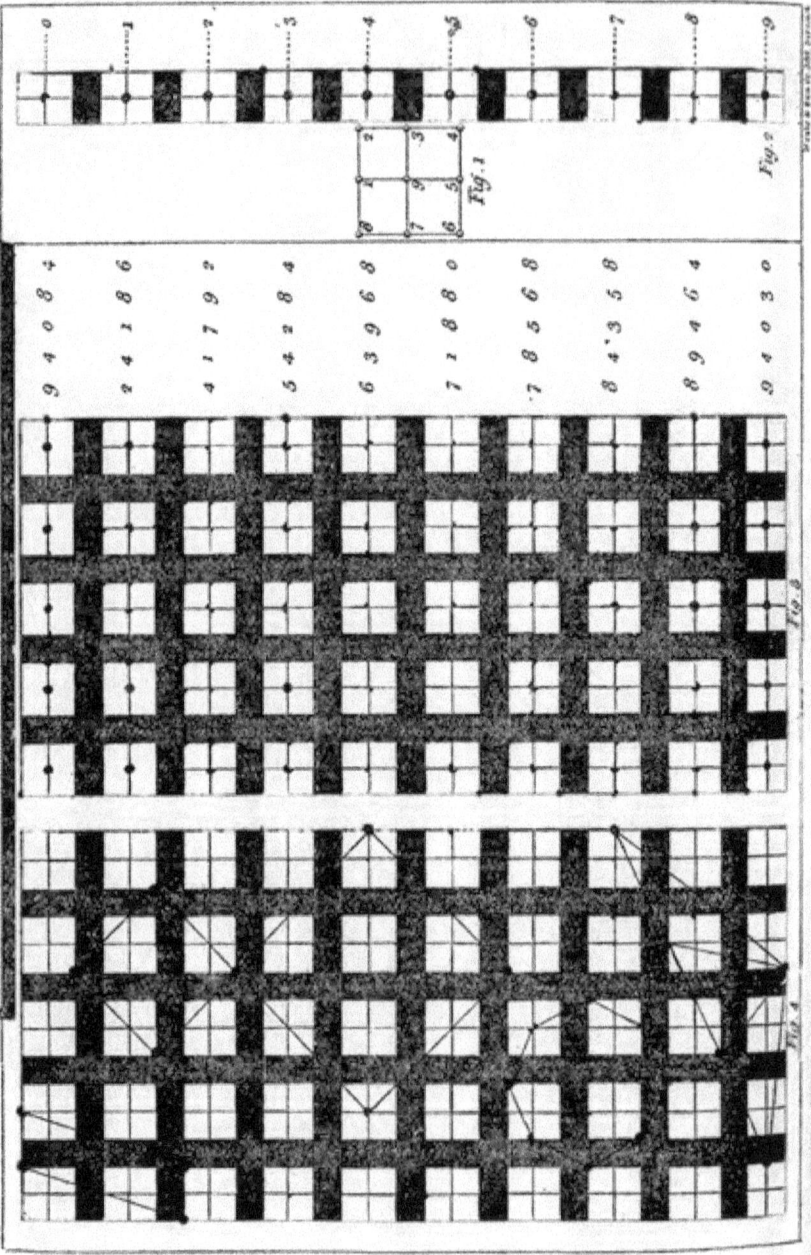

TABLES OF SAUNDERSON.

Fig. 1

Fig. 2

Fig. 3

Fig. 4

above it. To express three, the zero must remain where it is, and the small peg be fixed to the superior angle towards the right. To express four, the small peg descends and follows the zero immediately. To express five, the small peg descends as far as the inferior angle to the right. To express six, the little peg must be below zero. To express seven, the place of the small peg is the inferior angle to the left. To express eight, the small peg ascends to the level of the zero. In fine, to express nine, the small peg occupies the superior angle to the left.

By this invention the ten numerical characters could be known without trouble, by means of the touch alone. But that the reader may form a more distinct idea of these characters, it will be sufficient to cast his eyes on Plate I., figs. 1 and 2.

The great pegs, or zeros, which are always in the centres of the small squares, and most commonly at equal distances from each other, served him for guides to preserve his line, to fix the limits of each character, and to prevent all the other mistakes that might have happened. As three of the perpendicular parallels suffice for a single character, three of the horizontal parallels suffice for another line, and so on without any danger of confounding them. In this manner, he would have at once on his board some lines of characters one above another, and, consequently, divide with ease one number from another.

Besides, he placed and displaced his pegs with inconceivable quickness.

The patterns of this arithmetic, reduced to vulgar numbers, consist in arithmetical tables, which he had calculated and kept for his own use. But one cannot conjecture what object he had in view in calculating them. They seem to have some relation with the tables of natural sines, secants, and tangents, and consist of four pieces of solid wood, having the form of rectangular parallelopipeds, and about eleven inches long by five and a half broad, and sometimes half an inch thick. The two opposite faces of each of these parallelopipeds are divided into small squares, precisely like the board described above, but have holes only in the necessary places, the pegs being fastened. Every face contains nine little arithmetical tables, each of ten numbers, and each number is composed of five characters.

The figure No. 3 is the model of an addition, the numbers of which are represented on the right side : the same board became, if wanted, geometrical, and served to demonstrate the properties of rectilinear figures. He placed each of his pegs, or pins, in the angular points, and by surrounding them with a silk thread, he made all the figures apparent which he wished to form, as is seen on the figure No. 4. By means of the table we now use at the Institution, and the ciphers that have been contrived, the blind calculate in the same way as those who have their sight, and without any arbitrary convention.

Saunderson's touch was so perfect, that by running over a suit of metals he could distinguish the true from the false. He perceived the least vicissitude of the atmosphere. Assisting one day at some astronomical observations, he perceived whenever a cloud passed between the sun and him ; which was the more extraordinary, as he was not only deprived of sight but even of the organ.

He had some good qualities; but his morals did not correspond with his talents : he is even reproached with some shameful excesses, unworthy of a great man. He died at Cambridge, in 1739, at the age of fifty-six.

Sir Henry Moyes, a Scotchman, who lived in our days, lectured extremely well on the Newtonian philosophy. He was a good chemist and musician, and an excellent mathematician.

Dr. Blacklock, of Edinburgh, born blind, is considered in England as a good poet.

M. Pfeffel, of Colmar, who lost his sight when very young, in consequence of a violent ophthalmia, has composed some very pretty poems, principally fables,[1] some of which have been translated into French by Degerando. He was privy councillor of the Margrave of Baden ; and

---

[1] 6 vols. 8vo. Colmar, 1791.

established at Colmar a military school, where
people of the first families sent their children.
The Prince of Schwartzenberg and the Prince
of Eisenberg, who were brought up there, are
proud of having had this learned blind man for
their master. M. Heilman, now a pensioner of
the Quinze-Vingts, was also his pupil, and does
him the greatest honour. M. Pfeffel died at
Colmar in 1809.

Weissembourg, of Mannheim, became blind
at the age of seven. He wrote perfectly well,
and read with characters he had contrived for
himself before he had ever seen any. He was
an excellent geographer, and composed maps
and globes, which he used for studying geography. He had also invented an arithmetical board, which differs but little from that of
Saunderson.[1]

The blind Du Puiseaux is too well known to
render it necessary to enter into many details
concerning him. Everybody has read Diderot's
Letter on the Blind, and is acquainted with the
knowledge of that extraordinary man. He was
the son of a professor of philosophy in the University of Paris, and had attended, with considerable proficiency, the lectures on chemistry and
botany, in the king's garden. After having dissi-
pated a part of his fortune, he retired to Puiseaux,
a little town on the Gatinais, where he established

---

[1] *Journal de Paris*, April 1784.

a distillery of liqueurs, which he used to go and sell every year himself at Paris. He was original in all he did : it was his custom to sleep during the day, and rise in the evening : he worked all night, because, he said, then he was disturbed by nobody. When his wife got up, she found everything perfectly well arranged. He spoke very sensibly of the qualities and defects of the organ he wanted, and answered with great exactness the questions that were put to him. Being asked what idea he had of a looking-glass ? 'It is a machine,' said he, 'which places things in relief far from themselves, if they are properly placed with respect to it. It is like my hand, which I must not put by the side of an object when I want to feel it.' He put some whimsical questions on the transparency of glass, on colours, etc., to Diderot, who visited him at Puiseaux. He asked if it was only naturalists who could see with the microscope, and if astronomers were the only people who saw with the telescope ? if the machine which enlarges objects was bigger than that which diminishes them ? if that which brings them nearer was shorter than that which makes them farther off ? He thought that astronomers had their eyes differently formed from other men, and that one could not pursue the study of such and such sciences without eyes that had particular faculties for that purpose. 'The eye,' said he, 'is an organ, on which the air should have the same effect as my stick on my hand.'

He had the memory of sounds to a surprising degree, and recognised by their voice persons whom he had only heard once. He could tell if he was in a street or a blind alley, in a large or a small room. He estimated the nearness of fire by the degree of heat; the fulness of vessels by the noise which the liquid poured into them makes in falling; and the nearness of bodies by the action of the air upon his face. I knew a blind man at the Quinze-Vingts (Levé), whose hearing is so perfect, that on going into his room he can perceive if any of his furniture has been displaced, any curtain taken down, etc.

Somebody once asked Du Puiseaux, if he would not be very glad to have his sight? 'If it were not for curiosity,' said he, 'I would rather have long arms; it seems to me that my hands would teach me better what is passing in the moon than your eyes or your telescopes; and besides, the eyes cease to see sooner than the hands to touch. It would, therefore, be as well to improve the organ I have, as to give me the one I want.'

Being out of humour one day with questions which inquisitive persons were putting to him: 'I perceive very well, gentlemen,' said he, 'that you are not blind; you are surprised at what I do; why are you not astonished to hear me speak?'

He made use of characters in relief, to teach his son to read, who never had any other master.

M. Hubert, of Geneva, an excellent naturalist,

author of the best history of bees and ants. On reading the descriptions which this learned blind man has given of those insects, one would suppose them to be the composition of a clear-sighted man, very well versed in this branch of natural history ; Hubert, however, had no other assistant in this great work but his servant, who told him the colours of the insects, whose form and size he afterwards perceived by the touch, with the same ease as he knew them by their buzzing when they flew in the air. This laborious writer has also published a work on education, very much esteemed.

Lesueur (Francis), born at Lyons, the 5th of August 1766, of very poor parents, lost his sight at the age of six weeks ; he went to Paris in 1778, and begged at a church door, when M. Haüy, discovering he had a disposition for study, took care of him and taught him, promising him a sum of money equal to what he got by charity.

Lesueur began to study in October 1784. Six months after, he could read, compose with characters in relief, and print ; and in less than two years had learned the French language, geography, and music, which he knew very well, for his intelligence and penetration were wonderful. This astonishing young man was for the blind what Massieu afterwards was for the deaf and dumb. He was successively repeater to his companions, head of the printing concern, and

steward of the Institution.   He died a few years
ago, a pensioner of the Quinze-Vingts.

It is painful for us to say, that Lesueur was
ungrateful towards his benefactor and master, to
whom he owed everything, and that he deserved,
from his conduct, the reproach of ingratitude,
which is made, with some foundation, against all
blind persons.

Avisse, born at Paris, was one of the most
distinguished pupils of the Institution.   His
father, who kept a furnished hotel in the *rue
Guénégaud*, destined him for the sea.   He went,
when very young, on board a vessel that was a
slave-ship, in the quality of secretary to the captain.   He was struck by a blast of wind on the
coast of Africa, and lost his sight by a violent
inflammation that followed.

His parents got him admitted into the Institution for the blind, where, in a few years, he became professor of grammar and logic.   He wrote
a comedy in one act, and in verse, entitled *La
Ruse d'Aveugle*, which was acted in Paris ; also
a scene in verse, the title of which was *L'Atelier
des Aveugles-travailleurs*, and several other
pieces, printed in one volume 12mo, second
edition, 1803.   He died scarcely thirty-one years
old, regretted by his family and friends, at the
moment when he gave the greatest hopes.

Were we not afraid of hurting the modesty of
several blind men now living, we should have
cited with pleasure M. le Chevalier Pougens, who

is now concluding a great work begun at Rome in 1777, which contains the most curious and most interesting researches on the origin of the French Language; M. Isaac Roques, of Montauban, the more surprising, as he formed himself; and many others, chiefly pupils of this house.

CHAPTER II

*Of the Blind who have distinguished themselves
in the practice of the Arts*

THE number of the blind who have distinguished
themselves in the arts is almost as great as of
those who have excelled in the study of the
sciences.   It is not less surprising to see these
unfortunate beings, deprived of a sense so necessary to the exercise of the arts, succeed perfectly
in divers mechanical professions, and to a certain
degree, rival those who have sight, in promptitude
and dexterity.   If we except painting and the
application of colours, there are few things they
cannot do, either singly or together, especially
when they are directed by well-informed and
intelligent persons who have their sight.

It is very desirable, therefore, that the repug-
nance people have to employ the blind could be
got over, and that they might be employed in the
different works in which they succeed.   It would
be at once an act of charity, and a means of
improvement for them, which would turn to the
advantage of those who employed them.

We shall now give a succinct account of the

blind the most distinguished in the arts, as in the
preceding chapter, and thus complete the biography of celebrated blind men.

Stengel relates, that in 1602, a young cabinet-
maker at Ingolstadt, who was polishing a bronze
tube, inadvertently laid it down on some powder,
which exploded and destroyed his sight. He
was carried to an hospital full of old infirm
people, where he fixed himself in a retired spot,
in order to work at his ease, and formed a little
room of boards round his bed, which he decorated
with pictures. He afterwards made, without
any other instrument than a coarse knife, two
pepper-mills, with wheels and teeth, and every
thing necessary for grinding. One of these mills
was so well made, that it was judged worthy of
being sent to Munich to be placed in the museum
among other rare and curious things, and where
it may be seen at this day.[1]

Sir Kenelm Digby relates some extraordinary
things of his son's tutor, who was so completely
blind that he did not perceive the light of the
sun. He could beat the cleverest chess-players,
and knew almost all other games. He went,
without a guide, all through the house, and sat
down at table with so much ease and confidence,
that it was impossible for strangers to perceive
he was blind. When he heard anybody speak
for the first time, he was never mistaken with

---

[1] Laurentius Stengelius, *Lib. de Monstris*, cap. 16, § 10.

respect to their size and shape. When his scholars were reciting before him, he could tell what posture they were in, and what gestures they made, and could easily distinguish a dark day from a clear one.

We have already observed in speaking of Saunderson, that the blind (those even in whom the organ is destroyed) distinguish light from darkness, and a fine summer day. Those who have preserved the globe of the eye, but do not see, *amaurotics*, for example, call this *un point de vue*. They think themselves very happy with this advantage, which is much envied by their companions in misfortune, though it is of no use to them. On what can this extraordinary phenomenon depend, which we observe every day in this house? It is difficult to tell; for we are far from thinking that the blind see by the skin, as a modern philosopher has asserted, who certainly was no great physiologist.

A butcher of Bologna, mentioned by Aldrovandus, could tell by the touch the weight of the beast he had to kill. He knew weights and moneys; rode on horseback, and performed all the other business of a butcher.

De Piles saw in Italy a blind man, about fifty years old, full of genius and intelligence, and an excellent drawer. He met him in the Justiniani palace, modelling in wax a statue of Minerva. This man could, by the touch, discover precisely the forms and proportions of the originals.

The Duke of Bracciano, who saw him at work, had some doubts of his being completely blind; and to be certain of it, he made the blind man take his picture in a dark cave; but it was a perfect resemblance. It being objected to him that the duke's beard helped him to know him, he offered to take the portrait of one of his daughters, which he also drew perfectly like.

I saw, says De Piles, by this famous blind man, the portraits of the late King of England, Charles I., and of Pope Urban VIII.; and in France, that of M. Hesselin, all perfectly well executed. He found some difficulty in representing hair, because it is moveable, and all his art was in drawing.

We have seen in our days, M. Buret, one of the ablest sculptors in the Academy, who, falling blind at the age of twenty-five, in consequence of the small-pox, did not cease working.[1]

Gambasius (John), of Volterra, lost his sight at the age of twenty, and remained ten years in that state, without having the least knowledge, even of the elements of sculpture. All at once, he felt a desire to try and make a statue, and having felt all over a marble statue, which represented Cosmo de Medici, he made one of clay, so like as to astonish everybody who saw it. His talent for statuary improved so much, that

---

[1] Derbyshire lately afforded an example of a blind surveyor and able constructor of roads.—TRANSLATOR.

Prince Ferdinand, Grand Duke of Tuscany, sent him to Rome to model the statue of Pope Urban VIII., which was also very like. He afterwards made many others with equal success.

A Dutch organist having become blind when very young, was only the more expert in his profession. He acquired, besides, the habit of distinguishing by the touch different kinds of money, and even colours:[1] those of playing cards could not escape the fineness of his fingers, and he became, by that means, a formidable player, for in handling the cards he knew those which he gave to others as well as those he kept for himself.[2]

Chauvet, born blind, was for several years organist of Notre Dame de Bonne-Nouvelle, at Paris. The amateurs of good music were always eager to have him.

Miss Paradis, of Vienna, who lost her sight at the age of two years, in consequence of an apoplexy, was the admiration of all Paris at the spiritual concert in 1784. She had a great talent for composing, and had found a means of writing herself what she composed, by figuring the harmony. She first began with cards, which

---

[1] I shall mention hereafter how the blind ascertain some colours; but it is not by the touch. Boyle was wrong in saying of a man at Maestricht, from testimony undeserving of credit, that he distinguished colours by the touch, which is impossible. The blind do not discover the colour, but the effect which it produces on coloured bodies.

[2] Lecat, *Treatise on the Senses*, p. 11.

she pricked with needles ; but this first attempt proving unsuccessful, suggested to her the idea of another process, our ignorance of which we regret the more, as it was infallible, and of easy execution.

Among the objects of curiosity in the Museum at Copenhagen, are medals struck by the blind, and a superb sideboard of ivory and ebony, made by a Norwegian artist, who was blind.

In Italy one frequently meets with blind people, who offer travellers pretty baskets, which they make with rice-straw, and beads that are made with cherry-stones, very prettily worked.

I saw a milliner's shop in Paris, where blind girls, directed by a mistress who had her sight, made gowns and other sorts of work. In the *Ephemerides Naturæ Curiosorum* is a history of a blind man, of Würzburg, who sewed very well. At Halberstadt also, there was a blind man who, among other tricks, would thread a needle perfectly well.[1]

---

[1] *Ephem. Germ. cur. dec.*, secundo anno, 1, obs. 71.

PART III

OF THE INSTRUCTION OF THE BLIND

———•———

FIRST SECTION

———•———

CHAPTER I

Origin of the Paris Institution

IT was a fine thought of that monarch who, on
his return from a war which he thought necessary
for the glory of religion, instituted an asylum for
three hundred knights who had lost their sight
in Egypt.[1]   This house, owing to the piety of
Louis IX., escaped the revolutionary vandalism,
and still subsists at this day, under the denomination of the Royal Hospital of the Quinze-Vingts :
three hundred poor blind persons, of all ages,
successors of the three hundred knights, are

---

[1] In 1260.   The Quinze-Vingts were then in the *rue Saint
Honoré*, facing the *rue de Richelieu*.   In 1780, the Cardinal de
Rohan, then Grand-Almoner, had them transported to the ancient
hotel of the *Mousquetaires Noirs, rue de Charenton, faubourg
St. Antoine*, where they now are.

maintained and lodged there, at the expense of the state.

The creation of the Institution of the Young Blind, by Louis XVI., under very difficult circumstances, excites, perhaps, more admiration than that of the Quinze-Vingts. Louis XVI. owed nothing to the young blind; St. Louis was bound by gratitude towards those, who having abandoned their country to follow him into Asia, had participated in his reverses and bad fortune.

The generous heart of Louis XVI., pitying the lot of the young blind, had no other motive than to snatch from wretchedness, and from the contagion of vice, unfortunate beings, whose only crime was the misfortune of their birth. His noble mind suffered at the sight of so many of his subjects being exposed to want, and forced, in order to prolong a painful existence, to implore the compassion of the public : he thought their situation would be meliorated by affording them instruction,—and the Institution was created.

Penetrated with gratitude for this benefit, we have neglected nothing to fulfil the wishes of the founder. It will appear from the following exposition of the studies and labours of the young blind, and from the augmentations and meliorations made by our predecessors as well as ourselves, whether we have done all that depended on us to render the establishment confided to us worthy of its royal origin.

If we had not already, in different parts of this

work, spoken with sufficient detail, of the manner of instructing the blind, we should have prefixed to this third part a special chapter on the mode of instruction to be followed ; but this mode being only the application of the processes we are going to describe, we have preferred reserving for each of the following chapters the observations which the practice of teaching has given us occasion to make, in order that there may be more connection and precision in the details.

The order and distribution of the chapters are indicated in the following table, which is conformable to the progression we observe in the studies and works.

FIRST SECTION.

Instruction.

Chapter I. Of characters in relief, and of reading.
    II. Of the impression of books in relief.
    III. Of books for the use of the blind.
    IV. Of writing.
    V. Of geography.
    VI. Of languages.
    VII. Of mathematics.
    VIII. Of vocal and instrumental music.
    IX. Of the means of communication between the blind and the deaf and dumb.

SECOND SECTION.

Manual Labours common to both Sexes.

Manual Labours peculiar to the Boys.

Some other trades which had been attempted
for the blind, such as the art of making models
in plaster and wax, the binding and boarding
of books, the manufacture of cloth, joining, etc.,
have been given up, either because they were
too difficult to learn, or because they would not
have been very useful.

CHAPTER II

Of Characters in Relief, and of Reading

ALL those who have wished to instruct the blind, and have performed it with success, were convinced of this truth, that the objects we wish to make them acquainted with, and the form of which those who have eyes perceive by their sight, must be rendered sensible to them by the touch. Consequently, the object of all such attempts has been to make them acquainted with the letters that we use ourselves, or to compose for their use arbitrary figures, to which a conventional value may be assigned; for it was only at a much later period that the teaching them our alphabet was thought of.

The first signs were nothing but the Illyrian or Sclavonian alphabet modified, which begins like most of the ancient alphabets, by *a*, *b*, *g*, *d*, *è*, *z*, etc., of which the invention is attributed to St. Jerome, because he made use of it for the translation of the Vulgate. This alphabet had undoubtedly been preferred to all the others, on account of the square form of the letters, which, it was thought, would make them better to be known by the touch than ours. I am

sorry I cannot give here the figure of these
singular characters, which were soon abandoned,
as they did not offer more advantages than
common characters.[1]

Afterwards moveable letters were made on
small thin tablets of wood, about eighteen lines
high by six broad. They were placed on a
board with grooves, and were made to slide on
it, by the side of each other, in the same way as
has been since done for the small figures of reading by echo. This process, very defective for
teaching the blind, is well enough for enabling
them to teach persons to read who have their
sight.

It was with similar letters that Usher, arch-
bishop of Armagh, who died at Camberwell towards the end of the seventeenth century, was
taught by his two aunts, who were blind.[2]

As early as the sixteenth century, letters in
wood had been cut to instruct the blind; but
instead of making them project, they were made
hollow : the fingers could not feel the circumference of the letters as with those in relief;
they plunged into the hollow, and the blind perceived, though with more difficulty, the form of
the letters. When an impression was made with

---

[1] The figure of these letters may be seen in the excellent
Typographical Manual of Fournier, vol. ii. p. 226, No. 68.
Edit. 1766.

[2] *Biogr. Brit.*, London, 1773.

these plates, the letters remained white, and all
the rest appeared black.[1]

Rampazzetto had published, in 1575, examples
of letters carved in wood, which he dedicated to
St. Charles Borromeo; but these plates, which
were not preferable to those of Francis Lucas,
offered the same inconvenience, that of the cohe-
sion of the letters, and consequently the necessity of engraving as many plates as pages, as
is done at present with stereotype impressions.[2]

In 1640 a notary at Paris, called Peter
Moreau, had moveable leaden characters cast
for the use of the blind; but disgusted by the
difficulties he met with, or not caring to advance
the money necessary for this undertaking, he
gave it up, and merely undertook to make
punches and matrixes of new characters, in the
style of writing; a discovery which has procured
him a name in typography.

Other persons had attempted to give the blind
an idea of letters by figuring them on large
pin-cushions, with inverted needles. The blind
derived a double advantage from this method,
as he learned the form of the letters and exercised his fingers in running over the extremity of
these points; it was by this ingenious process
that Miss Paradis had learned to read.

---

[1] *Arte de Escrivir de Francesco Lucas*, dedicated to Philip ii.,
King of Spain, Madrid.   4to, 1580.
[2] *Essemplare di piu sorti di Lettere di M. Gio Francesco
Cresci*, Milanese, scrittore in Venezia.   4to, 1575.

Moveable letters of wood have also been made, like those which printers use for bills to be posted up; but all these insulated letters had the inconvenience of not being able to be collated in great numbers, and could only serve, at most, to make the blind acquainted with the alphabet.

As people cry very loud to make the deaf hear, they think it is necessary to present to the blind objects of very great dimension, that they may be more easily felt, which has given rise to the great letters I have already mentioned. We do not sufficiently consider that the blind, who can only have successive ideas of the objects which he touches, must necessarily at first form different opinions of things, which, though identical in their form, differ in size. He must perform a secondary operation in order to bring together his first ideas, and finally to judge by comparison, after having run through the whole series of intermediary ideas. Do not we do the same thing when we see a drawing in miniature? We do not recognise it always immediately, and we should not even recognise it at all if the reduction were carried too far: *because the cessation of a colour is to the eye what the cessation of resistance is to the touch.*[1]

The blind Du Puiseaux made use of wooden letters with a tail, which he connected together

---

[1] *Of Signs, and of the Art of Thinking,* vol. iii.

by means of a metal skewer, which traversed each tail, as blacksmiths join the iron letters that are used for tamping barrels.

This form of letters and the method of uniting them was already a great improvement; but as a substitute for writing it still remained to discover the possibility of making these letters so far independent of each other that they could be taken off separately, and replaced when required, by others.

The first characters were cast by a pewterer, but were very imperfect, as he had neither punches nor matrixes, and cast them in sand. In 1783 the Philanthropic Society had punches engraved and matrixes struck, with which characters were cast by Fournier. M. Rouillé de l'Étang, then treasurer of that society, paid the expense of them.

Without falling entirely into the error of those who formerly attempted to make the blind acquainted with our characters, the letter-founders, who forty years ago cast the first letters in lead, made them much larger than was necessary (about six lines high), always supposing that they would be more easily recognised than those of two lines, for example, which we now use. Experience has since proved that it is not the size but the perfection of the form of the letters which helps the blind to distinguish them, for they recognise completely the smallest printing type (the *nonpareil*). When their fingers are

ALPHABET ENGRAVED ON WOOD.

a b c d e f g h i j k l m n
o q p r s t u v x y z &

CAPITALES.

A B C D E F G H I J
K L M N O P Q R
S T U V W X Y Z

insufficient they touch the objects they wish to ascertain with the point of their tongue, and are then never mistaken.

These first characters being found to be of too large dimensions, new punches were cut, and an assortment of characters was cast in the foundry of Vaflard, nearly similar to those which we make use of at this day.

To give an idea of these characters, which are read from left to right like common writing, while printing characters are read, on the forme, from right to left, we have had the twenty-five letters which compose the alphabet of the blind engraved on wood, placing them in a direction suitable for printing.

In adopting this form of letters, which is very remote from the ordinary form, no regard has been paid either to custom or regularity; the only object has been to make them easily known by the touch, thinking that whatever difference there may be between these letters and common letters, this alphabet was, nevertheless, much more suitable than any that had been made down to our time, and the letters of which were foreign, or connected with nothing like those I have spoken of above.

We have made considerable changes in the new punches, which the administration has lately had engraved by Lyons, an engraver and caster of characters, and for that purpose we have consulted the oldest blind pupils, and combined their

observations with ours, in order to render this
reform as useful as possible.

The *e* is now more rounded than in the preceding casts, so that the blind no longer confound
it with the *c* and the *o*. The two sides of the
u are a little more separated, which prevents
this letter being confounded with the *a*. The
upper part of the *k* has been lengthened, and the
external angle is more open. By means of this
correction it will no longer resemble the *h*, etc.
In general the letters are more opened, and
their dimensions in breadth has been a little
augmented, which has prevented the former mistakes, and at the same time has given them more
elegance and solidity.

The metal of the first cast was too soft, and
accordingly the characters that were produced
were afterwards rounded off. In the materials
of the last cast there was a much greater quantity
of regulus of antimony than in the first. The
common proportion is from fifteen to eighteen
pounds of antimony to a quintal of lead for
printing types. The proportion varies according to the size of the type ; it increases for very
fine ones, and diminishes for those that are less
so. Ours, which are subject to strong pressure,
should be composed of one part of antimony to
three of lead, the better to resist the frictions.

Our characters differ from those of printing
types, not only because the letters are turned in
another direction, and are not proper for printing

PLATE II.

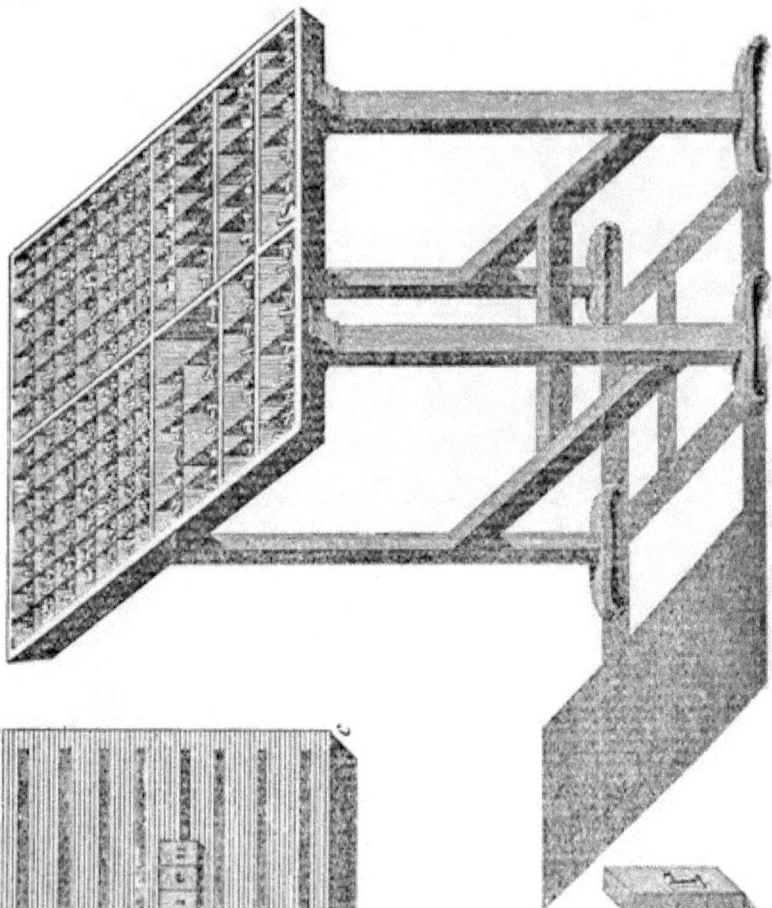

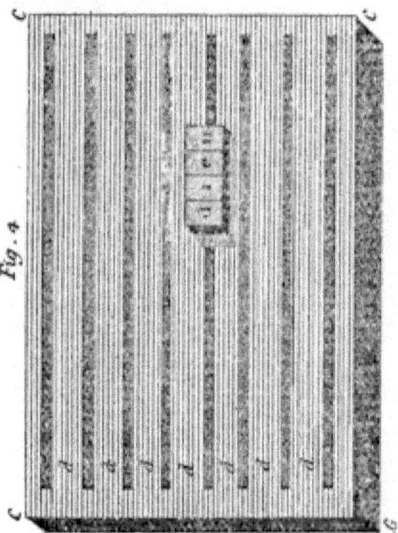

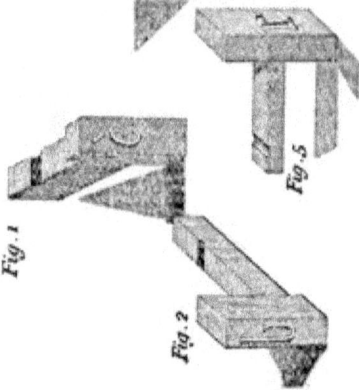

Fig. 3

Fig. 4

Fig. 1

Fig. 2

Fig. 5

black ; but also because the tail (*see fig.* 1) is much larger than it commonly is to support a letter of that size (*French canon*), and because the letter rests on a transversal part (*fig.* 2) equalling in extent two-thirds of the length of the tail. The object of the transversal part is to stop the letters that are placed on the composition board, which I shall describe hereafter.

In the beginning, the letters, similar in the inferior part to common letters, had no transversal chevron, and not being supported on the board, they only rested on the bottom : this hindered the boards from being transported from one place to another, as may be done at present. The chevron has another advantage, that it offers a support to the extremity of the fingers, and affords, by the contrast of a plain with an elevated surface, the means of ascertaining the relief.

The letters are placed in two cases (*see fig.* 3), divided into divers small squares, perfectly like a printer's. Every square, which is called a *box*, contains one sort of letter. The *boxes* are larger or smaller, according as the letters in them are more or less frequently used. The lower case (*see fig. a*) contains the small letters ; the upper (*see fig. b*) contains the capital letters, algebraical signs, accented letters, figures, etc.

These cases are commonly placed on frames (*see fig.* 3), and bent from before backwards, forming an angle of about forty-five degrees, in order that the compositor may easily reach the capitals in the upper case, without being obliged to make any great motion, and also that the letters may not slip from one box into another.

When the letters are taken from the boxes, they are immediately arranged on the composition board (*fig.* 4) ; while in printing, the compositor arranges his letters in a composing-stick, which is lengthened or shortened according to the extent which the line ought to have, and is called *justifying*.

On the stem of our characters, as well as on those of the printer, there is a nick (*see fig.* 5), which serves to point out the upper part of the letter : the blind person, on taking the letter out of the box, instead of touching it to ascertain the position of the nick, drags the stem along the lower part of the box ; if it does not catch, he knows that the nick is above, and that the letter is in the position in which he must place it on the board ; if, on the contrary, he feels that the nick catches it, he turns the letter between his fingers in carrying it to the board.

The blind never mistake in taking the letters from the case but when some have fallen from one box into another. The fault which results from this, and which those who have sight commit also, consists in the substitution of one letter for another, which everybody may remark even in the most accurate editions.

When exercised in this mode of composition, the blind acquire quickness enough to transcribe on the board in a quarter of an hour ten or twelve lines of a common 8vo. This process, which was used originally for teaching them to read, is now employed also for teaching them languages, and every part of their education.

The composition board we now use (*see fig.* 4) is far preferable to all the means hitherto contrived. This board may be larger or smaller, but should not be less than an inch thick, and of oak or walnut-tree. It is composed of a frame or case (*c c c c*) about eighteen lines broad, and of rulers (*d d d d*) separated from each other by an interval equal to the thickness of the tail of the characters, that they may enter easily, and be placed there like the word *dieu*, which serves as an example. The number and breadth of these horizontal rulers is proportioned to the dimensions of the board, which must be provided at the angles and underneath with square pieces of iron screwed in, which prevent the dislocation and separation of the frame which supports all the weight of the characters.

As to the replacing of the characters in the case, it is the same as for the common characters : the blind man takes between the thumb and first finger of his right hand, one or more words at a time, and putting his hand over each box, lets the letter fall in which he had taken for composing : this is called *distributing.*

Children who are sent to the Institution are exercised in recognising the letters ; but they do not begin the alphabet as with those who have sight, by *a*, *b*, *c*, etc., which would be creating unnecessary difficulties. They are first taught to touch the *full stop*, then the *comma*, by making them sensible of the difference between that stop and the stop with the *tail* below, which makes a *comma*, then the *semicolon*, the *colon*, the *mark of exclamation*, the *interrogation*, and the *parenthesis*. Care is always taken to compare one sign with another, and to make them touch from time to time, a *quadrat*,[1] in order to make the form of the signs more perceptible. They next proceed to the study of the letters ; beginning with the *O* of the capitals, and immediately after they perceive the *o* of the lower-case, with all the series of letters which we call *simple*, *l*, *b*, *i*, *j*, *d*, etc., and comparing, whenever that is necessary, one letter with another, in order to exercise their touch. Care must be taken that they do not read with their nails, that they do not press the letters too much, so as to harden the skin of their fingers, the ends of which should be soft and sensitive, in order to feel the form of the relief, when they are put into the hollows.

---

[1] A stem, or tail, of metal is so called, above which there is no letter, and which, consequently, remaining below the level of the other letters, leave neither mark nor colour on the paper. There are quadrats and spaces of different sizes. The *quadrats* serve to fill up the line of a paragraph ; the *spaces*, to make a proper division between the words.

The letters being known singly, they are taught to distinguish the vowels and consonants, and then to form syllables, words, and at last phrases. The tasks are then done with these characters as those who have sight do with writing.

CHAPTER III

Of Printing for the Use of the Blind

WHEN the means had been discovered of teaching
the blind to read, by the composition of a particular character, it was thought possible to print
books for their use with the same ; but till this
first essay of a new kind of printing appeared,
nobody would believe it was practicable.

The inventor took the idea of printing in relief
from seeing a sheet of paper just from the press,
on the back of which the letters appeared in
relief, from having been forcibly struck, but in a
contrary order.

Our printing letters are similar to those we
have described in the preceding chapter, with
this difference, that instead of being raised on a
transversal chevron, they rest on a stem of an
equal breadth in all its parts, like printing letters,
from which they differ only by having much
more white, and from its not being necessary to
interpose spaces to separate them.

The letters are placed on the forme from left to
right, and the imposition of the pages is, consequently, the inverse of the usual imposition.   In
black printing the lines are read from right to

left, because the paper being taken from above the forme, becomes reversed after having received the impression, and can be read from left to right.

At first, for printing in relief, a wooden press was used, like those for expressing oil, pressing cloth, etc. ; but when the board was rather large, the tablet which was to make the pressure on the paper was not uniformly closed by the screw, and the edges were less pressed than the middle ; so that the insufficiency of this process was very soon perceived. As nobody imagined at that time that a common press would serve for printing books for the blind, another method was contrived. This gave birth to the cylindrical press, made in 1784, by Beaucher, a locksmith. This press, which was very like that used by copper-plate printers, had, moreover, two iron bands, between which the formes were placed. A lever made the cylinder move, which rolling on the board caused a successive pressure, and produced a bad effect, because the paper was displaced by the rotation of the cylinder.

M. de Kempellen, inventor of the automaton chess-player, made a press for Miss Paradis, with which she printed German characters in relief; but of this press, and of the manner of using it, we have never been informed.

Fruitless efforts continued to be made for printingin relief, when M. Clousier, the king's printer, to whom the establishment has very great obligations, conceived that a perpendicular pres-

sure, given to the whole sheet at once, would
be preferable to successive pressures ; he used
such presses for printing in relief, and succeeded
completely.

A press was afterwards constructed with a
strong bar and a table in yellow copper, very
thick, able to support the strongest pressure.

The mechanism of printing in relief differs,
in many things, from common printing : in the
relief, the letter, pressed from above downwards,
incrusts itself in the paper by repelling it in a
contrary direction. To avoid tearing, the strongest
and best-made paper is employed ; and the *grand-
raisin* is commonly preferred to every other.[1] It
is steeped for several days, and must be almost
reduced to a paste before it is put on the forme,
and is carefully covered with several thick pieces
of flannel. A man draws the bar of the press
towards his breast, while another drives it back
violently in the same direction. A great pressure

---

[1] For some years past the printers have employed a sort of
paper called *machine-paper*, which seems pretty strong to the
touch, but has no substance, because, in the manufactories they
employ to pound the rags, hammers, put in motion by a mechanism
which cannot modify the strokes, and the linen is in a manner pul-
verised ; for this reason, when the paper is torn, one does not
perceive those filaments which are perceptible in that made in the
old way. This paper, which besides is very bad to paste with,
easily tears ; which has lately happened to us in printing an
English Grammar : when the pressure of the bar was too strong,
the characters went through the paper. Double *grand-raisin* well
pasted, or *carré* of large dimensions, called *carré des Vosges*, which
is much cheaper, should be employed.

PRINTING PRESS.

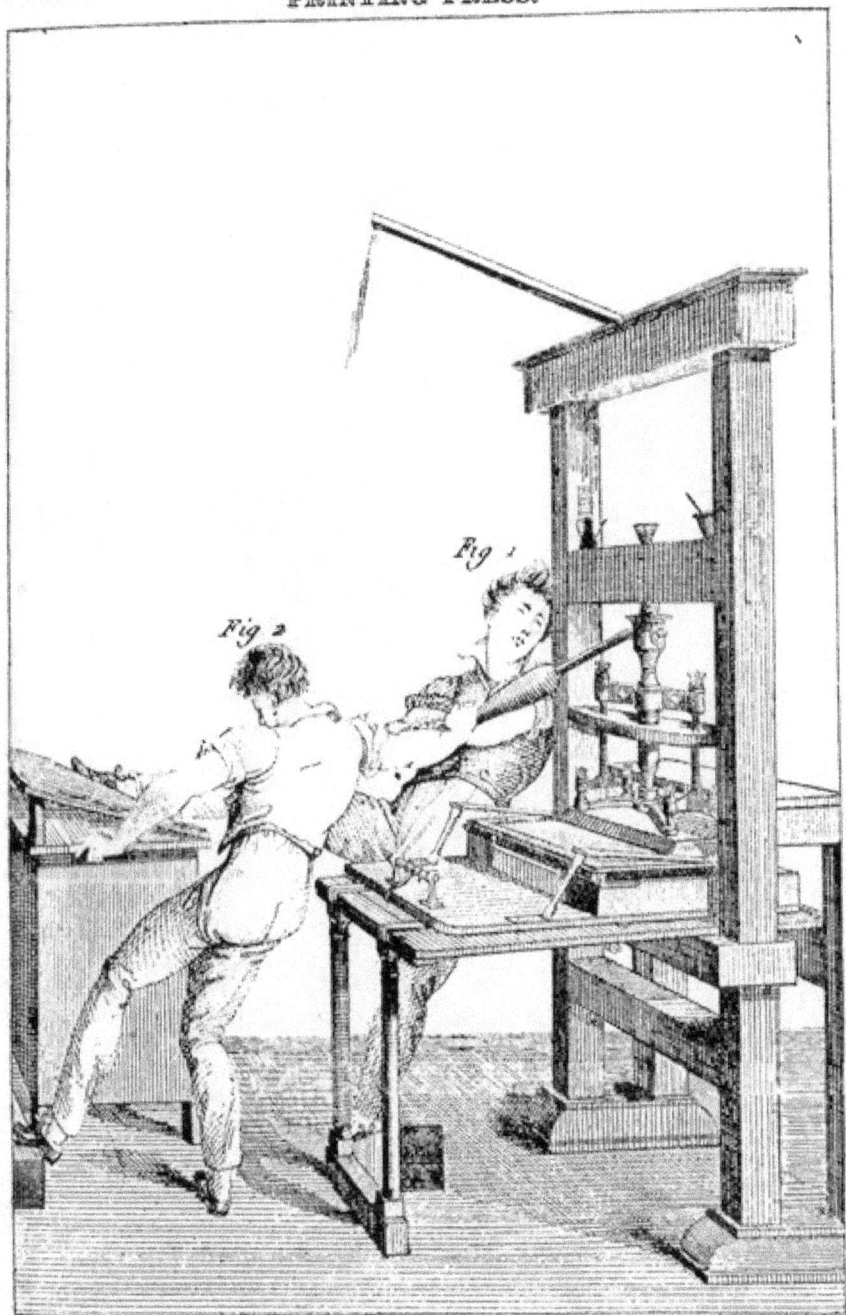

is not made immediately, which, to make use
of the expression among the workmen, would
astonish the paper.   They begin by a slight pressure, for which it is sufficient to make the bar
go over a quarter of a circle, or thereabout ;
when repeated it is increased ; and finally, after
resting an instant, the bar is brought as far as
possible, and they stay on the stroke four or five
minutes, in order to give the flannel time to
penetrate into all the hollows, and that the paper
may dry by the pressure of the characters, and not
grow flat after it is drawn from the forme, to which
it always adheres strongly, though the precaution
is taken to smear the letters, from time to time,
with dry soap, in order to prevent adhesion.

It is easy to conceive, from this explanation,
that it is impossible to print on both sides the
paper if we wish to preserve the relief.   If the
opposite side of the sheet were printed, the first
impression would be almost entirely destroyed by
the second.

When we wish to have the letters in relief and
black at the same time, a tympan is added
smeared with ink (for there is no frisket when
the printing is white), and by letting it fall gently
on the sheet, which is then pressed between the
forme and the tympan, the letters appear black.

The blind, who print all the books for their
use, can print also like those who have their
sight.   The business of a printer is even one of
those for which they show the most talent.   As

early as the year 1786, MM. Vincent, Clousier, and Saillant, certified that they had seen them *compose, justify the lines and pages, impose, touch the formes, make the margin, serve the press, distribute the characters, etc.*[1] The blind had made great progress from that epoch down to 1812, when their printing was unmercifully destroyed by the order of the director-general of printing and bookselling. In consequence of this act of cruelty, these unfortunate beings lost the means of learning a business, which put them in the way of gaining a livelihood better than any other.

Nevertheless, in order to prove that the business of a printer is very suitable for the blind, we continue to make them print before the company on public days, the prospectus of the exhibition : but, not to be in opposition with the regulations of the press, which forbid anybody but printers to have types, we send them to compose the board at a printer's out of the house, and send it back immediately after the exhibition is over.

---

[1] *Report of the Academy*, p. 15.

CHAPTER IV

Of Books for the Use of the Blind

WE should have wished to have been able to speak of books in the second chapter, immediately after having treated of reading : but as many things relative to the composition of these books are connected with the details of printing, we have been forced to invert the natural order of classification which we had adopted.

As soon as the sheets are taken from the press, they are spread singly on lines to dry, taking care that they are not damaged by friction.

The sheets are then joined together by pasting the margins only, the lines of the *verso* are made to meet with those of the *recto* ; finally, by stitching the leaves together, they are made into volumes, which are covered with thick pasteboard.

The method of executing this pasting has been altered several times ; it was thought, at first, that by interposing between the two leaves a compact matter capable of resisting the pressure of the fingers, the relief would be more durable ; and it was with this intention that, in the first books, the agglutination was made with paste thickened with powder of rotten wood, with which the hollows were filled; but the paste, the humidity of which could not evaporate, did not dry, and softened and swelled out the paper. It has since been found, that the air enclosed between each sheet was sufficient to hinder the relief from falling.

It appears, from what we have hitherto said, that many attempts had been made to teach the blind to read; but that all these painful efforts had ended in teaching them merely to learn the alphabet.   About the middle of the last century, a learned foreigner thought he had discovered a method of making books in relief.   His process consisted in writing on thick paper, with a viscous and corrosive liquid; this writing was sprinkled with very fine scrapings of wool, as is done for making the velvet of tapestries; but the letters thus made were heavy, the finer parts did not come out, and the friction soon destroyed them.

In 1783, MM. Adet and Hassenfratz attempted, unsuccessfully, to compose for the blind a thick ink, which, on drying, would have preserved the relief.   This attempt has been since renewed by M. Robertson; but also without success.

The discovery of printing books in relief is one of the most important for the instruction of the blind.   It is by the assistance of these books, which have no other inconvenience but that of being bulky, that they are taught the elements of languages, and fix in their minds the beautiful passages of history and morality which they have learnt; for they know much better what they have read than what they have heard: and we therefore augment, as far as our means will allow, the library of the blind with works which we think fitted for their instruction. They have already two Catechisms, the Office for Morning and Evening, French, Latin, Greek, English, and Italian Grammars. One would hardly believe with what rapidity they read in these books, if one did not see it at the public exercises.

Attempts were made to diminish the bulk of the volumes, by making abbreviations, which consisted principally in the suppression of the *m*, *n*, *u*, the double letters, etc.: but as, to indicate the abbreviation, a sign was necessary on the preceding letter, it greatly increased the embarrassment of the reader, and was, therefore, given up.

The following example will show how these abbreviations were made:

When the *o* was to be followed by an *n*, the bar was placed above. To indicate that a double letter was taken away, a stop was placed below that which remained. The *u* after the *o* was replaced by a bar under the latter letter, etc.

By means of books in relief, the blind teach young people who have sight to read, who are afterwards useful to them as readers. They begin by teaching them the letters by means of the books we have mentioned above. These letters, which are cut in pasteboard, and fastened on the book, are perceptible to the blind man, who can touch them ; and to those who have sight, who can see them. When the twenty-six letters of the alphabet are learned, the blind man, having in his hands a table of syllables in relief, similar to a copy in black that is under the eyes of the child, makes him spell, and thus the readers of our blind men have learned to read, and look with rapidity in the Dictionary.

CHAPTER V

Of Writing

As all men prefer those things the possession of which is difficult, before those which they can easily obtain, so the blind, who can only write by surmounting numberless obstacles, set a great value on it. Among the privations arising from their melancholy situation, they reckon the impossibility of writing as one of the greatest. It was, perhaps, to console them that attempts were made so long ago to teach them to form characters, and to enable them to hold a correspondence without the necessity of recurring to the intervention of a third person.

To discover the means of making a blind man write seems an incredible piece of dexterity; nevertheless, this study now rests on such sure principles, that it is become, we will not say easy, but practicable; which is proved in our public exercises, when the pupils write the phrases that are dictated to them.

Before we describe the process now employed for writing, we shall rapidly run over the series of attempts made down to this time for rendering it easy to the blind.

In the researches we have made on the instruction of the blind in general, we have found nothing beyond the end of the seventeenth century which indicates that they had learned to write. Saunderson himself, who lived at that period, could not write. Bernouilli, being at Geneva in 1676, taught Elizabeth Waldkirch to write, who had lost her sight two months after her birth ; but he never made known the method he employed.

Dr. Burnet, Bishop of Salisbury, has mentioned many particulars, in his *Travels in Switzerland*, of a Miss Walkier, of Schaffhausen, whose eyes were burnt at the age of one year. She had a prodigious memory, spoke five languages, and had learned by heart all the Psalms of David and the New Testament. She had learned theology and philosophy ; played very well on the violin, and was a good musician. To all these valuable qualities she added great piety and resignation in supporting her misfortune. This young woman had learned to write by means of characters cut out hollow in wood, which at first she felt with an iron point ; she next made use of a pencil, and when Burnet was at Schaffhausen, in 1685, he saw her write very quickly and correctly.[1]

Towards the end of the last century, when the minds of men, directed towards beneficence, were

---

[1] *Travels in Switzerland and Italy*, by Dr. Burnet, Bishop of Salisbury, vol. i. p. 218, Letter 2. Rotterdam, 1718.

PLATE III.

Fig. 1

Fig. 3

Fig. 2

seeking improvements in everything, the ink, which we have mentioned in the preceding chapter, for the composition of books, was thought of for the writing of the blind. This ink, which was expected to congeal immediately on the paper, congealed much quicker in the pen; and this method appeared so defective that it was given up almost as soon as it was tried.

Discouraged by the difficulty which they found in making the blind write, the first persons who taught them thought proper to give up the use of the pencil, and merely adopted an alphabet in copper, the moveable letters of which were touched with balls supplied with an ink made with gum. These characters applied on the paper, left on it the impression of the letters; but the blind man, who could not follow with the forefinger of the left hand the letters which he traced with his right hand, often printed these letters one upon the other, without perceiving it; and at other times he placed them at great distances: sometimes, also, not having taken ink enough, the letters were not visible. This process, though insufficient, might have been susceptible, perhaps, of some improvements; but when other methods more easy and more certain were found, it was set aside.

In the beginning of the Institution, they made use of a wooden board (see fig. 1) which was given up afterwards for another, that has been modified since. This first board is ten inches broad and sixteen high ; the edges are about three lines higher than the centre. These edges are furrowed with twenty-four grooves, three lines in depth, which makes the bottom level with the central part. At the external part of each of these grooves is a hole which traverses the board throughout ; in the internal and lower part is a long groove three lines in extent from within outwards, and about a line high. It is in this groove, which extends from one extremity of the board to the other, that the paper to be used for writing is introduced by making it slip in. A small rod of iron-wire is then placed transversely in the parallel holes, the two extremities of it being bent square like those of curtain-rods, and the blind write by following the rod, on which they draw their middle-finger. This board, be-sides many other inconveniences, which it is useless to enumerate, as it is no longer used, made it difficult to arrange the rod, which the blind often placed diagonally on their paper, especially when the board was very broad, or the lateral grooves were worn.

The second board, which M. Haüy contrived, is of a different form from the preceding (*see fig.* 2); it is nearly of the same size, and consists of a board as thick again, of which the bottom is fixed. Above is an opening, a parallelogram, in which is a frame opening with hinges on the left side, and kept shut on the right side by two small copper-bolts. This frame is furnished with several moveable rods of iron. Below the two great ascending panels of this frame, there is on each side a broad steel-spring, stretching from one extremity to the other, fixed at one end by two English screws, and at the other only stopped, at pleasure, by a turning bolt, like those which shut the frame. It is between these springs and the lower part of the sides of the frame that the paper is placed, which remains immoveable under the rods — such was the second board. That which has been made since differs from it in this, that instead of a wooden bottom, there is an opening equal to that of the frame, which, provided with a thick silk, gives the blind man the facility of reading what he has written, either with the stilet or the pencil, because the pressure is always strong enough to leave the trace of the letters on the silk. This improvement, and some minor meliorations, which it would be difficult to describe, have determined us to adopt this board, which was devised by Mr. Heilman, a blind man, who has also contrived a portable portfolio for the blind, by means of which they may write, and read directly what they have written, with the greatest ease.[1]

---

[1] We should always prefer, for the instruction of the blind, the means contrived by them : they perceive much better than we, as we have already said several times, what is wanting in our ordinary processes to render them useful to them.

Method to be followed in teaching Writing to the Blind.

The principles of writing for the blind are, with some small difference, the same as those for people who have their sight. The latter are exercised at first in making strokes ; and we also begin by giving the blind an idea of the elementary letters. They have, in this pursuit, a great advantage over those who have their sight, because, knowing already how to read, they know in part the form and the direction of the letters in writing.

Attitude of the Body.

It is of little importance what attitude the blind take for writing, they have none of the motives which determine us to observe the rules established by writing-masters, as it is not with the pen but with a point that they write. He has neither full nor fine strokes to make ; and would write as well on a table or against a wall. Nevertheless, we are in the habit of exercising them either on their knees or on a table, by placing them so that the light may come from the left side, in order that he who teaches may easily see the blind person's hand, whose left arm should rest entirely on the board, the hand closed, with only the fore-finger held out, to follow the stilet which traces the letters.

Way of holding the Stilet.

The stilet, or pencil, should be held with the thumb, the fore-finger, and the middle-finger; the two others are bent back and drag along the paper in the progression of the hand. The blind, in general, have the fault of holding the stilet too close between their fingers, and of pressing it so hard on the paper that they tear it. They must, therefore, be habituated early to bear on it as lightly as possible.

Motions of the Fingers and of the Hand.

It is rather difficult to make a blind person understand why the letters should not all have the same direction; why a letter inclined to the right is not as well as one to the left. To avoid, therefore, the irregularity that would necessarily result in the form of the letter from the ill-directed motions of the wrist, instead of allowing them to make strokes vaguely, in different directions, as is the practice with children in general, we begin with making them follow, with an iron stilet, on a tin or copper plate (*see fig.* 3) the form of the less compound figures, cut out hollow; first simple strokes, then strokes bent up from below (*ı*), which forms the *i*; two of these strokes near to each other (*u*), which forms the *u*; then strokes bent back in a contrary direction above and below (*ı*), which makes the second part of the *n*; afterwards the *c* and the *i*, which, joined together, form *a* ; the *c* and the *j*, which form the *g* by their union. We thus go successively over the whole series of the letters, passing from the most simple to the most compound.

Remark on the Alphabet.

One cannot adopt for the blind a particular sort of writing, such, for example, as the clerk's hand, the running hand, English writing, etc. It was necessary to discard the letters that would have been too difficult to form, and to select from each of these sorts of writing the letters that would suit the blind best. But the details which would be necessary to make this understood would probably appear puerile and of little value, and we therefore omit them in this place.

Of the joining Letters in order to form Words.

When the blind person has been long exercised on the copper table we have just described, and has practised all the remarks we have enumerated, we must make him write on the board (No. 2). For this purpose we make use either of an iron stilet, about six inches long, or of a pretty hard pencil. In the first case the white paper is put on the board of the writing-table : the frame being raised, on this white sheet is placed a sheet of paper blackened with grease and chimney-black on the side which corresponds with the white sheet; this second sheet is fixed against the lower part of the frame, all the motions of which it follows by the elastic spring I have already mentioned. The frame is allowed to fall on the white sheet. The blind man, by writing on the first sheet, takes the black colour out of the second in every part where he has leaned with his stilet. If he wishes to have several copies at once, it is sufficient for that to form, on his board, a sort of mattress composed of sheets alternately white and black; by writing on the first he will have written on all the others, an advantage which the pencil has not, which, besides, has the inconvenience of frequently breaking, and of marking no longer when it requires to be mended, which the blind person cannot do himself. For these reasons we have abandoned the pencil, and prefer the stilet and coloured paper, according to the method of Heilman.

The board being arranged, as we have just said, it is placed before the blind person, so that the left inferior angle touches the edge of the table, and the right inferior angle is about an inch from it. The person who gives the lesson must be standing behind the blind man, and, taking his hand in his,[1] he places his middle finger on one of the rods, to accustom him to feel it and slip over it. When the pupil is ac-

[1] See PLATE IV., Frontispiece.

customed to guide his stilet in a regular manner between the two rods, he is taught to make letters ; and that he may keep the necessary interval between each of them, the extremity of his left fore-finger rests against the point of the stilet, which it accompanies, and of which it measures all the motions. When he can place the letters at a proper distance, and write straight between the two rods, the separation of which is about eight lines, one of them is taken away, which doubles the interval, and he is then exercised anew ; afterwards a second is removed ; and all being taken away successively, he is made to write in the frame without any rod, and at last on a sheet of paper without either rod or frame.

The writing of the blind is never very regular, because they cannot keep a line with a uniform base ; the tails of the great letters go unequally beyond that line ; nor can they appreciate the dimensions of our letters witten with a pen, nor form an exact proportion in the form of their letters ; but still their writing is legible, and sufficient for their wants. They do not write very fast : but as they are never in a hurry, slowness is to them a trifling inconvenience.

CHAPTER VI

Of Geography

DOWN to the epoch when M. Weissembourg, of Mannheim, made maps in relief, the lessons of geography given to the blind were merely oral; consequently, they had made very little progress in that study. The first attempts of M. Weissembourg were not happy. He began by having the principal divisions of Europe engraved in relief, on a board of the size of ordinary maps, in the hope of being able to get such maps printed as books are; but the too-large hollow spaces destroyed the effect of the projections, and this defective plan was abandoned almost as soon as formed.

The second attempt consisted in spreading over all the illuminated lines glass beads of the same colour as the illumination, and in fixing them by means of a thread, which went through them, and which was sewed on the map; but these beads broke, or else did not keep their relation with the subjacent lines.

For the glass beads he afterwards substituted *chenille*, which he pasted before he sewed it. He

also made maps, at a great expense, which excited
more curiosity than interest, and were much
spoken of at the time : the seas and rivers were
represented on them by pieces of glass, cut with
great art, and the different countries were distinguished by sand of different granulations; the
towns were known by copper nails with round
heads of different sizes : but the rubbing soon
made the sand disappear, and these maps were
considerably damaged by the least handling;
they were of no use to those who had their sight,
who could not even guess the purpose of them
unless informed of it.

This learned blind man was not long before he
perceived the insufficiency of this process, notwithstanding the eulogiums that were lavished
upon him ; he therefore endeavoured to discover
more durable and less defective means, and at
last fixed on the following scheme :

He had common maps pasted on strong gummed
linen, as is done for folding maps that are shut
up in portable cases ; these were embroidered
with little chains, and by employing silks of
different sizes, he could make all the divisions
that he judged necessary, much better than with
the sand, which could only serve to indicate
great parts. By making use of coloured silk, he
could even make these maps useful to those who
had their sight : nevertheless, this plan, though
much preferable to the other, was still defective,
as the embroidering, after having served some

time, got loose, and, tearing the paper, lost the connection which it had with the illuminated lines.

The geographical maps of the blind were in this state when the inventor of those which we make use of at present thought of employing wire for making the divisions, which till then had been made successively with beads, chenille, or different embroideries. The following is the process for making them, which are not less solid than useful.

The map is pasted on a very thick pasteboard, and then on all the parts that are to be made apparent, is pasted iron-wire, well seasoned, easily bent, and folded in silk-paper, like that which the milliners use for ladies' hats : this pasting is easily done by means of a small hair-pencil, like those that are used for colouring with Indian ink, and the agglutination of the wire on the map is very solid, by means of the paper with which it is surrounded. As to the circumvolutions which this wire requires, they are done very exactly with very fine crane-beaked pincers, taking care to put it often on the illuminated lines, in order to be certain of the exactness of the different parts ; this wire is cut in shorter or longer pieces, according as the work requires ; nevertheless, too frequent cuttings are avoided, because the ends of them come over and tear the map laid upon them, or if the student hits his fingers against them, he might hurt them. The towns and islands are indicated by nails with demi-spherical heads of different sizes, which are nailed into the paste-board, which ought to be thick enough for the points not to go through.

Maps thus made would be sufficient for the wants of the blind, but would be disagreeable to the view, and fatiguing for masters who have their sight, who could not discover the parts covered by the wire, or hid by the paste ; and for this reason the first map is covered with a second perfectly similar.   All the wrinkles which the paste or other foreign bodies may have left on the pasteboard are taken off by scraping it with the back of a knife ; it is glued in all its parts, and the second map, which has also been moistened with a slight layer of paste, is then fastened on. The centre is first pressed, and while another person raises the edges, a slight pressure is made with a rag, proceeding from the centre to the circumference.   This operation ought to be done as quickly as possible, to avoid the desiccation of the paper, and prevent the formation of bubbles, which happens when the compression has not been made circularly and quick.   The centre application of the map being finished, partial pressures are made on the wires, that the paper may go in on each side, and leave the divisions apparent and well arranged together ; this is done easily enough while the paper is wet, as it then yields to the pressure of the fingers.   When the map is complicated, like that of Asia for example, it is necessary that many persons at once should press the iron wires, that the map may not have time to dry. When this first work is terminated, there still remain wrinkles on the map; but it would be wrong to try to make them disappear, as it would tear if the paper were too much stretched. It is placed, immediately afterwards, under a screw-press. If there be no press broad enough, it may be put on a very even table, covered with a thick flannel, and pressed down with a board and heavy weights, in order that on drying it may preserve exactly the divisions that have been made in it.

After having left it five or six days under the press, it is drawn from it perfectly dry, and is varnished with a very soft pencil, slightly moistened with a white varnish, made with spirit of wine, in order to prevent the humidity of the fingers from fretting the paper.

Maps thus prepared are very serviceable to the blind, and very commodious for their teachers, who can read them with ease. Nevertheless, when the divisions and cuttings are carried too far, they become confused; which has forced us to give up the use of the map by departments, as the limits, too often alike, could not be sufficiently appreciated. We make use of the division by provinces, and we indicate by partial divisions the number and relative situation of the departments which each province contains.

We have not spoken of the spheres, globes,

and planispheres, that we use ; it is always by
the same process that we turn them to our use ;
and it would be useless to repeat what we have
already said.

CHAPTER VII

Of the Study of Languages

In the beginning of our Institution, we confined ourselves to teaching the blind reading, writing, French grammar, and geography : languages were not taught.   It was not till long after that they were thought capable of learning them. They began by the study of the Latin language ; but what a labyrinth, what a wilderness for children deprived of their sight, was a dictionary, which they could only make use of by the assistance of another person!   Notwithstanding, they learnt in this way, with the feeble assistance of masters as inexperienced as themselves, to translate some elementary pieces ; but they were soon stopped, and it was then perceived that they could not be instructed like ordinary children ; and that the method of teaching must be proportioned to their infirmity.   This was, among us, the origin of mutual instruction, which, for the last two years, has been known by the name of the method of Bell or of Lancaster, though it does not belong to one any more than the other,

H

and came to us, according to all appearance, from the Indians.

This method, which is simple and natural, always appeared to us the best, and we had made use of it for a long time, when it was first introduced into public schools.

We are convinced that it would be impossible to instruct the blind collected together, or to teach them anything, especially languages, without the help of mutual instruction. We have not introduced, either venal recompenses which extinguish generous sentiments, nor those humiliating punishments which repress emulation, nor that desire of pre-eminence which so easily degenerates into pride; and in this respect, our method belongs, perhaps, rather to the system of Pestalozzi than to that of Lancaster.

We prepare our pupils for the study of languages, by confiding to their memory, at an early period, short phrases forming a sense; we have formed for them a sort of *phraseology*, in which all the words, distributed by families (nearly as in the spheres of Pestalozzi), class themselves naturally, as well as the combinations, the most usual derivations, the alliances of words with each other, etc. We are far from making an abuse of the memory of our pupils by making them retain lists of words. Languages are not studied in this way; to translate well is not to translate words, but to know their relative value, their different inflections, and the influence they have on each other. This is what we endeavour to teach them before we speak to them of rules ; for, as Dumarsais has said, there are no general principles which, to be well understood, do not suppose a knowledge of the particular ideas which have occasioned them. To begin by rules which are the result of general principles is to invert the natural order of things and begin where we ought to end.

For the translation of languages we have adopted the use of the interlineary methods ; for the Latin we make use of those of Frémont, a distinguished teacher. To a great fidelity in the translation of the text they add the advantage of being elucidated by very good notes. The Latin word is translated by the corresponding French word, which is found below. In the third line comes what is commonly called good French ; on the opposite page, the pure text ; below the text the literal translation, and below the translation the notes and explanations. It is impossible to find anything more exact and more philosophical than this performance, the efficaciousness of which is proved by the rapid success of our pupils.

Dumarsais, who first translated the Latin authors interlineally, the good Rollin himself,[1]

---

[1] I have always wished there were books made on purpose for beginners, in which they might find the application of the rules ready made, instead of being obliged to do it in themes, which are only calculated to torment them by a painful labour of little use.—*Treatise of Studies.*

Radonvilliers, and all the celebrated grammarians
who have appeared since, have expressed a
desire to see the use of these translations become
general. In fact, can we take too much pains
to save children from useless tears and vexations,
and above all, from the loss of a precious time
which might be so usefully employed at that
age?

We have made the application of this method
to the study of Greek; but as there are no
authors as yet translated interlineally, collabo-
rator, Mr. Dufau, by making use of the vulgar
characters, as several Greek scholars advised him,
has made partial translations on our composition
boards. Though long and troublesome, this
operation has enabled our pupils to understand
Æsop and Anacreon after a few months' study,
which they now easily translate at the public
exercises.

The same process is used for the study of
English and Italian, as we can derive no assistance from the translation of Boisjermain, which
are very incorrect. Our method sometimes fails,
I confess, with the pronunciation of English, but
these disappointments excite our emulation,
and we seldom leave our pupils without being
understood. We must do justice to their
aptitude and penetration, which are such that
some of them comprehend so exactly the manner
of an author after the first pages that they will
explain him afterwards, from one end to the

other, almost without any assistance. The girls have not so much readiness as the boys in learning languages; nevertheless most of them speak Italian with ease.

Two masters and one mistress are sufficient to teach eighty scholars, who learn reading, writing, and the French, Latin, Greek, English, and Italian languages; geography, history, the transcendental mathematics, and vocal and instrumental music in all its parts. So great a number of scholars taught, we have the confidence to say, with some pre-eminence by three persons, is sufficient to show the excellence of the plan of mutual instruction. We may add that this plan is here directed philosophically; we have rejected the idle and noisy walks, and all the trash of the automatical exercises of the Lancastrian schools, and have adopted only the spirit of the plan, perfected by observation and experience. We hold the first threads, and six professors taken among the most distinguished scholars are appointed to transmit to their companions the knowledge they derive directly from us; the most advanced amongst those taught by the masters are selected for repeaters, and finally, from those who receive instruction from the repeaters weekly teachers are selected, who, not being sufficiently advanced to govern long, only remain on duty a week. Thus, from him who reads Tacitus to him who begins to lisp the first series of the phraseology, all are professors and masters, and all advance, like giants, towards the object they have constantly before them. This, whatever name may be given to it, is in my opinion the real method of mutual instruction.

CHAPTER VIII

Of Mathematics

IF the privation of sight may, in some circumstances, prove an advantage, it is in the study of mathematics. The blind have a natural disposition for this science, and apply to it with a decided taste. When very young, they easily learn the most complicated operations of arithmetic, and without employing any of the means which those who have their sight make use of for geometry, they have an exact and precise idea of figures; which is proved by their success in algebra, trigonometry, and the other subsequent branches of mathematics. Their intelligence for this study is so comprehensive, that they are not only enabled to follow completely the demonstrations made on the board, and to profit by the public lectures given by the most distinguished masters, but even to carry off the first prizes in the colleges.

It follows from the principles hitherto established, that we must never use any arbitrary method for the instruction of the blind : it was this principle which determined the inventor of our present arithmetical board to give up that of

Saunderson, which, though very ingenious, necessarily gives conventional values to the pegs,
according to their size and situation.

The letters and ciphers which we make use of
at present are in no respect different from the
common ones, and it is in this that the perfection
of our method of instruction consists, that it is
the same for the blind as for those who have
their sight.

These ciphers are mounted like the letters on
a transversal chevron. (*See* Pl. v. *fig.* 1). The
fractions are mounted in the same manner, but
the upper part of the chevron is hollowed in a
square form (*fig.* 2), to receive a moveable cipher
in the form of a wedge, by means of which the
numerator and the denominator and ergo the
necessary changes. Strings, that may be placed
horizontally or vertically (*fig.* 3) serve to indicate
the divisions of the numbers. These ciphers are
placed in a case (*fig.* 4), distributed into eleven
broad cassetins, by the side of which others are
found for the numerators and denominators.
This case, more long than broad, should be placed
on an inclined plane, like the case for composition.

In the cast that has been lately made, the size
of the old ciphers has been diminished one half;
they were too heavy, and occupied too much
space on the board. The fractional ciphers,
which it was thought might be retrenched, were
not re-cast.

The calculating board (*fig.* 5) differs from the

PLATE V.

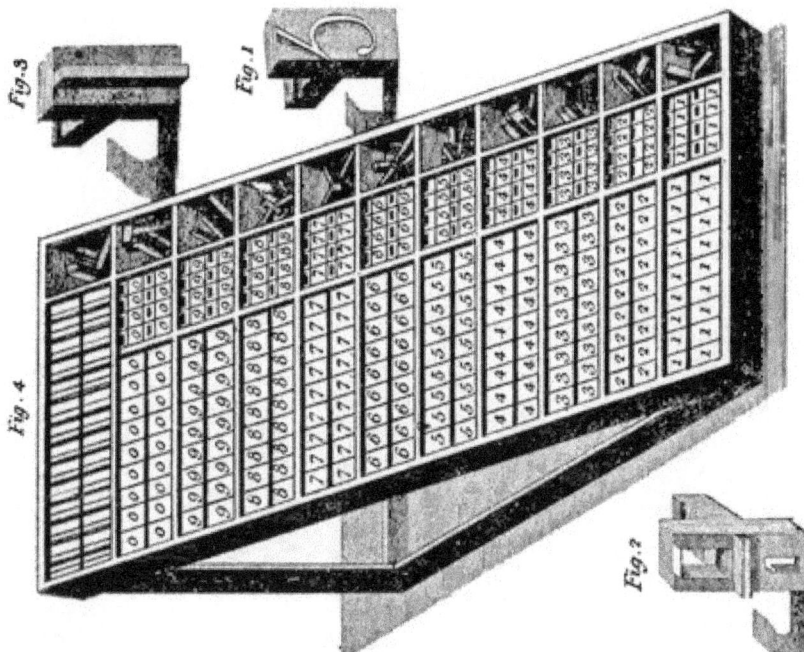

Fig. 3

Fig. 1

Fig. 4

Fig. 2

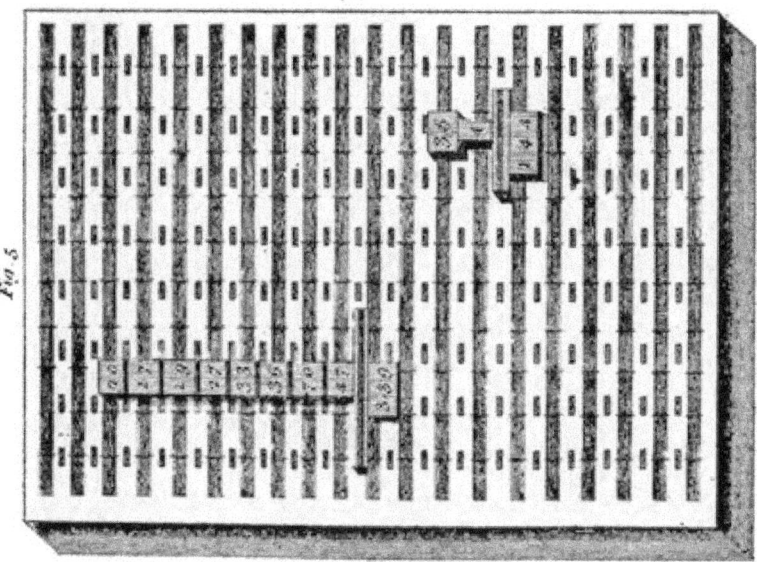

Fig. 5

composition board only by the transversal intervals being crossed by iron wires, which keep the ciphers in relation with each other. The same board becomes geometrical, when pegs are placed in the holes which are on the rods, and are surrounded by a silken thread, as Saunderson did.

It would be a mistake to suppose that we derive any great assistance in teaching geometry from the little wooden figures which are sometimes used for those who have their sight. I have already had occasion to explain why we did not adopt these means, which would be more prejudicial than advantageous, as they would materialise the thoughts of the blind, who ought to have the idea of these figures mentally. They may indeed assist themselves with some means of comparison : two points separated from each other, a stretched string, a rolling ball, may give them the idea of a straight line ; a slack rope may represent a curve, etc., but we must not found on these vague notions a theory which would have nothing real.

People are astonished to see our pupils go through a course of optics as well as those who see, and they admire their sagacity in speaking of dioptrics and catoptrics. As we do not wish to enjoy an admiration that is unmerited, we must declare, that what makes the demonstration of all the phenomena of optics easy to them is, that they reduce everything to lines. They perceive only palpable points where we see coloured prints ;

for they have not, nor can they have, any idea of colours.[1] If they distinguish some, it is not the colour, properly speaking, but the colouring matter ; and the best proof of this assertion is, that when they cannot guess the colour by the touch, they *taste* it. If in touching they confound blue with black, they are no longer mistaken when they taste it ; indigo and nutgalls do not appear the same to them, as our eyes, so apt to deceive us, often make us believe. The distinction of colours, analogous, not by their shade, but by the dye ; yellow and green, for example, appear difficult to them, while deep pink and light red, which appear to us almost identical, are to them much more striking colours than yellow

---

[1] One of our pupils translating at a public exercise, the first strophe of the second ode of the first book of Horace, was stopped at these words *et rubente dexterâ, etc.*, by the examiner ; who asked him the proper translation of the words *rubente dexterâ* ; the young man translated it *his flaming right hand*. Being pressed again to translate literally the epithet *rubente*, he gave the equivalent *red*. Being asked again what he understood by a *red arm* : he answered, that he did not think like Locke's blind man, that the colour red was like the sound of a trumpet ; but nevertheless he could form no direct idea of it ; but that he had at first translated *rubente flaming*, because he had been told that fire is red : whence he had concluded that heat is always accompanied by redness ; which determined him to mark the anger of Jupiter by the epithet *flaming*, because when one is irritated one is hot, and when one is hot, one *must be* red. This answer was made in 1814 by the scholar Fonsèque, who is still at the Institution. We thought it extraordinary enough to deserve being quoted, because it gives an idea of the secondary means which the blind employ to attain some vague notions of the theory of colours, which to them will always be a mystery.

and green. Respectable writers have declared
they knew blind men who could tell, by the
touch, the colour of the hair of certain animals.[1]
We are far from denying this assertion ; but we
do not understand how it can happen.

---

[1] De comite Mansfeldico cœco refert Keckermannus, *Syst.*
Physic. lib. 3, cap. 16, solo tactu album a nigro discernere ; de
equo fusco vel albo, item de columbâ nigrâ vel cæruleâ judicium
ferre potuisse.

CHAPTER IX

Of Music

IT is generally supposed that the blind are not
taught music by principles, and that they only
imitate the sounds they hear ; but this is a great
mistake. Nothing could be more wrong than
such a mode of instruction. Our processes for
teaching music are no other than those that are
employed for those who have sight ; it is by
the methods of the conservatory that our scholars
learn the elements of music, of composition, etc.
How could they know the measure ? how could
they execute great pieces with the precision they
do, if they were only guided by a blind routine ?
the signs of music would have no value to them
if their form was not rendered sensible ; and this
has determined us to have engraved on broad
boards of pear-tree wood, the figures of the notes,
the keys, the rests, and all the alternate signs,
with some lessons that serve as examples.

Music was formerly printed in relief ; but we
have ceased to make use of it, as it was very
expensive and of no use : the scholar could not
read (with his fingers) and perform at the same

time. The following is the way in which the
lessons are now given : a boy, whom the blind
themselves have taught to read music, being
placed in the middle of the orchestra, solfas some
measures of a division, which is before his eyes,
announcing beforehand for what instrument the
piece is which he sings. The memory of the
blind is so faithful, that it is seldom necessary
to repeat the same phrase to them more than
twice. After having thus learnt successively on
all the instruments an equal number of measures,
the (blind) music-master puts together what has
just been learnt : the boy resumes his solfa, and
at length, when from 150 to 200 measures have
been retained, in a sitting of about two hours and
a half, the chief of the orchestra makes them
be repeated several times, in order to give the
necessary shades and expression. This piece is
connected with the one that was learnt the preceding day, by executing them together. Thus
long pieces are learnt, and masses, choruses,
symphonies, etc., are so exactly retained, that
sometimes a single repetition is sufficient to bring
them forward again, though frequently neglected
for several years.[1]

---

[1] We have always considered this manner of learning music
preferable to many arbitrary systems that have been communicated
to us. We recollect having seen at Bordeaux, eighteen years ago,
a blind man, who played tolerably well on the violin, but having
been taught by masters who knew nothing of the way of teaching
the blind, and was ignorant even of the first elements. He had
invented a singular method of copying music ; he represented the

They have no masters but themselves for instrumental music ; notwithstanding some of them are capable of playing a concerto very well. Each blind professor has in his head the entire method of the instrument he teaches, and a great number of pieces, duettos, etc.[1]

No scholar is exempted from the study of music. The choice of an instrument depends on the use he is to make of it after he leaves the Institution. The administration has redoubled its efforts, since the removal of the establishment, to realise the project, long since formed, of giving useful professions to the blind ; it has done all in

---

measures by button moulds, the value of the notes by pieces of cork, more or less thick, a round one by a ring, a black one by a piece of money, the silences by indented straps of leather, etc. We cannot recollect the confused series of all these signs, which he distinguished, however, tolerably well ; but we could not help laughing, when having mentioned the second concerto of Jarnowick, which he was then playing, he went and took out of a cupboard a sort of string of beads, seven or eight fathoms long, formed of the articles we have mentioned, which he told us was his concert, and pointed out the most difficult passages in it. He had several cupboards filled with this strange music.

We have seen other blind persons who wrote music on boards, in which were ranges of ten or fifteen lines, like those which Rousseau proposed, with points of different sizes.

Is it not more natural to use methods known by every one, especially when they are easier and more certain ?

[1] It gives us pleasure to find an opportunity of expressing our gratitude to the Abbé Rose, who, for several years past, has composed, for the blind, a great number of pieces of music that have always been heard with the greatest pleasure. We have also many obligations to MM. Duport, Habeneck, Jadin, Dacosta, and Baudoin, for the advice they have had the kindness to give to our scholars, with equal zeal and disinterestedness.

PLATE VI.

PLAYING THE PIANO.

I

PLATE VII.

PLAYING THE HARP.

its power to prevent them from going, as formerly, when they left our house, to play in public places, which were not always respectable ; it was with this view that an organ was purchased, in order to enable those who inhabit great towns to gain a livelihood with this instrument. Those who are to reside in villages where there is no organ, learn to play on the serpent, for they play on all known instruments. They took lessons this year, for the first time, on the harp. It was not thought possible, till now, to teach them this instrument, so difficult, even for those who have their sight, from the painful position of the body, and the multiplicity of strings undistinguished from each other. This fortunate innovation, which has been completely successful, is owing to the zeal of the mistress of the girls.

CHAPTER X

Of the means of communication between the Blind and the Deaf and Dumb

ONE is astonished at the facility with which the blind communicate with the deaf and dumb, and one can hardly conceive how this communication can take place between creatures deprived of the organs the most indispensable for the intellectual functions.

The reader will learn with pleasure what was the origin of the relations that exist between these two degraded classes in nature, and by what means the blind and the deaf and dumb came to understand each other, long before it was thought of inventing a method for them. These details—fastidious, perhaps, to those who are strangers to benevolence—will not be uninteresting to those feeling and generous persons who delight in relieving misfortune.

During the time that the institutions of the blind and of the deaf and dumb were united in the convent, formerly of the Celestines, the pupils of the two establishments, brought together by their habitation, but separated by their infirmity, endeavoured to establish points of contact between each other. The heads of the two houses, far from disapproving of this connection, favoured it, being convinced that it could not but be advantageous to creatures whom a sort of confraternity of misfortune led to seek each other.

Both had already received some instruction; for I cannot imagine what mode of communication could be established between the blind and the deaf and dumb, who had learnt nothing. Their situation, I suppose, would be like that of a child without experience, that must be shown everything.   I am therefore going to speak, not of the blind in a state of nature, but of the blind who have been taught.

When the blind had learnt that the deaf and dumb spoke to each other in the dark, by writing on their back, they conceived that this method might succeed also with them, as in fact it did. This new language soon became common to the two families; the deaf and dumb who found it tiresome to have written on their back what they could see perfectly well, attempted to make the blind write in the air, as they do themselves : this means, which was as long as the former, appeared to them more uncertain, as the blind wrote ill in that way ; they therefore preferred the characters the latter made use of ; but as these characters cannot be easily transported, the dumb taught the blind their manual alphabet, and the one by sight, and the other by touch, easily found by the inspection of their fingers, the letters that are formed by their different combinations.

Nevertheless, this manual alphabet, only exhibiting words, slackened conversation amazingly. They felt the want of a more rapid communication, and the blind learnt the theory of the signs of the deaf and dumb : each sign thus representing a thought, the communication was complete. This study was long and tedious, because it supposes a pretty complete knowledge of grammar ; but the wish to talk got the better of all these difficulties, and in a few months, the signs being perfectly well known, took the place of all the other means till then employed. The exchange between them was performed in the following manner :—

When the blind had to speak to the deaf and dumb, he made the representative signs of his ideas, and these signs, more or less exactly made, transmitted to the deaf and dumb the idea of the blind.[1] When the deaf and dumb, in his turn, wished to make himself understood, he did it in two ways : he stood with his arms stretched out and motionless, before the blind person, who took hold of him a little above the wrists, and without squeezing them, followed all the motions they made ; or if it happened that the signs were not understood, the blind man put himself in the place of the deaf and dumb, who then took hold

---

[1] It is unnecessary to observe that the difficulty of these communications is increased by the want of the signs of the physiognomy, and of a part of the gestures and motions of the body, which the blind man cannot appreciate, and of which he has not even an idea ; for, in speaking, the blind remain without motion and expression.

of his arms in the same manner, and moving them about, as he would have done his own before a person who could see, he filled up the deficiencies of the first operation, and thus completed the series of ideas which he wished to communicate to his companion.

But the degree of instruction of the scholars not being the same, they could not make use of the signs equally well; and supplied them by all the means which their inventive imagination could suggest. It was an extraordinary sight to behold a pantomime acted in the most profound silence by 150 children, anxious to understand each other, and not always succeeding; tired out with long and useless attempts, and often ending, like the builders of Babel, by separating without being able to understand each other; but at the same time not without having given reciprocal proofs of bad humour, by striking as the deaf do, or screaming like the blind.

SECOND SECTION

—•—

CHAPTER XI

Of the Manual Labour common to both Sexes

THOUGH we have neglected nothing in order to carry the education of the blind to the highest degree of perfection possible, as any one may be convinced by the enumeration of the divers branches of study to which they now apply, we should have considered the work as very imperfect, if we did not give these unfortunate beings the means of a certain livelihood, by teaching them some mechanical profession; we should feel very deeply grieved if, after having instructed them in the sciences, they should lose all the benefit of their stay in the Institution, and be obliged to have recourse to public charity, or to solicit their admission into one of those asylums where misfortune and misconduct are but too often confounded.

We have profited by the experience of our predecessors, and our own observations, in the choice of the trades which are fit for the blind.

There is a great number which they might follow, but which would not be profitable to them. We have therefore thought fit, for this reason, to prefer those only which they can easily practise. We always take care to proportion the business with the physical constitution of the individual, with his intelligence, situation, and that of his family ; for it would be absurd to send a blind person into a village with a trade that can only be followed in a large town, and *vice versâ.*

We should have dispensed with the detailed description of the trades followed by the blind, had we not remarked in each of them certain peculiarities, which we conceive it may be useful to point out to those who at a distance from the capital may wish, with the help of this book, to instruct the blind, without removing them. Most of the descriptions are accompanied with explanatory figures, which are not intended as ornaments, but because we are persuaded that when things have not been seen, graphical descriptions are the surest way of making them well known.

CHAPTER XII

Of Knitting

WE shall not here repeat what we have said elsewhere of the facility which the blind have in teaching each other, and of their superiority in this respect over those who can see; but shall only remark, that besides the consolation they feel in being together, their emulation is much greater than that of other children. We have seen blind persons taught singly, who could never succeed in any manual labour. We receive every day children, twelve or fourteen years old, who at home could not learn to make a single stitch, while the youngest with us are able to make garters in a few days.

It is impossible to conceive how tiresome and tedious it is to teach the blind in general in the beginning; this difficulty is doubled again when they are to learn mechanical arts. Knitting, which is very simple in appearance, and which those who have sight learn easily, presents, nevertheless, great difficulties to the blind. It is, however, the best kind of work for exercising the suppleness of their fingers. They are taught to make garters, to exercise them in holding the needles, which they always push too far for fear of dropping their stitches. The blind person who gives the lesson must place himself behind the scholar, and hold his hands, in order to direct the motion of his fingers.

The reason of all the motions is to be explained to him, and his hands are held till he is able to take up the stitches, which is difficult for him because, instead of introducing the needle straight between two threads, he makes it pass through the thread, and thus divides it frequently into several filaments ; from this it happens that their knitting always goes on widening, till their hand is regular. To avoid this division, they give them very thick thread, well twisted, and blunt needles. As to the breadth, decrease, and augmentation of the stocking, they can only do it well by calculating the number of turns ; when, by habit, they have learned to take up their stitches, and to throw them with the needle in the left hand, without closing them, they go on extremely quick, knit very fine, made open work, etc., with as much dexterity as those who can see. Several pupils of the house knit for the hosiers at Paris elastic waistcoats, shirts, and petticoats, which give the greatest satisfaction.

All the blind have not the sense of touch equally fine ; there are some who hardly feel the point of the needles, who are very clumsy in turning the thread and taking the stitches ; such generally begin with wooden needles, of the same size as those for knitting with worsted.

CHAPTER XIII

Of Spinning

SPINNING does not offer the same difficulties as knitting ; nevertheless, the blind must have great practice to be able to spin evenly.   As they are always inclined to bend forward, it is proper to keep their distaff high, and as near the head as possible ; the left hand being placed above the yarn, as with those who can see.

This hand holds the distaff, not only to support it, but to distribute and cull the yarn, which passes through the left hand to be rounded off ; the two hands, being thus brought near together, can, much more easily than if they were insulated, stop any knots that are formed, without the spinner being obliged to suspend the motion of the foot.   He must make the wheel turn gently, in order that the thread may not be too much twisted, which would necessarily happen if the yarn was not given out in proportion with the motion of the wheel.   It is, consequently, better that the wheels of their machines should be a little smaller than they commonly are, that the rotation of the bobbin may not be more accelerated than is necessary.

Plate VIII.

MODE OF SPINNING.

Plate IX.

MAKING PURSES.

CHAPTER XIV

Of Purses

THE blind make purses in several ways, but especially with the frame, the figure of which is seen in Pl. IX., or with the indented mill. They find more difficulty in making use of the mill, because they are exposed to throw one stitch for another, and thus to destroy their own work without perceiving it.

The frame with rods has not this inconvenience. I should wish to describe the manner of using it; but that is rather difficult when it is not before one. Two strings must be stretched transversely, and at about three feet from each other, one at the top and the other at the bottom of the frame, the two ascending branches of which are separated by an interval of about three lines, which is sufficient for the passage of the rods. The silk is stretched on these two strings, while the hand always passes in front of the frame, and describes a motion in the form of the figure 8. From eighty to one hundred threads of silk are put on, according to the length of the purse; on the right side of the silk is placed a thread, which is taken into the tissue, and which serves, when the purse is finished, to recover the stitches, so as to sew the borders. There is a great variety of points;

but they always begin from right to left, by taking alternately a silk in front, which is carried backwards, and one behind, which is brought forwards, after having crossed it with that which follows, to form the knot: as the knots which are made would undo if they were abandoned when the work is come to the last thread, the blind man keeps them on his right forefinger, and stops them by substituting for his finger a thin flat rod, with which he presses transversely the lower stitches, because the work done by the hands alone is repeated at the bottom of the frame by the crossing of the threads; so that there are always two purses made at once.

This business is very proper for blind women, who have generally a finer skin at the end of their fingers than men, and whose hands, besides, being drier, are not exposed to let the silk slip. The combination of the point may be effected in an infinity of ways, and the blind are very ingenious in finding out new ones. Nothing is more common than to see them make flowers, birds, etc., in the tissue of purses. As to the variety of colours in this sort of purses, it only depends on the primitive arrangement of the chain, and the crossing of the threads. The blind who know the bobbins want nobody to set up their frames; they know, moreover, very well what are the colours which can or cannot combine; they do not bring together colours too glaring, and in this respect never offend our taste nor our eyes.

PLATE X.

MODE OF TEACHING NETTING.

CHAPTER XV

Of Girths and Netting

NETTING is more difficult to the blind : those who can see find great difficulty in forming the meshes. The blind have never yet made silk-net, on account of the extreme fineness of the threads. The obstacle would not have been insurmountable ; but the time that must have been given to the execution of this net would have greatly exceeded its value. We have confined ourselves to make fishing-nets with middling-sized packthread. We have no particular process to describe for this work, in which we employ those blind persons who are to live in places where fishing or hunting are practised ; we shall merely observe, that it is very essential to make them sensible how the mesh and the knot are formed, and that the packthread is not to be drawn too hard towards them, to have uniform meshes ; for it is in the knots being equal that the perfection of the work consists. Girths are made in the same way as ribbons ; the process is too well known to need a description ; and, moreover, it has nothing peculiar with respect to the blind.

CHAPTER XVI

Of List Shoes

THE most simple and most useful works are
what we have selected and preferred to teach
the blind. Of this number are list shoes, which
they make very well, quickly, and without the
assistance of anybody;—they teach this work
mutually to each other, like all the rest. It
would be difficult for them to fasten the strips at
an equal distance, if they had nothing to point
out the interval they are to keep ; for this reason they place on each side of the form a narrow
and long piece of leather, pierced with a greater
or less number of points, the head of which is
against the form and the extremity without.
Between each of these points they pass a strip
that has first been fixed above the heel by a
head nail, and which is fastened besides at the
end of the form by another nail. The perfection
of the work consists in afterwards passing the
list crossways, and tightening well on the form
(*see* Plate XI.), in order to fill up the vacancies
that would be left by the uneven edges of the
list, which can only be clipped on one side. By
the same process they make shoes of merinos,
stuff, and coloured skins, which are afterwards
lined with lamb's-skin ; which makes them at
once convenient and pleasant.

PLATE XI.

MAKING LIST SHOES.

CHAPTER XVII

Of List Carpets

IT is only of late that list carpets have been in the number of our manual labours. The mechanism of them, however, is so simple, that one would say it had been invented for the blind ; so that they perform this work, which is not laborious, as well as those who see, and young people of both sexes are trained to it.

As our frames differ a little from those which are used by the manufacturers of chip, it will be necessary to describe it. The workman must be standing, or sitting on a high seat. The frame, which greatly resembles that of the mattress-makers, consists of four moveable pieces ; first, a strong cross-piece of oak, twelve feet long, by three inches of *écarissage*, kept against the wall by two iron hooks ; this bar is furnished on its interior edge with hook-nails, which are fixed in it at the distance of two inches from each other. On each side of this first piece of wood are two other pieces, pierced with holes, at six inches distance, and fixed, by their extremities, by means of cords which facilitate the displacing, to the cross-piece, which they meet, forming with it an acute angle. The other extremity rests on two moveable trestles. Opposite the cross-piece, and above the lateral pieces, is a cylindrical roller, having an equal number of nails. The list is mounted on the two transversal pieces, by fastening it to the nails and hooks; the number of turns determines the breadth of the carpet, and the length varies according as the cylinder is more or less near the cross-piece, which adheres to the wall. This piece turns on itself, and serves to roll the work already done, by means of a wooden handle, which is fastened at pleasure with a cord, which, however, would not prevent the cylinder from rolling, if it were not stopped at its other extremity by a small iron peg, which goes into the holes of the piece. The list being thus stretched lengthways, and the colours properly arranged, there is nothing more to be done than to cross it with other pieces of list, passing alternately above and below from right to left, then from left to right, till we reach the hooks of the cross-piece. The carpet is then unfastened, and the last piece of list is passed crossways to stop it; this, which is the most difficult part, concludes the work.

Our scholars have made a vast number of carpets of all sizes. Many benevolent persons have already purchased them to excite their emulation, and to have in their possession some work of these industrious artisans.

PLATE XII.

MAKING LIST CARPETS

CHAPTER XVIII

Of Woollen-plush Shoes

THE list shoes we have described in Chapter XVI. are not warm, and cannot be worn without a trimming of felt or leather. Those of plush, thicker, and lined with fur, are much warmer. The process for making these shoes was communicated to us by a Dutchman, who sold great quantities of them in his own country, and in the north of Germany. The blind have succeeded completely in fabricating these shoes, which have a great sale, especially in winter. We shall attempt to give an idea of the manner of making them, by first pointing out the choice of the raw material.

For the setting they make use of common wool, which is spun rather thick. Packthread may even be substituted for wool, which makes the work more solid; but the shoe is not so warm. But though wool or packthread may be used indifferently for the setting, it is not the same with the web; for then the shoe would be composed entirely of packthread. The wool for weaving is the same as is used for the setting; but for plush, old carded wool is preferred.

The frame is composed of two pieces : first of a board, longer or shorter, according to the size of the foot ; but always a third longer and broader than the common forms. This board is rounded and denticulated in the upper part, to receive the woollen threads. The lower part is terminated by a stem an inch broad, pierced from before backwards ; this stem enters into an opening, formed in the midst of a piece of wood, rounded (*d*), and furnished all round with pegs more or less distant, according to the size of the frame. The wool being set on the frame is arranged on it. The part which is outward on the frame becomes inward when the shoe is turned, after being finished.

The woollen threads are passed transversely from one side to the other, and when they get to one of the edges, the thread is bent back on itself to go over the same in a contrary direction, taking care to interpose between the meshes, at about six lines distance, a flock of loose wool. When all the threads, stretched from one extremity of the frame to the other, are thus trimmed, the packthreads are cut level with the pegs, and are tied strong together, in order to close the heel. The upper threads are cut three lines from the meshes, and are made to go in below, that they may retain the threads and be hid. The wool that comes over the meshes is then combed with a fine card ; which makes a soft even fur-lining, much better than the skins

PLATE XIII.

METHOD OF MAKING WOOLLEN PLUSH SHOES.

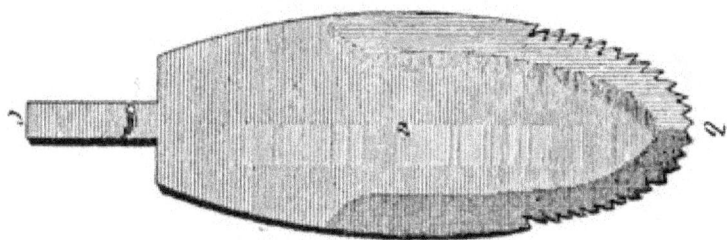

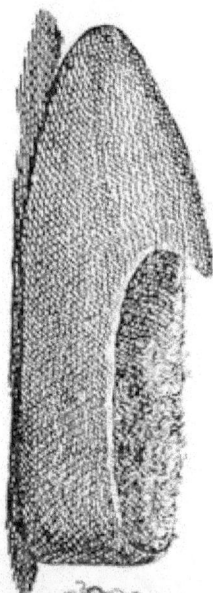

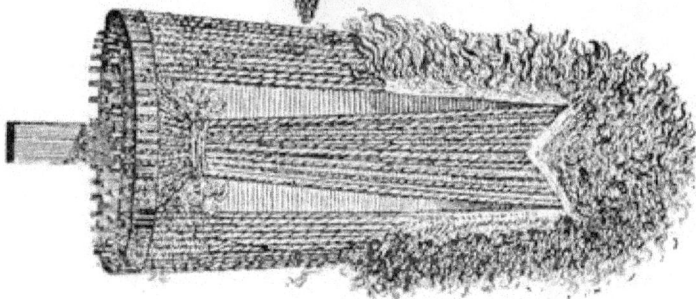

PLATE XIV.

MAKING PLUSH SHOES,

of rabbits and lambs, with which list shoes are commonly trimmed. Finally the shoe is turned when finished (see Plate XIII).

The best way of holding the frame is to place it between the knees, with the upper part resting against the breast. It must not be made so tight as not to turn easily, according as the shoe is trimmed, as is indicated in Plate XIV.

CHAPTER XIX

Of Catgut Whips

THE manufacture of whips in the loom is no longer lucrative, since machinery has been invented by which a single man can make a great many at once. Nevertheless, as the blind can never make whips with the machinery, without assistance, as they did formerly with the frame, we think proper to describe it, that those who wish to make use of it may be able to copy it.

Two parallel boards, fourteen inches in circumference, supported by vertical brackets fifteen or sixteen inches high, which, uniting them, form the *boisseau.* The interval between each bracket is filled with linen, or skin. This *boisseau* is supported by a foot, which is hollowed internally the length of a common whip. The thread or gut which is to cover the whalebone or cane is rolled on leaded bobbins, which hang on the sides of the frame. The whip is fixed in the tambour by a moveable bolt with a spring. By turning the *boisseau* alternately from right to left and left to right, the blind person covers the whip, by making the meshes he wishes, according as he

PLATE XV.

MAKING CATGUT WHIPS.

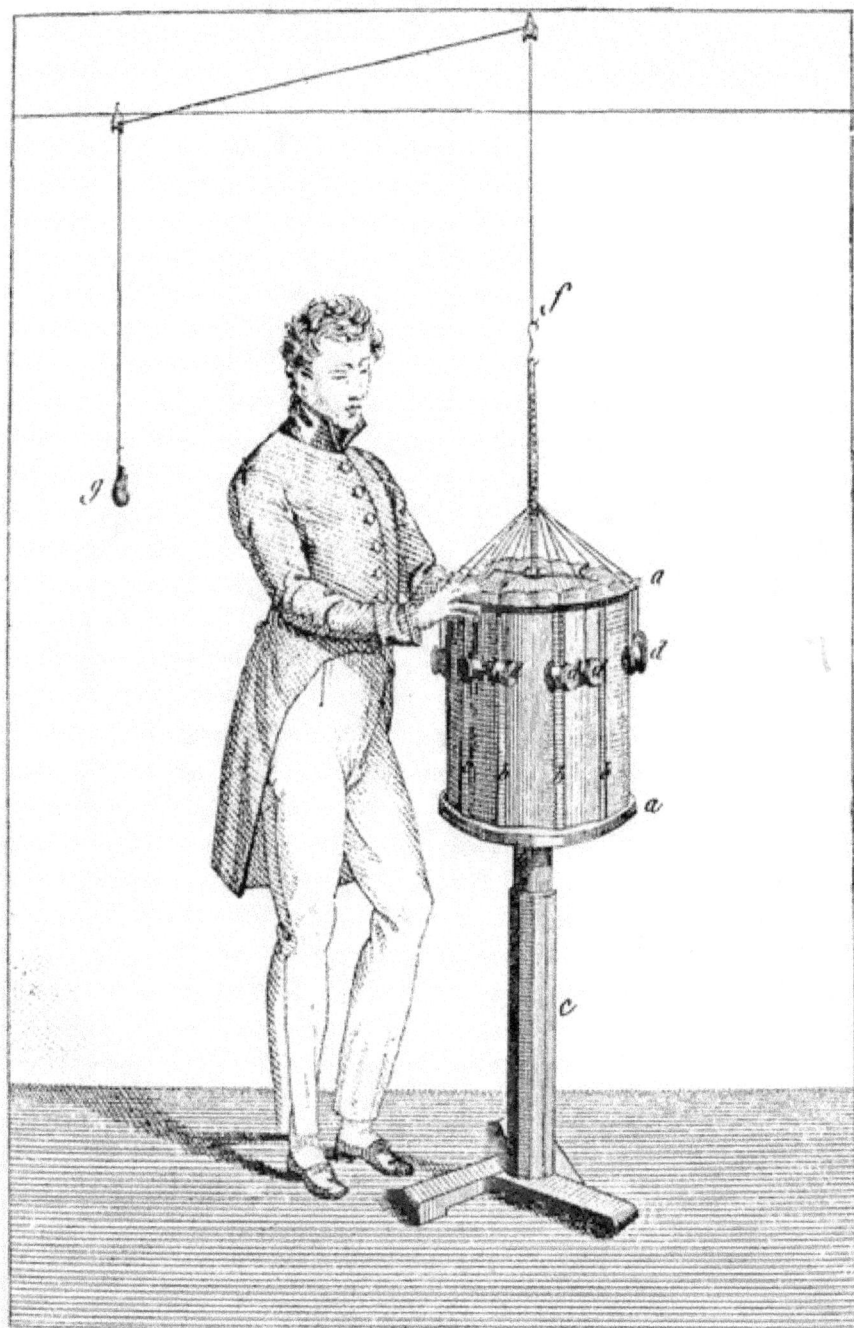

combines the threads, the mingling of which produces the variety of points.

The whip is fastened by the upper part to a
cord which is stretched by means of a weight
suspended to its extremity, by which means the
blind man has only to open the bolt to raise the
whip.

The blind are very clever in raising this frame,
which is at the same time an agreeable recreation
for them.   Some of them can make as many as
ten whips a day in this way, which, before the
establishment of the machinery, was a livelihood.

CHAPTER XX

MANUAL WORKS PECULIAR TO BOYS

Of Weaving

If there is any profession that is eminently suitable to the blind, it is that of weaving, which they have only been put to, however, since the translation of the establishment, though there had been for a long time, in the spinning house of the hospitals, among the other workmen, a blind man who supported his family by the produce of his labour.

Except setting the warp, for which sight is indispensable, there is no part of weaving which the blind cannot execute: they fix themselves the pieces on the looms: they prepare and dry the warp without burning the threads. They manufacture sail-cloth, of which sacks and sails are made, and worked napkins. We have even contrived to teach them to make cotton handkerchiefs of different colours. To prevent their making any mistake in throwing the shuttle, a packthread is placed on the right side of the warp, and is rolled with it on the beam, and

PLATE XVI

WEAVING.

has knots of different sizes, which indicate the change of colour, and the number of throws to be made with each shuttle. One, or several notches, at the extremity of the shuttle, according as has been agreed, serves to make the colours known.

Our frames differ from the common ones only by a denticulated wheel, which we have added on the right side of the beam, on which an iron hatch rests, rendered moveable by a cord by which the warp may be unrolled without changing one's situation, in proportion as the web is wove and moved off.

CHAPTER XXI

Of Straw Chair-bottoms

THE making straw bottoms for chairs is a mode
of industry which the blind perform with ease.
They are generally made with rye-straw dyed, or
of its natural colour.   It is wet and made into
bundles, and beat with a wooden hammer, in order
that the straws, coming nearer together, may be
formed into cords, more or less thick.   The chair is
placed on a tourniquet, with a double branch and
a screw, which rests on a stem fixed in a stone
heavy enough not to be overturned by the weight
of the chair.   The blind man being seated with
his hands on a level with the upper part of the
chair-bottom, he fastens the first straws on the
side of the back of the chair, and continues
turning it round every time he adds a straw.

The blind can work plain or coloured straw
equally well; but the work which suits them
best is that of the coarse chairs that are used in
the churches or public walks.

I have not mentioned straw hats, as the way
of making them is sufficiently known.   It has
much connection with other works in straw.

Plate XVII.

MAKING STRAW CHAIR-BOTTOMS.

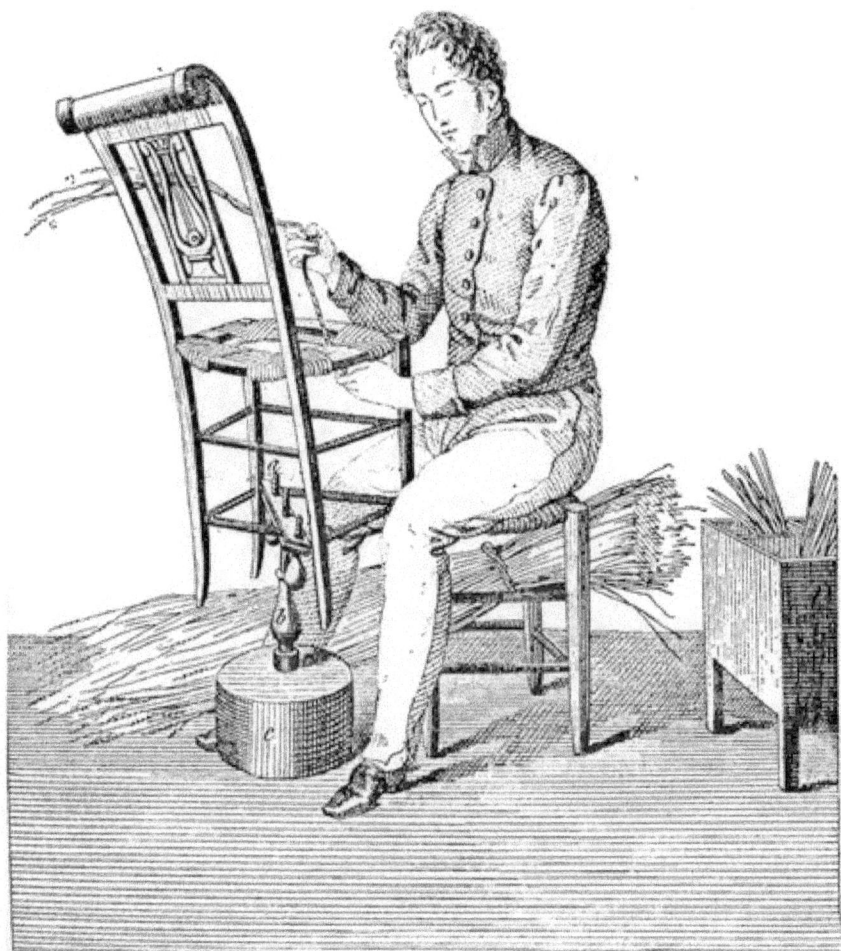

The blind make the flat straw very well, such as women's hats are made of in Switzerland ; but they take a long time to join the pieces together ; for which reason they have given up making the finer sort of straw hats, which, though more difficult to make, were neither more handsome nor more saleable.

CHAPTER XXII

Of Rope-making

THE blind easily learn the business of rope-making, which we teach, in preference, to those who are to inhabit sea-ports.

They are first employed with coarse tow, to accustom them to spin smooth. The right hand is placed before the left to stop anything which might render the cord uneven, as we have observed for the spinning of thread. It is necessary that the hemp should be much wetted, and the wheel turned gently, that the thread may not be twisted too much, because, of course, they separate the yarn more slowly than those who see.

They can make cord or common ropes, but not cables, as well as those who see ; but this part of the business is now done by machinery.

They are employed in combing hemp, even with the finest combs ; and the delicacy of their touch serves them better in this operation than our eyes do us.

They use the machinery for making balls of packthread with great address, and make them as well as those who can see.

PLATE XVIII.

ROPE MAKING.

Plate XIX.

MAKING BASKETS

CHAPTER XXIII

Of Basket Work

THE basket trade is only one of the dependencies of the chip-work, which we have already mentioned. It was one of the first trades given to the blind, because they can perform every part of it without assistance from those who see.

For some years past, however, we have had no workshop for baskets at the Institution, from the difficulty we found in disposing of them, and the capital they required in advance. The baskets, when made, occupied a great deal of room, and were damaged by drying up.

Notwithstanding, this business is completely suited for the blind, who, when they were employed in it, made very pretty articles, not only of osier, but also of rice and rye straw, and rushes, which were not in the least inferior to those made by the blind in London, who are almost solely employed in basket-making.

CHAPTER XXIV

Of Straw, Rush, and Spanish Plush Mats

WE have frequently said, the more easy the trades that are given to the blind, the more advantageous they are to them. Nothing is easier than to make them perform extraordinary feats, by accustoming them to conquer difficulties apparently insurmountable; but what advantage would such useless employments be to these unfortunate beings?

All the scholars, without distinction, learn to make straw and rush mats, as they are sure articles of sale in almost every part of France.

Straw Mats.—They are made with rye-straw, which is more solid than any other. They begin by wetting the straw, and beating it, to render it flexible; the braids are made with three stalks, and should be flat and very smooth. They are taught early to take them up below, that no ends may be seen on the upper part of the mat. They must not be made to wait for another bundle till they have entirely finished the first, as the mat would then be uneven. The straw is hung on a trestle, before which the workman is placed, seated or standing.

Rush Mats.—They are made with rushes gathered on the banks of rivers, which, always preserving a greenish colour, makes it unnecessary to dye them. These rushes are moistened and beat in the same way as the straw; but when the mats are made, they are carefully dried, for fear any moisture within them may make them rot. These mats are much easier to make than those of straw.

Plush Mats. — These mats, which are also called *gazon*, on account of their green colour, are made of a very fine rush which grows in Spain, on the shores of the Mediterranean. In that country they are used for making coarse mats for packing up the Alicante soda. We buy them of the druggists to get the rushes, which are picked out according to their length and size, and joined in bundles when they are to be used; they must be well tied together, in order to be beat with an iron bar, to bruise each stalk and divide it into plushy filaments. Thus prepared, it is formed into braids with five branches; but as it is commonly of a yellowish colour, it is necessary to dye it to make it green.[1] The braids being fastened to hooks

---

[1] This dye is made with three ounces of indigo, diluted in a quart of weak sulphuric acid, which gives at first a bluish solution; to make it green, a pound of the yellow root of *Curcuma longa* is added, in powder, which is diluted in seven buckets of cold water; —with this may be dyed about thirty-eight fathoms of mat.

fixed in two long cross beams, the blind man sits on these mats, and, with a long needle, and waxed packthread, sews them together, first two and two, then four and four, and so on progressively.

Plate XX.

MAT MAKING.

CHAPTER XXV

Games of the Blind

THE habitual state of concentration in which the blind are plunged from the want of objects to distract them, makes some diversions necessary for them ; this has induced us to make known a part of our games : too much cannot be done to alleviate their lot : and the intention, I trust, will excuse the description I here insert of some of their games.

The blind have long since played at cards with great dexterity, either with each other, or with people who see. Cards had been made for them in which the colour was raised a little ; but this soon rubbing off gave rise to mistakes, and it was found better to have them pricked. We shall select clubs, to show how such cards are commonly made : the king is indicated by a point placed at the junction of the upper third of the card with the two inferior thirds ; the queen, by a point placed at about the upper sixth and to the right ; the knave, in the same position, to the left ; the ace, in the upper sixth, but in the middle, and above the king ; the 10, in the upper third, to the right ; the 9, in the opposite direction.

The 8 is marked like the queen, and the 7 like the knave, except that the point is placed in the interval between the ace and the queen. The other cards are marked in the same way, and only differ by the number and position of the points. The hearts are indicated by two horizontal points (..) ; spades, by two points placed diagonally (:) ; diamonds, by two vertical points (:).

The pricking should be made from the outside inwards, that the rough may be felt on the same side as the colour ; and, if the blind play with people who can see, their cards may not be known. The pricks need not be very large, and may be done with a fine needle, which is sufficient for most blind persons.

Of Chess.

Chess is perfectly fit for the blind, as it requires calculation, and because, even in their recreations, they like to occupy their minds. But it is necessary to make the men solid by fixing them on the board, which we have contrived to do, by placing a round pivot at the lower end of each chessman, which goes into a hole formed in the squares of the board. The blind recognise their adversary's men by a little thin point almost imperceptible, on the knob at their upper end. By these means they can touch the men without overturning them.

PLATE XXI.

MANNER OF POINTING PLAYING CARDS.

DIAMONDS.	SPADES.	HEARTS.	CLUBS.
Roi. 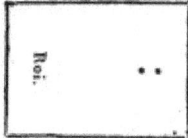	Roi. 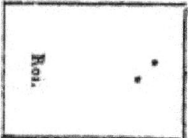	Roi. 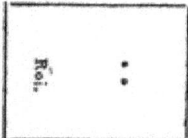	Roi. 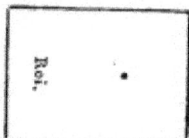
Dame. 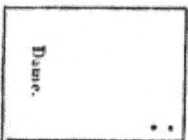	Dame. 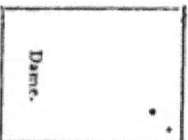	Dame. 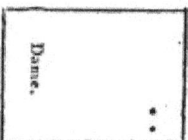	Dame. 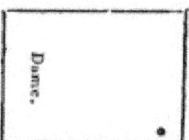
Valet. 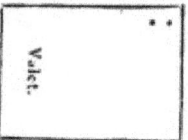	Valet. 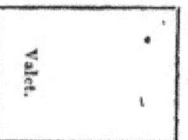	Valet. 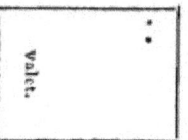	Valet. 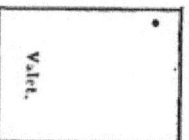
As. 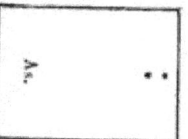	As. 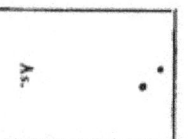	As. 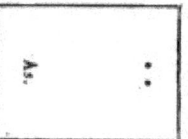	As. 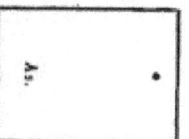
10 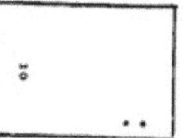	10 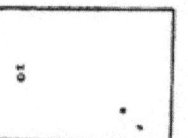	10 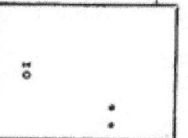	10 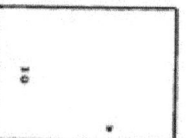
9 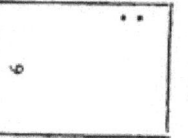	9 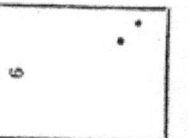	9 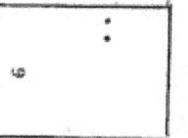	9 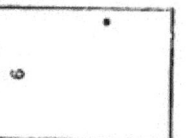
8 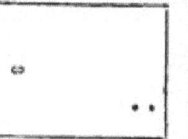	8 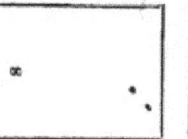	8 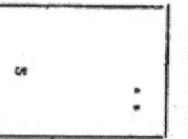	8 
7 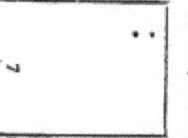	7 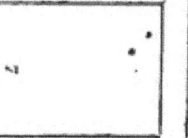	7 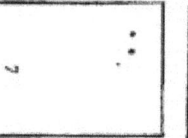	7 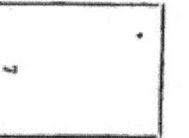

Of the Game of Drafts.

All that is necessary for the blind in this game is, that the men should be made of different kinds of wood. A draft-board, however, might be made on purpose for them, with the squares of one colour, a quarter of a line lower than the others, and the men might be distinguished by a notch on the upper part. A pivot also might be put under them to stop them.

The blind play with the same dexterity at trictrac (if the men are arranged for them), at dominoes, dice, and all other games, provided they are told exactly the numbers and colours, when they have no means of having them in relief.

CHAPTER XXVI

Conclusion

I HERE conclude what I had to say on the instruction of the blind. May the efforts I have made to make myself worthy of public esteem not be lost! I shall think myself happy if they contribute to excuse the imperfections of a work made in a hurry, in the midst of the laborious occupations of my employment.

The greatest part of this work is composed of descriptions of mechanical works which it is not easy to embellish. I have endeavoured to compensate, by the exactness of the facts, for what is wanting in regard to correctness of style, and purity of expression. I repeat, in concluding, to make the blind known, with their qualities and defects; to tell in what studies and occupations they may be usefully employed; to excite sentiments of benevolence and interest in favour of them; such are the objects I proposed to myself in writing this Essay. If I have attained them, my wishes are fully gratified.

Edinburgh: T. and A. CONSTABLE, Printers to Her Majesty.

REPRINT 1895.

EDUCATION OF THE BLIND

THE

NORTH AMERICAN

REVIEW

VOL. XXXVII.

BOSTON

CHARLES BOWEN, 141, WASHINGTON STREET

1833

LONDON

SAMPSON LOW, MARSTON AND COMPANY
LIMITED
St. Dunstan's House
FETTER LANE, FLEET STREET, E.C.

1895

Some Books and Papers about the Blind

REPRINTED BY

Messrs. SAMPSON LOW, MARSTON & COMPANY

LIMITED

St. Dunstan's House

FETTER LANE, FLEET STREET, LONDON

1774

THE EDUCATION OF THE BLIND. A LETTER IN THE EDINBURGH MAGAZINE AND REVIEW for NOVEMBER, 1774. Price 1s.

1793

TRANSLATION OF AN ESSAY ON THE EDUCATION OF THE BLIND by M. HAÜY. Dedicated to the King of France in 1786. Price 1s.

1801

HINTS TO PROMOTE BENEFICENCE, &c., by Dr. LETTSOM, with an account of the Blind Asylum at Liverpool. Price 1s.

1819

TRANSLATION OF AN ESSAY ON THE INSTRUCTION AND AMUSEMENTS OF THE BLIND by Dr. GUILLIÉ. Published in Paris, 1817. Illustrated, 5s.

1837

RECENT DISCOVERIES FOR FACILITATING THE EDUCATION OF THE BLIND. By JAMES GALL, of Edinburgh. Illustrated. Price 2s.

1842

THE EDUCATION, EMPLOYMENTS, &c., AT THE ASYLUM FOR THE BLIND, GLASGOW. By JOHN ALSTON. Illustrated. Price 2s.

1861

TRANSLATION BY REV. W. TAYLOR OF THE MANAGEMENT AND EDUCATION OF THE BLIND. By J. G. KNIE, of Breslau. Price 1s.

OBSERVATIONS ON THE EMPLOYMENT, EDUCATION, AND HABITS OF THE BLIND, with a Comparative View of the Benefits of the Asylum and School Systems. By THOMAS ANDERSON.

REPRINT 1895.

EDUCATION OF THE BLIND

THE

NORTH AMERICAN

REVIEW

VOL. XXXVII.

BOSTON

CHARLES BOWEN, 141, WASHINGTON STREET

1833

LONDON

SAMPSON LOW, MARSTON AND COMPANY

LIMITED

St. Dunstan's House

FETTER LANE, FLEET STREET, E.C.

1895

LONDON :

PRINTED BY WILLIAM CLOWES AND SONS, LIMITED,

STAMFORD STREET AND CHARING CROSS.

ART. II.—*Education of the Blind.*
1. *Essai sur l'Education des Aveugles ;* par M. HAÜY, Paris. 1786.
2. *Coup-d'Œil D'un Aveugle sur les Sourds-Muets.* Par ALEXANDRE RODENBACH, *Membre du Musée des Aveugles de Paris et de plusieurs Sociétés savantes ; Auteur de la Lettre sur les Aveugles faisant Suite à celle de Diderot,* &c., &c. Bruxelles. 1829.

IT has long been to us a matter of surprise that the blind have been so much neglected. Our age, compared with those that have passed away, is truly a humane one ; never has more attention been paid to individual man than now ; never has the imperative duty of society to provide for the wants of those whom nature or accident has thrown upon its charity, been more deeply felt, or more conscientiously discharged. Philanthropy has, in fact, been pushed almost to folly, and well-meaning enthusiasts, in their eager zeal to find new objects, seem half disposed to create suffering for the sake of relieving it : or, at least, would relieve one class at the expense of another : like the good Las Casas, who, in his blind enthusiasm for the Aborigines of South America, tore thousands of Africans from their homes, and made them slaves, that his darling Indians might go free and walk upright in lordly indolence. England and the United States are peculiarly characterised by associations for aiding the cause of humanity. Every infirmity, every misfortune, every vice even, has a phalanx of philanthropists to oppose its effects—every rank of society, every age, from the cradle to the grave, is provided with associated aiders and supporters. . They begin before the birth of the object by the preparation of lying-in hospitals, and sometimes even rescue the victim from the grasp of death, as is seen in the admirable and not unfrequently successful labours of the Humane Society.

That this spirit of humanity has not always been well directed ; that extraordinary efforts and great expenses have been lavished upon one class of unfortunate persons, while others more deserving and afflicted have been left neglected, is apparent in the case of the blind, who have been almost entirely overlooked in the general and eager search after new objects of philanthropy. The very efforts which have been made to lighten the burden of their woes have only added more weight to it, and those whom nature has bowed down under a load of affliction have been farther crushed by a sense of humiliating dependence. The cry of the blind has not been merely for bread, it has not been for alms ; these are not their only wants, but they claim our sympathies and our patient assistance to enable them to exert their own faculties, to develop their own powers, and to do something to break the listless inactivity which constitutes for them the *tædium vitæ*. But instead of administering to their wants, instead of striking at the root of the evil, and preventing blindness from necessarily entailing misery on the sufferer, men have increased its ill effects by diminishing the incentives to action ; and the hand of charity has wounded while it soothed the sufferer. The post of the blind has always been by the highway, in the humble attitude of the beggar ; their dwelling-place has been the alms-houses, where men try to hide and perpetuate much misery, which, by patient attention and resolute perseverance, they might entirely remove.

Discouraged by the apparent incapacity of the blind, men have only endeavoured to administer to them physical comfort in the shape of food and clothing. Even the philanthropist has shrunk from the task of endeavouring to combat the ills which blindness entails upon the sufferer ; and until within a few years no establishments existed in Europe, where the blind played any other part than that of listless drones and melancholy dependents. It is a little curious that a Pagan nation should have set a good example to enlightened Christians in this respect. It is said that in Japan the blind were long ago made to fill a comparatively useful sphere. The Government keeps a large number of them in an establishment, and their business is to learn the history of the empire through all the remote ages, to arrange it systematically by chapter and verse in their memories, and to transmit it to the young blind, who are to hand it down to the next generation, and thus form a sort of perennial walking and talking library of useful historical knowledge. It would be singular and interesting to enter this library of living books, and consult these breathing archives ; to go up to a man instead of pulling down a folio ; to hear him repeat his index, and then to turn over the tablets of his memory like the leaves of a volume until he comes to the matter in question.

We shall touch but lightly in this article on the physical and moral effects of blindness upon its victim, but confine ourselves to a practically useful view of the subject. We shall discuss the question of the capacity of the blind for receiving such an intellectual and physical education as will enable them to fill useful and ornamental places in society ; we shall notice the system pursued in the different European institutions, and point out the changes and improvements which, in our opinion, may be introduced in the treatment of the blind.

The effects of blindness upon the physical man, whatever they may be upon the intellectual, are decidedly pernicious ; not directly and necessarily, but, nevertheless, almost inevitably. The mind is not called into action, the muscular power is not developed by exercise and labour, the sufferer dares not run about and play with his comrades ; he cannot work in the open air, nor get the healthful movement which is necessary to bring the frame to the temper that will enable it to wear well in after life, and it consequently soon wears out. Hence we see so many of the blind, who were comparatively intelligent and active in childhood, gradually drooping through youth into premature old age ; becoming first inactive, then stupid, then idiotic, and finally going down to an early grave with the light of intellect completely extinguished, and enveloped in both physical and intellectual darkness. This is purely the effect of physical inaction, and this inaction always must have this effect ; hence so few strong men are found among the blind, hence so many weak and helpless ones.

The development of some of the particular powers seems also to be affected by blindness : this is particularly observable in regard to the sexual propensity, which, while it is particularly strong in the deaf, is weak in the blind ; and for the very obvious reason that the imagination is fed in the one case by the sight, and in the other is not. The same principle which causes the physical inability of the blind contributes mainly to the perfection of the senses which they possess, for these are called into strong and continual action. The touch, the hearing, and the smell of the blind, sometimes become so acute that they differ as widely from the same senses in the state in which we possess them, as does the scent of the spaniel from that of the greyhound.

It is a popular, but unphilosophical saying, that when " we are
of one sense bereft, it but retires into the rest." The blind man
does not hear any better, merely because he has not the sense of
sight ; but because his peculiar situation and wants oblige him to
cultivate his ear ; just as the sailor acquires a power of descrying
vessels at a distance, which is unattainable by the eye of a lands-
man. Few men are aware of the nature and extent of their own
powers ; few are aware that they are endowed with senses capable
of almost unlimited amelioration. When we reflect upon the
astonishing change which culture and attention effect in the
physical powers, we are inclined to believe stories like those of
" him who of old could rend the oak." We once knew a man
who had served for thirty years as a sort of telescope and
telegraph for the island of Hydra ; he used every day to take his
post with a glass upon the summit of the island, and look out for
the approach of vessels ; and although there were over three
hundred sail belonging to the island, he would tell the name of
each one, as she approached, with unerring certainty, while she
was still at such a distance as to present to a common eye only a
confused white blur upon the clear horizon. We hardly dare
recount some of the feats of vision performed by this man, or
give the number of miles at which he could distinguish ships,
for it would seem incredible to those who are accustomed to see
through our heavy atmosphere " as through a glass darkly " ; it
convinced us, however, that the old Athenians might have been
able, as is said of them, at twenty miles' distance from their city,
to discern the point of Minerva's spear as it glittered from the
Parthenon, the loftiest point of the lofty Acropolis.

The blind are obliged, both from inclination and necessity, to
pay as much attention to the cultivation of their senses as our
telescope of Hydra, and the result is still more astonishing. The
hearing is the sense which seems to us the most changed in the
blind, although we are aware that many people, and even many
of the blind themselves, say it is the touch. May we not, however, call all the senses mere modifications of the sense of touch ?
What is *touch* ? Lexicographers call it the sense of feeling ; now
this sense of feeling is inherent in a greater or less degree in
every part of the surface of the body ; in the lips it is very acute,
in the ear it is still more so, and the undulations of the air,
striking upon the apparatus of hearing, are felt, just as the pressure

of a hard substance is by the rest of the body. Is not the power
of vision, too, dependent on the touch? The rays of light strike
upon the *retina*, and we *feel* colour. The taste is decidedly a
modification of touch, though we are not aware that it is capable
of such change by use as the other senses. The power of distinguishing the physical qualities of bodies by the lips and
tongue is very striking in the blind, and the notorious fact that
they can pass a thread through the eye of a fine cambric needle
is much less surprising than some others which we shall have
occasion to adduce : but, as we said, we do not know that the
other kind of *touch*, which we call *taste*, is sensibly improved.
Perhaps, however, it arises from the fact of the generality of
mankind tasting so much, and drawing so much pleasure from
the use of the sense, that the blind cannot outdo them. This at
least is certain, the blind are not often *gastronomes*.

Diderot, in his ingenious dissertation, remarks, that "of all
the senses the sight is the most superficial ; the ear the most
dainty ;* the smell the most voluptuous ; the taste the most
whimsical and inconstant ; the touch the most profound and
philosophic."

But we will leave metaphysical discussion, and consider the
improvement of the senses, in the light in which it has the most
direct bearing upon the situation and the education of the blind.

And first, of the hearing : people are not generally aware of
the powers of the ear, and instances which we may quote of it in
the blind may at first appear incredible ; we have known blind
men, for instance, who could not only ascertain the shape and
dimensions of an apartment by the sound of their voice, but
who could, on entering one with which they were familiar, tell by
striking their cane on the floor, and listening to the echo,
whether any of the large articles of furniture had been removed
from it, or shifted from their usual places. What seeing person
would think it possible, with his eyes bandaged, to tell which was
the tallest and which was the shortest of a number of speakers
merely by the direction in which the sound came from their
mouths to his ear ? Yet, many blind persons can not only do
this, but can ascertain very nearly the ages of the persons. We

* Diderot often used words for mere euphony, and sometimes for—he
could not tell what; this was probably the case when he talked about an
oreille orgueilleuse.

have made this experiment in more than fifty instances with the
blind, and in the great majority of cases they came as near the
mark as we did, aided by the eyes. There is no doubt that the
voice is changed with every changing year ; we seize only upon
the extremes of the chain ; we can tell the shrill scream of the
child from the rough firm voice of manhood, and the trembling
tones of old age ; but besides these,—besides the difference in
the volume and pitch which exists between the voices of different
persons, there is another produced by the course of years ; and
time stamps his impress upon the voice as surely as upon the
face. The blind man tests these by his practised ear, and not
only can ascertain with tolerable correctness the age of the
speaker, but pronounce upon his height, the dimensions of his
chest, and so forth.

Nor is this the most extraordinary part of the discriminating
power of some blind men, who seize upon the slight variations
of the intonation of the voice as we do upon the changes of the
countenance, and judge by them of what is passing in the mind
of the speaker. We all of us wear at times a mask upon the
countenance, and draw the curtain of hypocrisy over this window
of the soul, to conceal what is going on within ; but we seldom
think of the voice ; and it is upon this that the blind man seizes,
as upon a thread, to direct him to the seat of the passions.
Hence it is that some of them can ascertain on so short an
acquaintance the disposition and character of persons : they are
not imposed on by the splendour of dress, they are not prejudiced
by an ungainly air, they are not won by a smile, nor are they
dazzled by the blaze of beauty or led captive, as many are wont
to be, by the fascination of a lovely eye. The voice is to them
the criterion of beauty, and when its melodious tones come
forcibly stamped with sincerity from the soul, their imaginations
at once give to the speaker a graceful form and a beautiful face.
It is recorded of the father of Fletcher, the novelist, that he was
long continued in the post of Judge in the Police Court of
London after he became blind ; and that he knew the voices of
more than three thousand of the light-fingered gentry, and could
recognise them at once when brought in.

The ear of some animals is surprisingly acute, and there is no
doubt that it is improved by blindness ; we know of a horse who,
after becoming blind, evidently had his hearing very much

sharpened, for when feeding in the pasture with others, far from the road, he would hear the sound of hoofs, and raise his head and whinny out his salute, long before his companions betrayed any consciousness of the approach of the passing stranger.

So with the blind man, when he is walking along the street he can tell whether it is wide or narrow, whether the houses are high or low, whether an opening which he may be passing is a court closed up at the end, or whether it has an outlet to another street ; and he can tell by the sound of his footsteps in what lane, or court, or square he is. He goes along boldly, seeming to see with his ears, and to have landmarks in the air.

The accuracy of the ear gives to blind persons a very great advantage in music ; they depend entirely upon it ; and hence they harmonize so well together, and keep such perfect accord in time, that Paganini, after listening to some pieces performed by pupils of the Institution for the Blind in Paris, declared that he never before had an adequate notion of what harmony was.

The touch is capable of being equally perfected, and many remarkable instances are given of this. Saunderson, the blind Professor of Mathematics in the University of Cambridge, in England, became such a connoisseur of ancient coins that he could detect the modern counterfeits, even when good eyes were puzzled about them. There lived a few years ago a blind man in Austria, who executed very good busts by feeling the faces of persons and imitating them ; and there is now a bust of the late Emperor, executed by this blind man, and preserved in the Museum in Vienna, which is considered a very good likeness. Persons who have witnessed exhibitions at the institutions for the blind have been surprised at the ease and fluency with which they can read books printed in raised letters, by passing the fingers rapidly over them ; this, however, is by no means so extraordinary as many other instances which are notorious, though not well understood. A blind man, for instance, when walking in a perfect calm, can ascertain the proximity of objects by the feeling of the atmosphere upon his face ; it would seem at first that the echo given back, were it only from his breathing, might be sensible to his ear ; but we have ascertained by experiment that a blind man with his ears stopped could tell when any large object was close to his face, even when it was approached so slowly as not to cause any sensible current of air.

It is a common supposition that the blind can distinguish colours, but after much research we are convinced that this is impossible ; all the blind whom we have consulted on the subject have replied that they had no such power, and they did not believe that any blind person ever had it. Indeed, what tangible quality can there be in a substance so ethereal that it passes unobstructed through dense glass ? There was an instance of a girl in England, who was generally believed to have this power ; and the trials and tests which she successfully underwent somewhat puzzled us, until an explanation of the difficulty offered itself in the chemical properties of the different coloured rays of light. She could ascertain the colours of different pieces of cloth by applying them to her lips in succession ; and she must have learned that some colours radiate heat more rapidly than others, so that she could tell white from black by the different degree of warmth which it imparted to her lips. This is perhaps one of the most extraordinary instances of nicety of touch which can be quoted. The same girl used to astonish incredulous visitors by reading the large letters of the maker's name, written in their hats, while they held them behind her back.

We shall not dwell upon the changes which take place in the sense of smell, great as they are, particularly in those unfortunate beings who are both deaf and blind ; nor upon those of the taste, for neither of these senses are much depended upon by the blind in the acquisition of knowledge.

We have been thus particular in showing the superiority of the senses of touch and of hearing in the blind, because it is this superiority which compensates them in some measure for the want of sight, and puts them more nearly upon a par with seeing persons, in the attainment of knowledge : a subject which we shall now consider. And first, we shall endeavour to establish the position, that there is hardly a subject in the whole range of science which may not be mastered without the aid of the sight ; this fact, if it be not deducible from a consideration of the nature of the senses, may be established by numerous instances in history of blind men having raised themselves to eminence in various professions. How little do men in general learn by the sight, that they could not learn without it ? How vast and varied is the knowledge of some men, who seldom go beyond the bounds of the city in which they were born, and whose knowledge is obtained from books! But cannot the same knowledge be obtained by hearing books read by another? Nay, does not the mind grasp it more firmly, and hold it more tenaciously? The very facility with which we can glance over a page, and the ease with which we can refer to it, causes us to be negligent and inattentive ; the eye often travels listlessly over sentences, while the mind is travelling elsewhere ; and sometimes, even when performing two simultaneous operations of reading and repeating aloud, we may be thinking of something else. But the blind man has the greatest inducement to attention ; he knows that he cannot refer to the passages he hears, and he therefore arranges and stores them away in his mind with the greatest order, and can refer to them with ease.

The knowledge which we obtain from books, however, will not be long beyond the reach of the blind man, since ingenuity is fast bringing to perfection a system of printing for his use ; but even if it were so, there is a still more vast and valuable mine of knowledge which is to be explored by conversation and intercourse with the world, and to this the blind man has free access. There are a great many shrewd and intelligent men in the world who are as blind to books as he is, and who can hardly sign their names.

How did Malte Brun acquire his knowledge of the geography of the countries about which he wrote so fully and so well,—was it by visiting them? No! it was by a process of study which he might have followed as thoroughly, though not quite so easily, had he been deprived of sight. How do we learn the geography, the history, the language, the manners and customs of different countries which we never saw,—is it not by means which are perfectly within the reach of a blind man, provided the necessary pains are taken with him? In mathematics, do we not close our eyes, the more completely to shut out external impressions, and the more intensely to bend our faculties to the contemplation of the question? And in every mathematical calculation whatever, has not the blind man an immense advantage over us, provided he be furnished with the means of putting down his results in a manner to be read by himself? Now we shall see that such means are provided for him, and that he can go through arithmetical and algebraical calculations with greater ease than seeing persons. All kinds of problems may also be solved by the blind, since tangible diagrams can be prepared for them.

The languages, the classics, the long range of history, the wide
field of letters, are all open to the blind man ; we see no obstacle
at all in the way of his becoming an able counsellor at law, or
occupying the pulpit with ability and advantage. As for music,
and her sister poetry, it would be an idle waste of words to try to
prove that the blind can become their successful votaries,—for
there stand a long array of sightless bards, headed by the 'blind
old man of Scio's rocky isle,' whose verse has charmed every age,
and been repeated in every tongue. In music, the names of
Stanley, Gautier, and Chauvain are already conspicuous.

But, after all, the best argument in favour of the capacity of
the blind for receiving a high degree of education is to be found
in the number of those who have raised themselves to eminence.
Ancient history abounds with them ; the names of Didymus of
Alexandria, Eusebius and Aufidius are well known, and Diodotus,
the master of Cicero, who lost his sight, still pursued his studies
with great success ; his illustrious disciple says of him, " Is vero,
quod credibile vix esset, cum in philosophia multo magis assiduè,
quam antea versaretur, et cum fidibus Pythagoraeorum more
uteretur, cumque ei libri noctes et dies legerentur, quibus in
studiis oculis non egebat, tum, quod sine oculis fieri vix videtur,
geometriae munus tuebatur verbis praecipiens discentibus, unde,
quo, quamque lineam scriberent." Achmed Ben Soliman, one of
the most beautiful Arabian writers and poets, was blind from his
infancy.

But we need not go back to distant ages to find examples of
men who have raised themselves to eminence, in spite of the
obstacles which nature has placed in their way. Saunderson, who
flourished in the last century, and filled so ably the professorship
of mathematics at the University of Cambridge in England, had
lost his sight in infancy, and is known to every one. He published a volume called the Elements of Algebra, an extraordinary
work, filled with singular demonstrations which a seeing person
would not perhaps have hit upon. But the most wonderful of
Saunderson's performances were his dissertation upon optics, light
and colours, with which he used to delight and astonish his
audience.

The Rev. Dr. Blacklock, too, gave extraordinary proofs of the
power and correctness of the imagination, for though he never
saw the light, he has left us some most beautiful delineations of

nature, in the volumes of poems which he published—as in his Wish :—

> On rising ground the prospect to command,
> Untinged with smoke, where vernal breezes blow,
> In rural neatness let my cottage stand;
> Here wave a wood, and there a river flow.
> Oft from the neighbouring hills and pastures near
> Let sheep with tender-bleat salute my ear, &c.

And again,—

> Let long lived pansies here their scents bestow,
> The violet languish and the roses glow;
> In yellow glory let the crocus shine,
> Narcissus here his love-sick head recline ;
> Here hyacinths in purple sweetness rise,
> And tulips, tinged with beauty's fairest dyes.

Contemporary with Blacklock was Dr. Henry Moyes, the eloquent professor of philosophical chemistry in Manchester. "Though he lost his sight in early infancy, he made rapid progress in different sciences ; he acquired not only the fundamental principles of physics, music, and languages, but he plunged deeply into the most abstract sciences, and displayed a minute knowledge of geometry, of optics, of algebra, of astronomy, of chemistry, and, in a word, of most of the branches of the Newtonian philosophy. Every time he entered into society, he first passed some minutes in silence : the sound enabled him to judge of the dimensions of the apartment, and the different voices of the number of persons present. His calculations in this respect were very exact, and his memory was so faithful that he was seldom mistaken. I have known him recognise a person the instant he heard him speak, although more than two years had elapsed since they had met. He could ascertain with precision the stature of persons by the direction of their voices ; and he made tolerable hits at their character and disposition by the tone of their conversation." *

The instances which we have quoted are but a small portion of those which may be adduced in favour of the facility of giving to the blind an education. These were men who were endowed with genius ; but great as were their powers, their minds would

---

* Memoir on Blindness, by Mr. Bew, of the Philosophical Society of Manchester.

have been left in darkness as total as their bodies, had they not been fortunate enough to possess friends of a philosophic turn of mind, whose affections prompted them to great efforts to overcome the obstacle of blindness. The zeal of the subjects more than requited them.

We will now adduce one example of astonishing powers of another kind, in a blind man, who was entirely neglected in his youth : it is that of John Metcalf, about whom ample evidence and information may be obtained from the transactions of the Philosophical Society of Manchester, and from the Memoir of Mr. Bew. Metcalf was a native of Derbyshire, in England, and he early became so well acquainted with the roads, that he took up the trade of a teamster, driving his cart from one place to another. During very dark nights, he used to act as guide to those who had eyes, but could not see : in this, however, he was not entirely singular, for there is a well-known instance of a blind guide in Switzerland. But Metcalf gradually rose in the world, and having acquired a most exact knowledge of the situation, size, and shape of every hill, rock, and tree about the Peak, he undertook to correct the direction of the routes ; and having, by the help of a compass, laid out several plans, which were adopted, he took up the business of a surveyor.

Mr. Bew says, " He is now occupied in projecting and laying out roads in mountainous and almost inaccessible districts. I have often met him with a long pole in his hand, crossing roads, clambering precipices, descending into valleys, and feeling out their different dimensions, their forms and situations, so as to be able to make out his designs most correctly. He makes his plans, and estimates by a peculiar process which he cannot communicate ; nevertheless, his talent is so decided, that he constantly finds occupation. Most of the routes on the Peaks of Derbyshire have been changed in consequence of his suggestions, principally those in the neighbourhood of Buxton. At this moment he is employed in planning and putting in operation a new road between Winslow and Congleton, so as to open a communication with the great London road, which will obviate the necessity of crossing the mountain." *

---

* We have not been able to procure an English copy of Mr. Bew's Memoir, and are obliged to re-translate it from a French copy.

It will require that a person shall have reflected much upon the nature of the senses, and known some instances of the astonishing increase of their powers in the case of the blind, to give full credit to the statements about Metcalf; but for our part we have no hesitation in believing them, for we have had personal knowledge of some of the blind, whose powers were almost equally great. We have known young men who rode fearlessly on the high roads on horseback; who could wind their way with speed and certainty through the streets and alleys of large cities; and who could mingle in society, and waltz with ease and grace. There is in our own neighbourhood a young man who accomplishes, every year, long journeys on foot and alone; going from Massachusetts to Main. There are in the Institution for the Blind in our city, several persons who go feeling about alone; and one, who though but six months resident here, will go readily to any street or house to which he has once been led; and can even find a house which he never entered, provided he is told on which side of the street it is, and many doors from the corner. His manner of finding his way is singular, and affords a striking proof of the delicacy of his senses; for he does not go groping along with a cane, and feeling of the houses and corners; but marches with head erect, avoiding persons whom he hears approaching. When he comes to an opening, he measures its sound with his ear to ascertain if it be the one down which he is to go, and if not, turns short on his heel, and marches until he comes to another opening. When he has arrived at the street in which is the house where he wishes to go, he either counts the doors from the corner, or goes on until he judges that he is near it, and then, finding some object which he knows, for a landmark, he makes up to the door and rings.

Now we say, it is strange, that, notwithstanding the obvious facilities which are given to the blind for the attainment of knowledge, in the superior acuteness of their remaining senses, so little has been done for them; and that, from examples such as we have quoted, a favourable inference was not sooner drawn in regard to the whole class. But such men as Saunderson, and Moyes, and Metcalf, were regarded as prodigies, and people paid them the passing tribute of admiration, without reflecting that they were members of a large class who were left in utter ignorance and neglect.

The benevolent and enthusiastic Haüy, who has generally been considered the inventor of the apparatus for educating the blind, established the first school for them in his own house at Paris, about forty-five years ago. He does not, however, appear to have done so much in the way of inventing apparatus as has been generally supposed, for, according to the report of the commissioners of the French Academy, "his system resembles that of the blind man of Priscaux ; his method of teaching geography is about the same as that of Mr. Weinemburg ; and Mr. Hamoroux had formerly invented tangible musical characters." The Abbé Haüy, however, merits the endearing title which has been given him of "the father of the blind "; a reward richer than a crown,—a title more truly glorious than that of conqueror. He invented a method of printing for the blind, by pressing the type strongly on sized paper, so as to produce a bold relief in the shape of the letter upon the reverse of the page, which relief the blind feel with the ends of their fingers. He produced a great sensation in the French capital by exhibitions of his pupils ; all classes of society became interested ; and it was for some time an absolute rage ; each one strove to outdo the other,—donations poured in, and upon the strength of this passing enthusiasm an institution was got up and filled with young blind persons. But in a short time the enthusiasm of the public subsided (as it ever will,) the institution could not be continued on the scale upon which it was commenced, the pupils were in want of even decent clothing, and the establishment was at its last gasp, when the Constituent Assembly of the Revolution took it up. It has since been supported at the expense of the Government.

The good Abbé Haüy, however, knew how to keep up public enthusiasm, by applying the torch in another place, when the combustible matter was exhausted in the first, and he had the satisfaction of being summoned by the Autocrat of Russia to found an institution for the education of the blind in St. Petersburg : thither he repaired with one of his accomplished pupils ; and having raised there a second monument to his own glory, and that of humanity, and a third in Berlin, he returned to Paris, and was gathered to his fathers. The generous impulse which he had given was communicated to other countries, and Institutions for the education of the blind were got up in

Amsterdam, Vienna, Dresden, London, Liverpool, Edinburgh, and even in Madrid. Some of these schools were founded in a moment of passing enthusiasm, but like seed thrown upon the rock, they found no genial earth, and have sadly dwindled ; those at Amsterdam, St. Petersburg, and Madrid are in this situation ; and even the others, though planted in a propitious soil, and watered by copious showers of patronage, have not attained that lofty and luxuriant growth, which their nature seemed to promise them.

We propose to examine the system of education followed in these different seminaries ; and if our remarks shall appear to be in a tone of severe criticism, let it be understood that, in making them, we have in view the good of those institutions which are rising in our own country ; that we wish them to avoid the dangerous error of copying every thing from the European schools ; that we wish them to consider the latter as beacons to warn rather than lights to guide ; and finally, that while we find much fault with the details of the foreign system, we pay our sincere tribute of admiration to the humane spirit and generous philanthropy of those who are interested in these Institutions.

L'Institution des Jeunes Aveugles (formerly styled *Les Aveugles Travailleurs*), is sometimes confounded with the Hospital of the *Quinze Vingt :* but this is a very different establishment, and one of the proudest monuments of humanity of which France can boast ; it was founded by St. Louis on his return from the East, for such of his soldiers as had lost their sight ; as its name imports, it receives and supports *fifteen score* or three hundred adult blind persons : but no attempt is made to educate them or administer other solace than that of food, raiment, and a comfortable home.

The Institution for the young blind, however, is intended solely for their education, and none but children between ten and fourteen years of age are admitted ; there are one hundred of these interesting beings in the establishment, and a more delightful spectacle cannot be imagined than a view of its interior. You see not there the listless, helpless blind man dozing away his days in a chimney nook, or groping his uncertain way about the house ; but you hear the hum of busy voices,—you see the workshops filled with active boys, learning their trades from others as blind as themselves,—you see the school-rooms crowded with eager

C

listeners taught by blind teachers. When they take their books,
you see the awakened intellect gleam from their smiling faces,
and as they pass their fingers rapidly over the leaves, their varying
countenances bespeak the varying emotions which the words of
the author awaken :—when the bell rings they start away to the
play ground,—run along the alleys at full speed,—chase, over-
take, and tumble each other about,—and shout, and laugh, and
caper round with all the careless heartfelt glee of boyhood. But
a richer treat, and better sport awaits them,—the bell again
strikes,—and away they all hurry to the hall of music ; each one
brings his instrument, and takes his place ;—they are all there,—
the soft flute, and the shrill fife,—the hautboy and horn,—the
cymbal and drum, with clarinet, viol, and violin ;—and now they
roll forth their volume of sweet sounds, and the singers, treble,
bass, and tenor, striking in with exact harmony, swell it into one
loud hymn of gratitude and joy, which are displayed in the
rapturous thrill of their voices, and painted in the glowing enthusiasm of their animated countenances.

Such is the scene which presents itself to the delighted visitant
of the Parisian Institution for the young blind ; and he comes
away with a feeling of unqualified admiration for that spirit of
humanity which, guided by science, is there accomplishing so
much in defiance of the apparently insurmountable obstacles of
nature. But he who goes again, and again, and examines not
only the foliage and the flower, but waits for the season of the
fruit, finds his admiration dwindling into doubt ; and feels at last
the painful conviction that all this display is of comparatively
little good, and that not one half the benefit that might be
derived from such splendid means ever accrues to the unfortunate
inmates. He asks the question, How many of those who leave
the institution at the expiration of their time are enabled to gain
their own livelihood ?—and is startled at the answer of "not one
in twenty." What then ? Must they relapse into their original
inanition ? Must they take their places by the highway, and beg
at the corner of the streets, with the pangs of dependence sharpened to torture by increased sensibility ? Alas ! it is almost as
bad as this with many. And how is it proposed to remedy this
evil ? how do they hope to prevent the glimmering which the
blind here catch of happiness from being followed by a futurity
doubly dark and wretched ? Why, instead of looking for the

cause of the evil, instead of suspecting the system, and correcting that, they propose to establish a place for the permanent reception and support of those who come out from the institution, and who cannot provide for themselves. This is very like educating men for the almshouse.

We were painfully affected by this conclusion, which seemed like the destruction of one of the fairest fabrics that ever blessed the dream of the philanthropist ; and were led to examine again and again the system in detail, until we discovered, or thought we discovered, most apparent causes for the meagre harvest of good, which is reaped from such a promising soil. We looked in vain for the improvements which ought to have been made in the apparatus of Haüy, during the thirty years which had elapsed since his death ;—we looked in vain, for none existed. A narrow and illiberal jealousy ; an attempt at secrecy and reserve met our endeavours to examine the nature of this apparatus: and when we inquired whether some obvious and simple changes might not be made for the better, we were repelled by the sapient and reproving answer, that surely, if any improvements could have been made, such great and good men as the Abbé Haüy and his successors would not have overlooked them.

But before exposing the faults of the system of education pursued at the Institution for the Blind at Paris, we ought, perhaps, to explain it as it now exists. Pupils are admitted from the age of ten to fourteen, and are expected to remain there eight years. During this time they receive a very good intellectual education ; they have much attention given to the cultivation of their musical powers ; and are taught also many kinds of handicraft work. Their library consists of about forty different works, which have been printed in raised characters, and are legible with the fingers ; among them are Latin, English, and Italian grammars ; Extracts from Latin, English, and Italian authors. They have maps constructed by a very expensive and clumsy process ; they paste the map of any country upon stiff pasteboard, then, having bent a wire into all the curves of the coast, and laid it along the courses of the rivers, and in the line of the boundaries, they sew it down to the pasteboard, and taking a second map of the same dimensions, paste it immediately over the first, and pressing it down all around the wire, leave its windings to be felt. Here it is obvious to any one, that

c 2

common ingenuity could devise material improvement. Some have in fact been devised and put in operation at the Institution in our city, where the maps, made at one tenth of the expense of the Parisian ones, present the most obvious and important advantages over them.*

They have also in Paris music printed in the same way as the books, that is, by stamping the notes through the paper and producing their shape in relief on the opposite side. It is not found very advantageous, however, to print music in this way, for the memory of the blind is so tenacious that they can learn very long pieces.

Mathematical diagrams are made in the same way as the maps, but in defiance as it were of common sense, they retain the old ones of Haüy, which are very large and clumsy ;—so large, that the hands of the pupils must be moved about in all directions to feel the whole outline of the forty-seventh proposition of Euclid, whereas the smaller the diagram is made, the more easily it is felt and studied, and the less does it cost. The blind are indebted, we think, to the Rev. Mr. Taylor, of York, in England, for a plan of embossing mathematical diagrams: † but even his are larger than they need to be, and many of the problems would be more rapidly learned by the blind student, were the diagrams so small that he could feel the outlines of them with his fingers, without moving his hands.

The children are taught arithmetie, not merely orally, but the use of the slate is supplied to them by a very clumsy contrivance similar to that of Saunderson : a board is filled with numerous square holes arranged symmetrically ; and into these holes types are made to fit, on the ends of which are the shapes of the figures of the units,—as one, two, three, &c., so that when the learner wishes to put down 25, he searches among the types for the one which has the figure 2 upon the end ; this he places upright in the square hole so that the figure is above the surface of the board, and then he searches for the figure 5, which he

---

* The improvement consists in having a metal plate engraved with all the lines, elevations, boundary marks, positions of towns, &c.; from this plate impressions are struck in pasteboard, which produce a perfect embossed map.

† The Diagrams of Euclid's Elements of Geometry, arranged according to Simpson's Edition, in an embossed or tangible form, for the use of blind persons who wish to enter upon the study of that noble science. By the Rev. W. Taylor, Vicar of Bishop Barton, York, 1828.

places in the hole to the right of it, and then, feeling of both, he reads 25. And thus any number or any combination of numbers may be put down, and any arithmetical process may be performed. This method, however, has been much simplified by a contrivance of one of the pupils in the Edinburgh school, where they use but two types instead of ten. There the types, instead of having the form of the figures at the end, have a point on one corner ; and if the type is placed in the square hole, in such a way that this point is felt on the left hand corner of the upper line, it signifies *one*,— if the type is turned, and the point is on the right hand corner of the upper line, it signifies *three*, if on either of the other two corners, it signifies the other two odd numbers : thus we have four figures with one type. Now there is on the other end of this type a point in the middle of one of its edges, instead of being on the corner, and this, turned to one or the other of the four sides, signifies one or the other of the four even numbers—two, four, six, eight ; thus we have four odd and four even numbers with one type turned to different sides of the square hole. Then there is a second type which has a point in the centre of one end to signify *five*, and which is smooth on the other end to signify *zero*. Now, suppose one wishes to express 5073, he searches for the type with a point in its centre, and puts it into the square hole, so that the point is felt above the surface of the board ; he then finds another type of the same kind, and putting it into the hole, the other end first, he has the smooth end of the type above the surface, which is zero, he then has down, 50 ; now, he takes one of the other kind of type, and feeling for the point at the corner, he places it in the hole, so that the point is felt in the right hand corner of the lower side, or the side towards him, to the right of the zero, it then reads 507 ; then taking another of the same kind of type, he puts the other end down, and leaves above the surface the point in the middle of the upper side, in the situation in which it signifies 3.

Now it is evidently a very great advantage to be able to work with only two kinds of type, instead of selecting from ten ; but the Parisians never dream of adopting the Scotsman's improvement ; and perhaps the Scotsman will be as slow in adopting an improvement of his method by an American, but which is as evident as his improvement of the Frenchman's. It will be

perceived that in running the fingers over the surface of a
number of types it may be difficult to ascertain whether the
point is upon the corner or in the middle of one edge of the
type, and a mistake in this respect will ruin the whole process.
In the Institution in this city this is obviated by having an
entirely different mark on the end of the type ; instead of distinguishing the sign 3 from the sign 4, by its being on the corner
instead of the middle of one side of the type, it is marked by two
points on the surface of the type ; and the figure for 5, instead
of being marked by a type which differs only from the rest by
having its point in the centre instead of on the corner, is marked
by a sharp line drawn diagonally across it, so that the types differ
from each other not only by their position, but by such a marked
difference in the feeling of them, that they cannot be confounded.
The arithmetical board itself has been improved by being made
much more compact, by the holes being brought much nearer
together, and the bulk and weight of the whole apparatus considerably diminished.

Printing for the use of the blind is carried on in the establishment at Paris, and the composition, the press work, the stitching
and the binding are all performed by the pupils, with very little
assistance from *les clairvoyans*. In setting up and distributing
the types they are very expert, and though in the first they
require to have a seeing person to read to them (unless they
reprint from a page in relief), yet in the latter they work perfectly well without any assistance.

The books printed by the blind have attracted much attention
and excited much observation ; but to us it is really astonishing
that so little should have been done towards improving them ;
indeed we cannot perceive that they are in any respect superior
to those issued from the press in the very infancy of the art. It
is a beautiful and most valuable invention, which enables the
blind

> "to look
> Along the pages of a book ";

but our admiration is qualified by regret when we think of how
much improvement they are susceptible—to what a comparative
degree of perfection they might be brought, and reflect that
nothing has been done towards it. The books now used are
exceedingly bulky and expensive, and the New Testament would

be extended to at least ten volumes of folio size if printed entire for the blind. The French seem to have been arrested in the progress of improvement by a blind adherence to the false maxim established by the Abbé Haüy, that in all things, "*il faut autant que possible rapprocher les aveugles aux clairvoyans*"; hence, say they, we must make their books resemble those of seeing persons, and print them with the same shaped letter. Now, this is a foolish adherence to the letter of the rule, without regard to its spirit, even were the spirit of it correct, *which is not the case*. It is not possible, as it respects their books, *de rapprocher les aveugles aux clairvoyans :* because a blind man never can read the books of seeing persons, and seeing persons never will read those of the blind, be they printed ever so like his own : it is, therefore, ridiculous to adhere to our clumsy and ill-shaped letters in printing for the blind. They are quite aware of this in Scotland, and Mr. Gall, of Edinburgh, with a praiseworthy zeal, and at great expense, has made many experiments, and succeeded completely in avoiding the error of the French, by running into one on the opposite extreme. He has succeeded in bringing the lines much nearer together, and saves something in space on each page ; but he founds his principal claim for improvement upon the change in the shape of the letters, which he makes entirely angular ; and distinguishes one from the other by the different positions of the angles,—for instance, a triangle with the acute point turned to the left, shall signify one letter, and the same shaped triangle, with the point turned to the right, shall signify another letter. Now in this way Mr. Gall overlooks what we maintain to be an indisputable maxim in printing for the blind,—viz., *make the letters to differ as much as possible from each other in shape, and do not let the difference be in position merely;* and for this obvious reason, that if an acute-angled triangle shall signify *a* when its angle is turned to the left, and signify *b* when it is turned to the right,—then you require two mental processes to be carried on in the mind of the blind man before he can tell *a* from *b* ; first, he has to feel the shape of the letter,—he finds it is an acute-angled triangle,—and having ascertained this, he must feel whether the acute angle is turned to the right or to the left, before he knows whether it is *a*, or *b*. Now it is true that the operation is carried on in an inconceivably small space of time, but nevertheless it is a space

of time, and if it be multiplied by the number of letters on a
page, it amounts to something ; the principal objection, however,
is the double mental operation which is required.   Mr. Gall
asserts that he has tried the experiment upon blind children, and
found that they could learn his system of letters much quicker
than the common shaped ones ; this may be, and still his system
may be a very imperfect one ; but we do not place much confidence in such experiments, unless they be tried upon great numbers and with most marked results.   We have also tried the two
systems, and the children who learned only one each, seemed to
learn them with equal rapidity, while those who learned both,
declared that they learned them with equal ease.   Let us grant,
however, for the sake of argument, that Mr. Gall's angular
characters may be more easily learned ; this by no means proves
that they should be adopted.   It by no means lessens the regret
which every enlightened friend of the blind feels, that so much
expense has been incurred, and so much pains taken to introduce
a system of printing, so manifestly imperfect, since this is an
objection to changing it ; and we think the persons connected
with the Edinburgh Institution were right in withholding from
Mr. Gall their countenance and support to his plan of printing
the New Testament for the blind in a character which supplied
none of the *desiderata*.

Another system of letters has been devised by Mr. Hay, a blind
man, teacher of languages in Edinburgh ; but there exist as
powerful objections to it as to that of Mr. Gall, viz. the size and
similarity of the characters ; his may be called the right lined
system, while Gall's is the angular one.

But the clumsiest and most uncouth system which ever was
devised, is that practised in the Glasgow Asylum, where they have
letters made by different kinds of knots tied on a string, which,
of course, must be wound up in a ball, so that the pupil must
unroll the whole ball before he comes to the part he wants.   A
chapter of the Testament makes a ball as large as an eighteen
pound shot ; and the whole Bible would require a store room as
large as a church.

The art of printing for the blind is a most important and interesting subject ; and there is nothing on which the man of
science and ingenuity can turn his thoughts with more hope of
accomplishing a desirable end, and bestowing an immense benefit

on an unfortunate class of persons. The principal objection to the books now in use is their bulk and consequent expense, and the grand *desideratum* is to condense them ; now this can only be done by throwing away our common letter entirely, and adopting a system of stenography. In this system three principles must be kept in view ; *first*, to make the letters differ from each other as much as possible in shape ; *secondly*, to adapt those figures or shapes which most resemble each other, to letters which do not often come together in writing, as *p*, *q* ; *thirdly*, to express the letters which occur most often, as *a*, *e*, *i*, by those signs which occupy the least space as a point.

We look confidently for the time when books may be printed for the blind in the stenographic system, which shall be nearly, if not quite as commodious and portable as those designed for our use ; and we would earnestly invite the attention of those who are so nobly and so eagerly engaged in putting the Scriptures within the reach of the benighted heathen, to the claims of hundreds and thousands in our own land, who are denied the privilege of reading the Word of God, and whose situation is much more forlorn than theirs. It may be said, that the blind can have the Scriptures read to them, and therefore that they have not so much need of having them printed for their own use ; but such an excuse comes with an ill grace from those who object to the Catholic religion, for the reason that it does not put the Scriptures within the reach of every one, and who believe that the welfare of an immortal soul may depend upon the construction of a few sentences. But besides the importance of allowing every one to read and judge for himself, let it be considered what a treasure a copy of the Bible in raised letters would be to a blind man ; how, deprived as he is of other books, he would pore over it, and study its every line and every precept ; how it would be the companion of every solitary moment ; how its divine and consoling doctrines would cheer and illuminate the dark night of his existence ; and how he would bless and pray for those who had kindled this beacon to throw a light across his dreary path. The lowest estimate must give more than five thousand blind persons to these United States, and surely it is as much an object and a duty to print the Scriptures for these unfortunate beings, to whom any book would be a treasure, as to print them for the heathen. As yet, only St.

John's Gospel has been printed for the blind; although many attempts have been made in France and England to get the means for printing the whole New Testament; let it be then for America to effect this; let her bestow this inestimable blessing upon the blind, and their prayers will be her rich reward.

But there is another powerful motive for printing the Scriptures in tangible characters, and that is, that there are many people who, from age or some affection of the sight, are unable to use their eyes; to such persons, a copy of the Scriptures, which they might read with their fingers, would be an invaluable blessing, especially as they may learn to read it in a week.

But we have wandered insensibly from our subject, which was a consideration of the causes which operate to prevent the French Institution from accomplishing the object proposed in educating the blind. In enumerating all of them, we might dwell upon the faults in the detail of their apparatus; but these are of minor consequence,—there must be more important causes; and one of these is the uniformity of the system, which is applied to all, without taking into consideration the disposition, talents, or the station in life of the pupil. Among an hundred who are admitted, there may be some who might make excellent mathematicians, but can never excel as weavers; there may be others who can become fine composers of music, but who never will make good baskets; on the other hand, we may see some who would become very expert at different mechanical arts and handicraft works, but who never could learn, and teach the languages. Little regard, however, is paid to this, and as little to the pecuniary circumstances, and station in life of the friends of the pupil. If a boy is taken from the highway, where he had been a beggar; and if at the end of eight years he is sent out of the Institution with a tolerable knowledge of music, mathematics, and general science, and a superficial acquaintance with four or five different kinds of handicraft work, but without a decided dexterity and excellence in any one; if, we say, such a youth be without friends, then his situation is more desolate and miserable than when he was in a state of ignorance and indifference. He has drunk at the fountain of knowledge long enough to create a painful thirst for its waters, which cannot be gratified; he has lived in ease only long enough to make penury doubly dreary; and his mind has been so elevated as to make a feeling of dependence the source of wretchedness. If, however, he had spent the most of his time in musical, or mathematical or classic studies, he might have attained such an excellence as to have taught them successfully ; or if the tenor of his mind had been unequal to this, he might, by devoting himself wholly to some *one* handicraft work, have become so expert at it as to compete successfully with his seeing rivals. But neither in the Parisian, nor in any other European Institution that we are acquainted with, is this principle properly regarded. At Paris, they class the pupils without any regard to it ; all are obliged to study a certain number of hours a day, to work a certain number, and to give the rest of their time to music ; and if they have no ear at all for it, they must study it without an ear.

Then, their time is frittered away by an extremely minute subdivision ; they give half an hour to one study,—and then they are called away by the bell to another class room, whence, after losing fifteen minutes in arranging themselves, and fixing their minds upon the subject, they are summoned in less than an hour to a third, and to a fourth.

Another great fault is, that they all devote five hours a day to handicraft work : now, this is a great deal too much for a blind man, whose object is intellectual education, and it is far too little for one who means to live by the labour of his hands. But what is worse than this, they are obliged to try to learn so many different kinds of work, that they succeed in none ; they devote a few months, or a year, to making whips, another similar term to weaving, a third to net-making, and a fourth to braiding ; so that in learning how to braid, a boy forgets how to weave. Now if men, with all their senses, must give their undivided attention for seven years in order to learn any art or trade, how much more necessary is it for a blind man so to do ?

We would apply the same remarks to most of the European Institutions, with the exception of that of Vienna, which has not fallen under our notice. But we have yet a word for the Parisian School ; and we feel constrained by a sense of duty to say it, with the hope that, considering the absolute dearth of any publications about the education of the blind, this paper may fall under the observation of those who are interested in the welfare of the Institution in Paris. There pervades that establishment a spirit of illiberality, of mysticism, amounting almost to charlatanism,

that ill accords with the well known liberality of most French
Institutions.   There is a ridiculous attempt at mystery,—an effort
at show and parade, which injures the establishment in the minds
of men of sense.   Instead of throwing wide open the door of
knowledge, and inviting the scrutiny and the suggestions of every
friend of humanity, the process of education is not explained, and
the method of constructing some of the apparatus is absolutely
kept a secret !   We say this from personal knowledge.   The same
spirit leads to ungenerous treatment of those pupils who leave the
Institution, who cannot procure the books which are for sale there
without paying an enormous advance on the cost,—while those
who remain, be their age or character what they may, are not
allowed to go into the city to give lessons in music, the languages,
or in anything else.   We have known some of them to study the
English language secretly in their leisure hours, because those
having the direction of the establishment had in their wisdom
discovered that it was an improper study for the blind !

With regard to the rest of the European Institutions, we shall
not enter into a minute examination of the system followed in
them ; a few general remarks and criticisms will apply to all
those on the continent.   Before making them, we would again
pay our most sincere tribute of admiration to the benevolent
individuals engaged in these establishments.   Their zeal and
labours have been productive of immense benefit to the blind.
But they have had much to contend with ; they have been labouring in a new and unbroken pathway to usefulness ; and it is in
the hope of profiting even by their errors that we point them
out.   What they have done well and successfully will serve us as
models and guides ; in what they have erred or failed, they will
serve us as warning beacons.

Those Institutions, endowed and supported by the governments,
in general aim too much at show and parade ; their object seems
to be to teach the pupils to perform such feats at the exhibition
as will redound to the credit and glory of the government, rather
than to their own good : there is an attempt to make them obtain
a smattering of many things, rather than a thorough and useful
knowledge of a few.   The Institutions at St. Petersburg and
Amsterdam have dwindled into mere Asylums, and that at
Madrid, if we mistake not, into nothing at all.

. Those establishments, which are supported principally by the zeal and humanity of individuals, thrive much better. The one at Berlin is under the direction of Professor Zeun,—a liberal and enlightened man, who is however cramped in his operations by the prejudices of others : he believes, for instance, that the blind, when educated, make the best teachers of the blind ; but he is not allowed to employ them as he would.

The Institutions in England are not under the direction of scientific men, nor is their object a scientific or intellectual education of the blind : the one in London is merely for indigent blind, and they are taught only handicraft work and a little music ; no books are used in the establishment, and no intellectual education is given. The one in Edinburgh is less objectionable in this respect, but the Liverpool and Glasgow Institutions are conducted on the same principle. It is alleged that the pupils, being all indigent, must depend solely upon the labour of their hands for a livelihood ; but we maintain that this is a false view of the subject, and we shall endeavour to show that, on this principle (which has been followed hitherto in all the Institutions,) fewer blind persons will be made competent to their own support, than might be by following an opposite one. The great obstacle to the successful competition of the blind with the seeing man, for a livelihood, is the want of sight. What is the occupation then in which sight is least wanted? Is it handicraft work? Decidedly not. Can a blind man ever work so fast or so well at any trade as a seeing man, *caeteris paribus ?* By no manner of means ; but he may become, to say the least, as good a musician, as profound a mathematician, as thorough a linguist ; and he may teach these branches of knowledge as well. If then the pupil has a decided talent for music, for mathematics, for languages, let him apply himself with all his might, and during the whole season of his youth, to these studies ; let him be assured that he will be more likely to attain excellence and gain a livelihood by them, than by making carpets or rugs, though he make them ever so well.

Manual labour should be considered as the *dernier resort*, the forlorn hope of the blind, and such only should be put to it, as cannot expect to attain excellence in the occupations we have already mentioned ; when, however, it is resorted to, let it be with constant attention, and let not this attention be distracted by a variety of callings. There are some kinds of work in which a blind man can nearly compete with a seeing one, as in weaving ;

but unfortunately for him, he has not man alone as a competitor, for machinery here defies competition. There is, however, the coarse rug-weaving, and the making of mattresses, both of which are carried on successfully in the Asylum for the Indigent Blind in Edinburgh. The mattresses, mats, and baskets, which are manufactured in the establishment, have quite as good an appearance as any made in the city ; and, enjoying a well-merited reputation of being stronger and more durable, they command a higher price in the market.

The Institution in Edinburgh is decidedly of a higher order than any other in England ; and it is one of its merits, that the fabrication of the articles we have just mentioned chiefly occupies the attention of the inmates. In London they attempt to teach the pupils to make shoes ; and they do make them strong and well ; but it is an occupation by which very few blind persons can earn even half the wages of a common journeyman ; and as common journeyman in England can hardly get wages enough to keep soul and body together, it is easy to conceive that their situation must be very uncomfortable.

One word more, and we have done with the European Institutions. The blind are there treated too much as mere objects of pity ; they are not taught to rely with confidence upon their own resources, to believe themselves possessed of the means of filling useful and active spheres in society.

It will be perceived, from what we have said, that the European Institutions fall far short of what should be the aim of the philanthropist in educating the blind, viz., *to enable them to pass their lives pleasantly and usefully in some constant occupation, which shall ensure to them a competent livelihood.* But far be it from us to despair of this great result ; there are innumerable difficulties in the commencement of every establishment, which perseverance and well directed experiments may remove ; the subject is new even in Europe, and most of the Institutions are but in their infancy.

In this country, however, not only will our Institutions reap the full advantage of all the experiments in Europe, but they will have much less to contend with. In Europe, the gains of the labouring man are so small, that he would starve if they were diminished one third ; but here, thank God ! the sweat of the poor man's brow does not all go to increase the wealth of him who is already rich ; and if a blind man were to gain a trifle less than his neighbour, he might still procure not only the necessaries, but the comforts of life.

In Europe, too, strange as it may seem in this age, the blind man has to struggle against stubborn and cruel prejudices ; people are so accustomed to consider the blind as ignorant and degraded dependents, that if two organists, equally well qualified, should apply for a place in a church, and one of them be blind, he would probably lose it. Here, it is to be hoped, the misfortune of the claimant would be the strongest argument in his favour.

Of the works whose titles we have placed at the head of this article, the first is well-known ; and the second is remarkable as being the production of a blind man, the author of *Lettres sur les Areugles faisant suite à celle de Diderot.* Alexander Rodenbach, member of the Belgian Chamber of Deputies, and one of the most active and conspicuous patriots of the last revolution, lost his sight in infancy, and was one of the pupils of the Abbé Haüy, who engrafted upon his bold and original mind an excellent education : he has a ready wit, and a happy delivery, and he forms one of the principal supports of the democratic party in the Chamber, which he often makes to ring with his original and eloquent speeches.

The title of his book is a singular one, *A glance by a blind man at the condition of the Deaf and Dumb;* and we might make many amusing extracts from it, were space allowed us. The most interesting chapter is that on the comparative situation of the blind and the dumb. Is it a greater misfortune to be blind or to be deaf ? It is as remarkable as fortunate, that each class decides this question in its own favour ; but it appears to us evident that abundant reasons might be given why blindness is the less evil were this not rendered unnecessary by the well-known fact that the blind are generally much more happy and contented with their lot than the deaf. We would recommend this book to those engaged in the education of the deaf and dumb ; they will find in it some proofs of the imperfection of the system in common use, some allusions to the quackery that has been imposed upon the world, and from which the Abbé de l'Epée was not entirely free. We fully agree with Mr. Rodenbach on the importance of teaching the deaf to articulate sounds, and we are sorry that this plan has been abandoned in the Hartford school, which (otherwise) is one of the best in the world. We have known deaf persons in Germany who could express their thoughts by articulate sounds, so as very easily to be comprehended by anyone ; and when we reflect that the world will not learn their system of signs, and that they are often placed in situations where they cannot write, it becomes to them a matter of moment to make themselves understood by speech.

While on the subject of the deaf, we may observe that, strong as are their claims upon humanity, those of the blind are still stronger, for the blind are much more dependent ; a deaf boy can learn any kind of handicraft work or trade, while a blind one can learn nothing without a system of education entirely adapted to his situation.

The efforts of human ingenuity to overcome the obstacles which accident has placed in its way are nowhere more visible than in the successful attempts of the blind and deaf to converse together. As the blind cannot perceive the signs of the deaf, nor they hear the words of the blind, each must seek a new language, and they communicate their ideas by tracing the forms of letters on the palms of each others' hands. When more familiar, the deaf may be seen teaching the blind the language of signs by holding up their hands, and placing their fingers in the position for the signs ; and when the blind have learned the signs, they read those which the deaf make by feeling their hands and fingers, and ascertaining the position in which they are placed.

In writing this article we have been insensibly led from one subject to another, so as to have lost sight of the arrangement we had marked out, and have already occupied so much space that but little remains for a consideration of the moral effects of blindness upon the sufferer. The blind have been considered in all ages as of necessity cut off from participation in the business and pleasures of life ; they have been made the *parias* of society, and although the hand of charity has ever been open to their cry, yet men have shrunk from an attentive examination of their situation. They have often been accused of a disposition to atheism, but we think without sufficient reason : surely the increased sense of dependence must be conducive to a feeling of reverential awe for a Power, about whom the imagination is ever busy. That many eminent blind men have been atheists is certain, but it is certain, too, that their scepticism arose in a great measure from the improper light in which they have been regarded. The dying Saunderson said to his clergyman, "You talk to me of the wonders of creation, but how often have I heard you express your wonder at my performing things which are to me perfectly simple; how then do I know that your wonder is more reasonable in the one case than in the other?"

With regard to what are called feelings of modesty, the blind possess them in a very high degree, the speculations of Diderot and others to the contrary notwithstanding; they are from their situation led to be particularly scrupulous in their regard to *les convenances* of society. They are exceedingly orderly, as well in the arrangement of their ideas as of their property, hence, perhaps, their horror of theft and their respect for the property of others. The method of classification which they adopt enables them to bring the memory to a very high degree of perfection, hence the astonishing instances which we have of blind men retaining several thousand words without meaning and without connexion. It is related of Dr. Moyes that he would recognise by their voice persons with whom he had had but a slight acquaintance, and whom he had not met for more than a year.

The want of sight makes the blind insensible to the infinite variety of beauteous aspects which nature puts on, when she comes forth blushing with the hues of morn, or arrays herself in the silver mantle of moonlight, or decks herself out in the gorgeous robes of sunset. If, then, all the grandeur and glory of nature are lost upon them, how much more insensible must they be to the ridiculous display of human pomp and pride; and how much ought this circumstance to influence our treatment of them! The necessity of this may be understood from the anecdote related by Diderot of the young blind man who was brought to trial for having thrown a stone which struck another person in the head, and for various misdemeanors: "He appeared before the judge as before his equal; nor could any threats intimidate him. 'What can you do to me?' cried he to M. Herault. 'I will cast you into a dungeon,' answered the magistrate. 'What then?' returned the blind. 'I have been living in one all my life time.' What an answer! What a text for a man who loves to moralize! We take our leave of the world as of an enchanting

D

spectacle ; the blind man goes out of it as from a dungeon ; if we have more to enjoy in living than he has, at least he has less to regret in dying."

But Diderot here (as is very common with him) displays more ingenuity than observation : the blind do not die with less regret than we do ; the love of life is not lessened by the want of one sense, any more than it is in the case of the poor by the want of wealth ; many blind men possess high moral courage ; some display a degree of independence of character, which at times degenerates into obstinacy, and excessive egotism ; but they are seldom possessed of much physical courage.

Nor is the world to them a less enchanting scene than it is to us, provided they have occupation. Blindness is not the sole, nor the principal cause of the unhappiness of the blind ; and, were they not continually reminded of their inferiority by our officious and unnecessary expressions of sympathy and compassion, they would not feel it. They cannot conceive how the sense of sight can be the source of any positive pleasure to us, otherwise than as it enables us to ascertain the physical qualities of objects at a greater distance than they can by the feeling. Hence they look upon the want of it as a loss of advantage, and not of enjoyment. There is a great deal of philosophy and of good sense in the answer of a blind man to the question, Whether the possession of sight would not increase his happiness ? " I cannot conceive that it would," said he, " in a very material degree. I suppose your eyes serve with you the same purpose that my hands and cane do with me ; that is to ascertain the shape and other physical qualities of bodies. The only advantage you have, is the ability to do this at a greater distance than I can ; now if I were to choose, it would be rather to have my arms so constituted that I could reach any object which you can see, than to possess what you call vision." Hence it is that we seldom find those who are born blind repining after sight ; but we do see them sitting bowed down under a sense of humiliating dependence : with their faculties undeveloped by action, and their minds gradually degenerating into imbecility, from the monotonous torpor of their existence.

With regard to the number of the blind, we have no means of knowing it very accurately in this country, for no correct census has been taken ; but from researches made by the Trustees of the

New England Institution for the Education of the Blind, it is quite evident that the returns made by the general estimates are far too low. The only document we have met with is one lately published in Philadelphia, apparently taken from the general census, in which the number of the blind in every State is given, and which makes the sum total a little over five thousand.*

---

* TABLE *showing the number of Blind persons in the United States; also the relative proportion to the population, &c.*

STATES.	BLIND.			Proportion to whole population.. 1 to	Proportion of blind whites to whole white population.. 1 to	Proportion of coloured blind to whole coloured population.. 1 to	Proportion of coloured to the whole population.
	White.	Coloured	Total.				1 to
Maine	159	1	160	2497	2505	1177	1 in 339
New Hampshire.............	105	0	105	2565	2559	—	1 443
Massachusetts.............	218	5	223	2737	2768	1409	1 86
Rhode Island	56	8	64	1518	1672	447	1 27
Connecticut	188	7	195	1526	1540	1152	1 30
Vermont	51	0	51	5503	2585	—	1 317
New York	642	82	724	2650	2918	547	1 43
New Jersey.................	205	22	227	1413	1464	734	1 16
Pennsylvania	475	28	503	2580	2758	1369	1 35
Delaware	18	11	29	2646	3205	1741	1 4
Maryland....................	147	124	271	1649	1980	1257	1 3
Virginia	355	438	793	1527	1956	1180	1 2
North Carolina	223	161	384	1922	2120	1647	1 3
South Carolina.............	102	136	238	2442	2528	2377	1 2
Georgia.....................	150	123	273	1893	1979	1789	1 2
Alabama	68	48	116	2668	2800	2482	1 2
Mississippi	25	31	56	2439	2417	2135	1 2
Louisiana...................	36	77	113	1909	2485	1640	1 2
Tennessee	176	37	213	3201	3044	3950	1 4
Kentucky...................	169	83	252	2729	3064	2050	1 3
Ohio	232	6	238	3940	3993	1596	1 98
Indiana.....................	85	2	87	3942	3887	1816	1 94
Illinois	35	4	39	4037	4443	596	1 66
Missouri	27	10	37	3796	4251	2566	1 5
Michigan	5	0	5	6327	6269	—	1 108
Arkansas...................	8	2	10	3038	3209	2358	1 6
Florida	3	16	19	1828	6128	1020	1 2
District of Colombia	11	8	19	2096	2506	1534	1 3
	3974	1470	5444	2363	2650	1584	

This table bears inaccuracy on the very face of it,—for example, Massachusetts is said to have 223 blind persons only,—whereas the imperfect statement, made several years ago by order of the House of Representatives, gave 245 blind, although only one hundred and forty towns, out of more than three hundred, made any return. It was ascertained that no returns were made from some towns where blind persons were known to exist; and Mr. Loud, chairman of the Committee of the House, estimated the total number of blind in the State at 500; an estimate which subsequent inquiries show to be rather high, but much nearer the truth than the one given in the above table.

According to this table, the proportion of the blind to the whole population in different parts of the Union, varies from 1 in 1413 to 1 in 6329; New

It is impossible, however, to form any estimate of the proportional number of the blind in sections of the country so small, as those in regard to which the writer of this paper attempts to do it ; nor do we agree with him in the causes which he assigns for the apparent variations. The fact is, that we cannot make any accurate calculation of the number of the blind which will be found even in a population of one million ; for it varies from temporary causes, and in different generations ; but we may calculate with some degree of certainty, how many blind persons

---

Jersey having the greatest, and Michigan the smallest number. There is a striking difference between the numbers of the *white and coloured* blind : the largest proportion of white being in New Jersey, viz., 1 in 1464; and the smallest in Michigan, viz., 1 in 6269; while the highest proportion of the blind among the blacks is in Rhode Island,—being 1 to 447; and the lowest 1 in 3950, being in Tennessee.

In the whole population of the United States, there is a considerable excess in the proportion of the blind among the blacks over that among the whites; it being among the blacks 1 to 1584; among the whites 1 to 2650; the proportion of blind persons, blacks and whites, in all the Union being, according to this table, as 1 to 2363.

In Tennessee, however, we find more blind in a given number of *whites* than in the same number of *blacks :* the former being one in 3044,—the latter 1 in 3950. In South Carolina, the proportion is about the same among *blacks* and *whites.*

How are these differences to be accounted for? Without examining in detail the theory which the compiler of the table has raised upon these calculations,—the whole fabric may be brought to the ground by knocking away the foundations, and showing that the table is manifestly incorrect, which we believe has been done in the text.

That the proportion of *blind* among the *blacks* should be greater than among the whites is perfectly natural and in accordance with the general principle which we have laid down, that the poor are more exposed to the causes of blindness than the rich, the blacks being generally poor.

In a statement of the number of blind in the different cities, which follows, the author of this table gives the number of blind in Boston as nearly three times greater than it really is.

It is important to ascertain the proportion between the blind who are of an age to receive an education and those whom age renders unfit for it ; we believe it to be much less than is generally supposed : the number of children born absolutely blind is very small ; but many become so in a few weeks or months ; fewer between infancy and youth, but still more rarely is the sight lost in youth or during manhood

Old age indeed dims the vision, but it is seldom thus entirely lost. The table we have quoted give the following proportions :—

			Total Number of Blind.					Over 50 Years.
Maine	...	...	159	...	...	...	...	11
New Hampshire	...	...	105	...	...	...	...	8
Massachusetts	...	...	218	...	...	...	...	8
Rhode Island	...	...	56	...	...	...	...	8
Connecticut	...	...	188	...	...	...	...	8
Vermont	...	...	...	51	...	...	...	9

will be found in a population of ten millions, the latitude and the climate being given.

How little dependence can be placed upon the calculations made in the paper to which we have referred, and in which the proportion in every county in Pennsylvania is attempted to be laid down, may be inferred from the fact that, in this city, there is but one blind person of the proper age for receiving an education ; while, in the neighbouring town of Andover, with less than one twentieth of the population, there are five ; in Cambridge four, and in some small towns on Cape Cod three. In the next generation, however, the prevalence of ophthalmia may give to Boston twenty or thirty : but though the laws of nature in this respect seem thus variable, they are in reality wonderfully uniform, and in every age the proportion of the blind to the whole population is about the same. Blindness appears to be more prevalent in the country than in cities, probably from the fact that people there can seldom procure medical assistance so seasonable or so efficient as to be of much use in the ophthalmia of infants. The poor are certainly more subject to it than the wealthy, partly from more exposure and partly perhaps from the hereditary nature of blindness. It is well known that blindness is very often hereditary, and we have instances in our neighbourhood of five children being born blind from the same mother ; now where such a scourge enters a family, it may readily be conceived how soon it will be reduced to poverty.

We have said that the general law of nature, by which a certain proportion of the human race are born with but four senses in perfection, is unfailing in its operation ; and in the want of any accurate statistics, we may correct our own by those of other countries similarly situated. As a general rule, blindness is more prevalent within the torrid zone, less in the temperate, and less still in the frigid ; in dry and sandy soils it is more prevalent than in moist ones. Egypt is the country of the blind *par excellence ;* different writers have estimated the proportion of the blind there very differently ; some say that one man in every hundred is totally or partially blind ; others one in three hundred. The latter calculation is probably the nearest to the truth ; but from our observation of the number of men with but one eye, or with distorted eyes, in the Egyptian army, we are inclined to think that the number of the blind in Egypt must be fearfully

great. The cause is probably the fine sandy dust with which the
air is continually filled in Egypt ; and which exists to such a
degree, that the first cotton machinery sent out from England for
the Pacha Mehemet Ali, was rendered useless by it in a very short
time. This difficuly is the greatest which his engineers have had
to overcome.

In several countries of Europe, the census gives accurately the
number of the blind. In the centre of Europe, it is about one to
eight hundred ; in Austria, one to eight hundred and forty-five ;
in Switzerland, one to seven hundred and forty-seven. Further
north the proportion is less : in Denmark, it is one to a thousand ;
in Prussia, one to nine hundred ; in France, one to a thousand
and fifty ; in England, a very little less. Now there seems no
sufficient reason why this country should be exempt from the laws
which operate upon others under the same latitude and with the
same climate ; and since we have shown how incorrect and ob-
viously low is the calculation by the census, which makes the
number five thousand, it may safely be calculated that there are
more than seven thousand blind persons in the United States.
This may seem incredible, and so did the number of the deaf
when it was first told ; but the blind, from their very misfortune,
are hidden from the world ; they sit sad and secluded by the firesides of their relatives ; the dawn of day does not call them into
the haunts of men, and they vegetate through life and sink into
the grave, unknown even to their neighbours.

But to be entirely within bounds, let us put the number even
lower than the absolute return by the census makes it, and call it
five thousand ; here are five thousand of our fellow-beings, with
the same faculties, feelings, and wants, the same pride, the same
ambition as ourselves, who are thrown entirely upon our charity
and humanity ; who are utterly unable of themselves to provide
for the wants of the body or the mind, and who appeal to that
sacred and fundamental law of society, by which we are bound to
provide for the wants of those whom nature or accident has made
dependent upon us. And how, we ask, has that appeal been
answered ? Have we not heard unheeded the cry of the blind
for assistance, and for *light ?* Have we not stopped our ears to
their cry, and thrust them into the almshouse instead of taking
them into the bosom of society ? Have we not shunned an
examination of their situation and wants, and hurried by them,

after bowing them still lower by the weight of alms? With the sun of science high in the ascendant, and the broad blaze of education pouring upon every class of men, have any of its rays been directed upon those who are sitting in physical and intellectual darkness,—who of all others have the strongest claim for assistance, and who, without instruction, are worse than idiots, because more miserable? We regret to say that till within a very short time, we have done nothing at all; with a population ten times greater than that of some of the European States, which have Institutions for the blind, there has not been a single school in the United States where a blind youth could go to receive proper instruction. But public attention has lately been aroused to the importance of the subject; one Institution has lately been put into efficient operation in Boston, a second has been organised, and is about commencing its operations in New York; and a third is in a state of forwardness in Philadelphia. We shall conclude this article with a brief notice of the present state of the first of these institutions, which is called the New England Institution for the Education of the Blind.

The first idea of this Institution was conceived by Dr. J. D. Fisher, in 1829. Several meetings of philanthropic individuals were held, and an act of incorporation was obtained the same year. The result of the investigations made at that time showed that there were more than 400 blind persons in the State of Massachusetts alone; and about 1500 in New England. But notwithstanding the publication of the melancholy truth, that so many of our fellow-citizens were left in degradation and ignorance, while the means existed of elevating their moral nature and enlightening their intellect, no effectual steps were taken towards establishing a school for them until 1831. It was no want of zeal or industry on the part of the gentlemen concerned that occasioned this delay, but the want of funds. The State now granted the unexpended balance of the fund for the deaf and dumb, amounting to fifteen hundred dollars, and about two thousand dollars were raised by subscription. Resolved to make an effectual effort, the trustees engaged Dr. S. G. Howe to organize the Institution, and put it into operation. A few days after his appointment, that gentleman sailed for Europe, visited all the Institutions for the blind there, engaged an intelligent blind teacher from the School at Paris, and another from that at

Edinburgh, and returned in August, 1831. Although the funds
of the Institution were almost exhausted, it was resolved not to
make any public appeal until some of the blind could be qualified
to plead their own cause : six children were accordingly selected,
and the school was commenced privately in September, 1832.
In January, 1833, the Treasury was empty, and the Institution
in debt. An exhibition of the pupils was then given before the
General Court, which afforded such complete and striking proof
of the capacity of the blind for receiving an intellectual education, that the Legislature, as it were by acclamation, voted that
$6000 per annum should be appropriated to the Institution,
for the support of twenty poor blind persons belonging to the
State.

The next public appeal was made in Salem, where several exhibitions of the pupils were held ; from which, and from the Fair
which followed, the Institution realised nearly $4500. Similar
exhibitions were given in Boston, the result of which was most
beneficial to the Institution, and creditable to the inhabitants.
About the first of May, the Hon. Thomas H. Perkins offered his
splendid mansion in Pearl Street, with all the land and buildings,
valued at $30,000, as a permanent residence for the blind ; and
enhanced the value of his offer by adding to it the condition,
that $50,000 should be raised as a fund for the Institution, before
the first of June. The ladies then united, and held a Fair on
the first of May, which was, perhaps, the most brilliant and
effectual one ever known. The proceeds, which, clear of all
expenses, exceeded $11,400, go to make up the Perkins' fund.
While this article is passing through the press (May 20), we are
informed that the necessary amount is already collected within
two or three thousand dollars, and that no doubt remains that
the sum will be completed within the limited time. Thus this
interesting Institution, which, on the first of January last, was
wholly destitute of funds, will possess on the first of June a large
and splendid building, worth $30,000, with a fund of $50,000 in
the Treasury.

The Institution may be said to merit this public favour ; the
progress of the pupils has been such as to astonish even those
who have visited the European Schools for the Blind. The
apparatus is not only as perfect as any one there, but several
important improvements have already been effected by native

ingenuity in the methods of teaching the blind. The pupils learn to read by raised letters ; they are also taught writing, arithmetic, geography, and all the branches commonly taught in other schools. Music occupies much of their attention ; and in a workshop attached to the house, they weave, and make baskets. The number of pupils is at present nearly twenty ; and they are as happy and intelligent children as can be found ; they spend twelve hours a day at their studies or work. It is intended to teach them all the higher branches of education, and the languages. The Musical Department is under the superintendence of Mr. Lowell Mason ; Mr. Trencheri, a blind man, teaches the intellectual branches; Mr. Pringle, who is also blind, instructs in the mechanic arts ; the whole being under the direction of Dr. Howe.

LONDON :
PRINTED BY WILLIAM CLOWES AND SONS, LIMITED,
STAMFORD STREET AND CHARING CROSS.

RE-PRINT, 1894

AN ACCOUNT

OF THE

RECENT DISCOVERIES

WHICH HAVE BEEN MADE

FOR

FACILITATING THE EDUCATION

OF

THE BLIND

WITH

SPECIMENS OF THE BOOKS, MAPS, PICTURES, &c.
FOR THEIR USE

PRINTED IN BEHALF OF THE

EDINBURGH SCHOOL FOR THE BLIND

EDINBURGH
PUBLISHED BY JAMES GALL
MDCCCXXXVII

LONDON
SAMPSON LOW, MARSTON & COMPANY
LIMITED
St Dunstan's House
FETTER LANE, FLEET STREET, E.C.
1894

RE-PRINT, 1894

AN ACCOUNT

OF THE

RECENT DISCOVERIES

WHICH HAVE BEEN MADE

FOR

FACILITATING THE EDUCATION

OF

THE BLIND

WITH

SPECIMENS OF THE BOOKS, MAPS, PICTURES, &c.
FOR THEIR USE

PRINTED IN BEHALF OF THE

EDINBURGH SCHOOL FOR THE BLIND

EDINBURGH
PUBLISHED BY JAMES GALL
MDCCCXXXVII

LONDON
SAMPSON LOW, MARSTON & COMPANY
LIMITED
St Dunstan's House
FETTER LANE, FLEET STREET, E.C.
1894

1894

Some Books and Papers about the Blind

REPRINTED BY

Messrs. SAMPSON LOW, MARSTON & COMPANY

LIMITED

St. Dunstan's House

FETTER LANE, FLEET STREET, LONDON

1774

THE EDUCATION OF THE BLIND. A LETTER IN THE EDINBURGH MAGAZINE AND REVIEW for NOVEMBER, 1774. Price 1s.

1793

TRANSLATION OF AN ESSAY ON THE EDUCATION OF THE BLIND by M. HAÜY. Dedicated to the King of France in 1786. Price 1s.

1801

HINTS TO PROMOTE BENEFICENCE, &c., by Dr. LETTSOM, with an account of the Blind Asylum at Liverpool. Price 1s.

1819

TRANSLATION OF AN ESSAY ON THE INSTRUCTION AND AMUSEMENTS OF THE BLIND by Dr. GUILLIÉ. Published in Paris, 1817. Illustrated, 5s.

1837

RECENT DISCOVERIES FOR FACILITATING THE EDUCATION OF THE BLIND. By JAMES GALL, of Edinburgh. Illustrated. Price 2s.

1842

THE EDUCATION, EMPLOYMENTS, &c., AT THE ASYLUM FOR THE BLIND, GLASGOW. By JOHN ALSTON. Illustrated. Price 2s.

1861

TRANSLATION BY REV. W. TAYLOR OF THE MANAGEMENT AND EDUCATION OF THE BLIND. By J. G. KNIE, of Breslau. Price 1s.

PREFACE.

THE Blind are now able to read nearly as fluently as those who see. Books are now printed for their use. They are also able to write letters to each other by post, and to read what is thus written. They can cast up accounts with no other apparatus than common pins ; and draw for themselves diagrams, with the same materials, for the study of geometry. Not only are books printed for their use, but also maps and music, which add greatly to their means of improvement ; and besides the invention for writing what they themselves can read, a very simple instrument has been invented, by which they are able to write the common written character, in a style as small, and even more elegant than is generally found among those who see.

As almost the whole of those discoveries have been made within a short time, and as they are so simple and available, that any blind person may avail himself of the whole of them for very little expense, it is important that they should be known, and their simplicity understood.

On account of the many applications which have been made for a description of these discoveries, along with directions for their use, the Author has been induced to draw out the following little Work for this purpose,—as he can describe them, by it, more minutely than he could always do in writing.

If this attempt should be the means of facilitating the mental culture of the Blind, of alleviating the unpleasantness of their unfortunate situation, or of even adding to the number of their accomplishments, he will not consider his labour misspent.

CONTENTS.

———

APPENDIX.

ILLUSTRATIONS.

THE

EDUCATION OF THE BLIND.

OF what use is education to the Blind ?—No one surely would ask
the question unless it were to answer by saying, that education is
of greater importance to the Blind than to those who see. But
alas ! the very reason why they need it most, is the reason why
they have been hitherto deprived of it.

Blindness *is* a difficulty in the way of education ; but it is not
an insurmountable one ; and it is the intention of this little book
to point out, not only effectual, but convenient and easy means, by
which that difficulty may be overcome. It is now considered an
established maxim in the economy of public charity, that it is
better to bestow upon an individual the power of providing for
himself, than to grant a continual supply of his wants, and retain
him in a state of dependence ; and upon the same principle, it must
be acknowledged, that it is better to raise the Blind by education,
to that state of intellectual and moral cultivation, by which they
would be able to occupy useful and trustful situations in society,
than to afford to them, by the cold hand of charity, the necessaries
and comforts of life which they might be enabled to earn for
themselves.

Of all the losses which the want of sight entails upon the Blind,
the inability to read must rank among the greatest. The man who
cannot read is generally an ignorant man. Blindness, therefore,
shuts out knowledge by its chief inlet. In solitude, reading performs two offices : it not only occupies and exercises the mind when
it would otherwise be idle, but it also gives knowledge at the same
time. The Blind, however, are deprived of this blessing. The
Bible itself is shut up from them, and the evil effects are apparent

in that morbid self-opinionativeness and metaphysical distortion of mind, which would be corrected by the enlightening influence of reading, as well as the contemplation of the simplicity and beauty of nature.

Reading is not dependent on the sight alone, because forms can be felt as well as seen ; and it is only because we can *see* better than we can *feel*, that we do not read with our fingers, and print and write in relief. If a printer were to press the large types very hard, we might feel their shapes on the other side ; and it is upon this principle that the printing for the Blind is founded, which we are now about to describe.

PRINTED BOOKS FOR THE BLIND.

Although Mr. Gall, in the present century, has revived the printing for the Blind, he was not the first who thought of it. It was attempted in Paris during the last century, and failed, not from any impossibility in the thing itself, but on account of the alphabet which was employed for the purpose. Mr. Gall perceiving that angles were more easily felt than rounds, and that the outside of the letter was more easily felt than the inside, modified the alphabet into its most simple form, throwing the characteristics of each letter to the outside, and using angles instead of rounds. After a long continued, laborious, and expensive series of experiments, by means of blind persons, he has produced the present Alphabet, which may now be considered the most simple, the most tangible, and therefore the most perfect Alphabet which can be constructed for the Blind.*

It is a curious fact, which has now been well ascertained, that the *finger*, even in an untutored state, can feel very small indentations upon surfaces ; and the reason why a person with his eyes shut does not easily know the shape by the feeling, is, that he is not in the habit of *receiving information* by such means. But after knowing what the letter is, he is able to perceive all the parts very distinctly by means of his finger.

---

* See Appendix, No. I.

As an illustration of the truth of this remark we shall take the
following diagram :—

This, by being written backwards, is not in itself less plain, but
has every turn as perfect as if it were written the other way ; yet
to the *unaccustomed* eye, it requires careful attention and reasoning
to perceive what the letters are. If it be supposed, that when
presented in the usual way it would not be easily read, one glance
at it, by means of a mirror, would dissipate every doubt upon the
subject.

This is the reason why we at first take a long time to feel the
letters before we can read them ; and yet the Blind are able to
skim over the letters with great rapidity in reading, in the same
way as we are able to read a written letter with great ease,
although, if it were presented to us in a mirror, we would scarcely
be able to read it at all.

So great is the facility with which the Blind are able to feel the
letters, that already they can read books printed with the common
English size of type. This is the same as is used in pulpit Bibles,
and papers printed for the Courts of law. And although this
surpasses all that was formerly hoped for, even this is not to be
considered the smallest size which the Blind will be able to read.

Mr. Gall has also added another improvement to the art, by
using fretted types instead of smooth ones. This gives the lines
of the letters better support, and makes a more decided impression
on the finger.

The Gospel by St. John was the first part of the Bible which was
printed in Great Britain for the Blind. At first it was feared, that
although the Blind might be able to feel the letters, they would be so
long in reading one verse, that all the pleasure they would get from
it would not be worth the trouble. Shortly after it was published,

a number of individuals began to teach the Blind to read, rather from a feeling of curiosity than from any hope of its being useful ; but they were surprised to find, that the Blind learned to read as fast, and in some cases faster, than children who see. Belfast seems to have been the first place where it excited any great degree of wonder. It had been adopted there in a Sunday school ; and the children improved so rapidly, that the school was generally filled with visitors ; and public interest was so much excited, that an Institution has been since built in that town for their education, along with the Deaf and Dumb. The Blind children in that Institution are decidedly the best readers at present in the kingdom.

The reading is now adopted with complete success in various asylums, but more especially by private individuals in different parts of the country. A school has also been opened in Edinburgh, the first which has ever been established exclusively for the education of the Blind.

TEACHING THE BLIND TO READ.

We have never heard of any of the Blind (except young children), who, when they began to learn, ever expected to be able to read ; and we have never heard of any who attempted to learn who were not successful.

The first object is to teach the alphabet ; and for this purpose, the first book which is put into their hand, is provided with a large alphabet, which enables them to feel all the parts of the letters. It is better to teach only one or two letters at a time, and to make them search for similar letters in the succeeding pages. When the alphabet has been learned, the short words which follow, enable the pupil to go forward without much difficulty, and to exercise his recollection of the letters and his spelling at the same time.

In reading, the pupil must use his right hand. The first, or the first and second fingers of which are made to feel the letters in their order ; while the forefinger of the left hand is allowed to rest at the beginning of the line which is being read ; and is brought down to the one below when it is finished. This plan enables the pupil to find the beginning of the next line without difficulty.

In a short time, the pupils are able to read by merely passing their fingers over the words; and so very plain do the letters appear to them, that they can read with a stout glove upon the hand, or a piece of linen laid upon the book.

WRITING BY STAMPS.

The writing by stamps, as we have already mentioned, enables the Blind to write, and to read what is written. The principle is very simple. If we prick a piece of paper with a pin, so as to form a letter, we feel the shape of the letter on the other side. Stamps with the letters set with pins, are used by the Blind to press through the paper; and in this way they are able to write a long letter upon a sheet of paper, to write the address by the same means, and when they have finished, they can read with their finger all that they have written.

At first, when the Blind addressed their own letters, it was feared that the postman would not be able to read the address; but in this they were very agreeably disappointed; for the letters went from one end of the kingdom to the other, with as much accuracy as if they had been addressed in the common way. There has been no instance yet known of their having miscarried.

It is exceedingly delightful to the Blind, to be thus enabled to correspond with their friends, and to receive letters which they can read without assistance. They are also in the habit of writing poetry and private memoranda, in which they take great pleasure. The frame upon which the writing is performed, is very simple, and costs about 5s. The wooden stamps cost about 6s. 6d., and the box for holding them arranged for writing, costs 3s. 6d., so that the expense of the whole apparatus is about 15s. This is the most expensive part of the apparatus for the Blind; but when once furnished, it is a source of much pleasure and convenience, as it enables the Blind to print their own books, and even to print music, as we shall afterwards shew. The Blind can write three or four copies of the same thing at once, by pricking through as many sheets of paper.

It is also to be remarked, that they may write on both sides of the paper, without producing confusion, even although the letters were to cross each other. That which is written on one side is not felt on the other side; so that although to the eye the letters are mixed, and appear in confusion, the finger feels only one series at a time.

TEACHING TO WRITE.

The Blind who can spell, may learn to write by the stamps in one lesson. The frame and stamps being laid before the pupil, he must first be taught to lay the paper on the frame evenly. In this he must be guided, by feeling whether the sides of the paper coincide with the sides of the frame.

The paper used is common writing paper, not very thin. The frame is adapted to foolscap; but any kind of *writing* paper will do. Common printing paper is thick enough; but not being *sized*, the points do not continue raised. When the paper is evenly laid on, the upper part of the frame must be laid over it for guiding the hand in using the stamps. It must be observed, that the paper must be written on the upper, and read on the under side; consequently it must be written either by beginning at the bottom of the page, and writing forwards line by line upwards; or, beginning at the top, to write backwards line by line downwards; the former of these methods is the more convenient, and is that which is now practised by all.

When writing in a book, or indeed in writing on any paper which has more than one leaf, it will be found a convenient rule always to keep the other leaf or leaves which are not being used, towards the *left* hand, and the top of the sheet or book *downwards*. When this is attended to, all the writing lies on the right side of the book, whatever page is turned up.

There are no capitals in the blind alphabet. The writing therefore must be all uniform. First, one letter is taken from the box, and brought to the lowest line, and towards the left hand. The letter itself on the stamp is turned upside down; but the index on the end of the stamp is not so. When properly placed, the person writing presses it down, or gives it a smart stroke with his wrist, so as to make it pierce the paper. Before putting back the stamp which has been thus used, the next letter is placed close by its side towards the right hand, when it also is struck down in the same manner. When this second has been struck, the first may then be removed, and a third struck down beside the second, and so on. When a word is finished, any of the stamps may be turned upside down, to keep the first letter of the next word separate from the word before it. This turned stamp should not be struck nor pressed. But even though it should be struck, having the pins turned upwards, it would not perforate the paper.

When one letter has to be used doubly, one of two plans may be followed. The first is when similar letters may be used. Instead of b d e m n p q u w 3 4 6 7 9, we may use q p 3 w u d b n m e 7 9 4 7, turned upside down. The second method is after using the stamp once ; it is taken out, and another of the same thickness put in its place, with the pins upwards. The stamp is then used again at its side.

WRITING BY THE TYPHLOGRAPH.

The Typhlograph is an invention by which the Blind can write a common current hand, as small and as elegant in its forms as that used by those who see. It consists of a board, a slide-rest, and a guide :—The board for holding the paper ; the slide-rest for enabling the writer to keep the line, and the guide to enable him to form the letters.

The *board* is a piece of common wood, a little larger than a leaf of common letter paper, and a quarter of an inch thick. A series of notches are cut down each side, at a distance from each other, corresponding with the proposed distance of the lines of the writing. Two pins are inserted near the top, to keep the paper from being moved, while the guide is used.

The *slide-rest* is made of two parallel pieces of wood, notched at regular intervals, and kept at a certain distance from each other. At each extremity, a wedge-shaped projection is placed so as to fit into the notches of the board. Two saw cuts are made across the under side of the slide-rest, to let it pass the pins of the board. The slide-rest is laid across the paper on the board, while the guide moves between the parallels.

The *guide* is a slip of brass which runs between the parallels from a cross piece of wood to which it is attached, and which lies across the slide-rest. The slip of brass is made narrower than the space between the parallels, so that it may either slide against the upper or the under one.

At one end of the brass slip, a long hole is cut, into which the pencil or point is placed, and along the sides of which it is made to move. By this hole, all the letters of the alphabet and the figures may be formed in the most beautiful manner, without the pencil having to leave the sides of the hole, except in a few instances, and even in these it is so slight, that it can be performed with great ease and precision.

The elegance of the writing by the Typhlograph depends almost wholly on the shape of the hole ; which, although exceedingly simple, requires great nicety of workmanship. The hole has an upper and under half, which are separated from each other on the right side by a small projection, which stops the pencil from going up or down from the one to the other on that side. When the *upper* half is used, the guide must rest against the *under* parallel ; and when the under half is used, it must rest against the upper one. In this way the line is kept straight.

The first lesson in writing by the Typhlograph, is to make lines of this kind, *〽* by means of the upper part of the guide, while it slides *〽* against the under parallel. The upper half of the guide is of this shape. *∩* When the pencil is put into the hole, it is slidden *∩* forward till it touches the pencil. The pencil is then moved upwards against the side of the hole round the top, and downwards on the right till it is stopped by the projection at the bottom of the line. While the pencil rests upon the paper at that point, the guide is again brought forward till it touches the pencil with its left side ; the pencil is again taken round to the projection, and so on.

The second lesson is to make these, by the under part of the guide, while it slides against the upper parallel. The under half of the guide is of this shape, and the pencil is made to move downward along the left side, and upwards along the right, till stopped by the projection. The guide is moved forward till it touches the pencil, and then it performs the same journey as before.

The third lesson is to make lines of this kind, by using part of both halves. He first uses the upper half, but does not bring the pencil further than the middle of the line thus He then brings the guide up against the upper parallel, and makes its left side touch the pencil, which is still at the middle of the line. The pencil is then brought down and up half way, to the middle again, thus : The guide is then brought down again, and the pencil takes the upper curve again, and so on ; so that the top half of the upper part, and the lower half of the under part of the guide, are used alternately.

The fourth lesson is the O, thus : This is made by first using the top of the upper half as before, only he brings the pencil back again to the left side, where he began (in the middle of the line). Then he uses the bottom of the under half in the same manner as before, reaching up to the middle of the line again. In this way the O is formed ; but in order to make the next letter a little distant, he moves forward the guide, till the left side touches the pencil, and then he draws the pencil across to the right side. The guide must be moved upward and forward again, to use the top of the upper part as before.

If the under half be parallel with the line when the guide is up, the upper half will be above the line ; and if the upper half be parallel with the line when the guide is down, the under half will be beneath the line. In this way the top parts of the b d i j h k l p t, and the capitals, may be drawn above the line when in the upper part, when the guide is up ; and the under parts of the f g j p q y and z may be drawn below the line when the guide is down.

From the preceding lessons the pupil will have learned the use of the guide in making the most common forms used in writing.

He may now proceed to learn to write the letters of the alphabet ; in which the teacher will scarcely require any help. But in any case of difficulty, he will find in the Appendix (No. II.) a description of the motions of the guide in writing each of the letters. There are represented the various parts of the guide which may be used at once ; and, by the marks attached to them, each letter is described by the parts of which it is composed.

A great variety in the style of writing may be obtained by a different formation of the Typhlograph. It may either be sloped or horizontal, thin or broad. Even the thickness of the pencil will affect the style of writing. When the point is small, the writing is large and broad ; when it is thick, the writing is smaller and very narrow.

We may either write with a black lead pencil, or with a steel point over black paper. When we use a black lead pencil, it is best to use a hard, but not a brittle one.

The steel point is the same as that used by copper engravers in etching, only it should be a little rounded at the point to keep it from cutting the paper.

The black paper is sold in shops, under the name of copying paper ; but as it is rather thin, and too much loaded with the blacking, it may be better to prepare *strong* paper in the same way. I am not certain which is the *best* way to prepare the paper : I have found paper rolled by the printer's ink roller, and then held to the fire for a short time, succeed very well. I might suggest also the snuffings of candles, or a thick salve of fine lamp-black mixed with butter, or some other unctuous substance rubbed thinly on the paper. If it be desirable to lay it on with a brush, it may be diluted with turpentine, without destroying the relative proportions of the other ingredients.

Having procured the black paper, the letter to be written is placed upon the board of the Typhlograph, and the black paper above it. The slide-rest is then laid over the paper, and made to rest in two notches of the board ; the guide is then placed within the slide-rest, and used as above directed. The point moving along the black paper, gives off the black to the paper below, and an indelible writing is thus produced, without the inconvenience of using a fluid ink, which must be supplied at intervals, of which a blind man has no means of reckoning. The black paper may be used a long time without being exhausted ; even when it is nearly exhausted, the change is indicated by faintness of the lines, not by the failure of the writing ; so that a blind man need never be afraid of labouring in vain. He produces legible manuscript long after the black paper has become unfit for proper writing. The price of the Typhlograph is 5s.

THE ARITHMETIC CUSHION.

Professor Sanderson, who was blind, and who was Professor of Mathematics in the University of Cambridge, invented a table for himself, by which he could cast up accounts. It consisted of a surface cut into squares, with grooves between, which crossed each other. Each square had nine holes, and according to the hole in which the pin was put, so was the figure distinguished. The squares being arranged in lines upwards, and also sideways, and each representing one figure, he was able to perform all the rules of arithmetic by its means.

An improvement upon this was a cast-iron board, with a great number of square holes. Each hole represented one figure, and that figure was indicated by one of two kinds of types which was thrust into it. One type had on one end a projection in the side, and on the other end a projection in the corner ; and as the type might be turned four ways, and might be used with either end turned upwards, this type could represent eight different figures. The other type had a projection in the centre at one end ; the other end had no projection at all, so that it indicated the ninth figure and the cipher.

In the Glasgow Asylum a further improvement was made, by which only one type was necessary. The holes, however, were made of a pentagonal form ; and as the type had on one end a projection on one of the sides, and on the other end a projection on one of the corners, each end could represent five different figures ; and thus ten ciphers might be represented by a single type. The great disadvantage of all those methods lay in the inconvenience of the apparatus. Without taking into account the great labour and expense of the materials, the Blind, after these were procured, could not cast accounts, or make any calculation, without being where they were ; and to have carried such an unwieldy apparatus about with them, would have been impossible.

The whole of this apparatus has been rendered unnecessary, by the method which we are now about to describe, and which requires no special apparatus at all. The figures are represented by pins stuck into a cushion or any soft substance, such as a chair, a bed, or a carpet. If the pin be stuck in obliquely, it may represent one of four figures, according as it may be turned to the right or to the left, to the top or to the bottom ; other four figures are represented in the same way, by two pins stuck close together, instead of one, assuming the same positions. If instead of being stuck in obliquely, they are thrust in perpendicularly, either singly or doubly, other two figures are obtained. The arrangements of the figures under this notation will be found in the Appendix, No. III.

The advantages of this notation must be apparent to those who can distinguish between that which is for *shew* and that which is for *use*. An arithmetical notation, which may be used in all places and at all times, without difficulty, without expense, and without any peculiar apparatus, is of a thousand times more value to the Blind, than any other which can only be used in the school-room, and by such an apparatus as the types and boards which we have already described.

Pins are in every house. They are cheaper than almost any other manufactured article which we know. They are very light, and are far from being bulky. They may therefore be carried about by the Blind in considerable quantities without inconvenience, and at a very little expense.

Cushions are easily procured, and even when they are not at hand their place may be supplied by a chair, or a bed, or a carpet, or indeed any thing into which pins can be thrust. Their very clothes may be used for calculating any little matter which might occur, when nothing more convenient presented itself.

When the Blind have been taught to cast accounts by means of the pin notation, they ought always to carry about with them a pin-cushion or a small box filled with pins, both for this purpose, and also for other purposes which shall afterwards be mentioned.

In business transactions the pin notation will be found to be most valuable to the Blind. It occupies the place of a scroll journal. Every customer has a small cushion appropriated to his accounts. These cushions have a loop of tape or ribband sewed to the corner to which it is to hang. This loop fixes the position of the cushion, and is always supposed to be at the top, on the right hand. The person's name being written with the stamps on paper, is pinned to the centre of the top; and when an article is to be charged against him, the name of the articles may either be written in the same way, or indicated by peculiar combinations of pins—a number of which are given in the Appendix. The quantities and prices are indicated in the same line by the pin notation.

The Blind ought always to be taught book-keeping. This is done first by making them cast the accounts on the cushion, and then *copy* them into the cash-book or ledger with the stamps.

GEOMETRY.

The pin-cushion is the universal album of the Blind. Not only are the arithmetical figures represented by its means, but any kind of diagram may be represented to the touch. In forming diagrams, the pins are thrust into the cushion to the very head, in lines corresponding with the shape intended to be felt. The heads of the pins therefore are the only parts which are felt—each head represents a point, and a succession of them represents a line.

It is necessary to have a pair of wooden compasses for the forming of geometrical diagrams. Instead of the limbs terminating in points, as in other compasses, there is a small nick at each extremity, into which the pin is placed before thrusting it down. The sides of the limbs are straight,—one of them having slight grooves cut at regular distances, for making straight lines by

rows of pins ; the other having the grooves cut at distances of
half-an-inch—every alternate groove being distinguished by a
larger indentation at the top.

The pin-cushion should never be awanting from the school, or
the study of the Blind. I have shewn how necessary it is to the
study of arithmetic and geometry. I shall now shew how it may
greatly assist in the acquisition of the other branches of a blind
man's education, and how it may become the interpreter between the
Blind and the Seeing, and even between the Blind and the Deaf.

In teaching the Blind the *alphabet*, we may use the cushion
with great advantage. By arranging the pins into larger letters,
they are able to feel them with great ease ; and the differences
between the letters may more easily be explained by the cushion
than by any other means.

When the Blind are beginning to read, we may make up sentences and short words upon the cushion with great ease and
considerable advantage. For although the same object may be
gained by using the printed spelling book, or by writing the same
words with the writing stamps ; yet, in the absence of all these, we
may, without using a particle of paper, teach a blind person to read.

In teaching the Blind to *write*, we cannot in a more convenient
way give the pupil an idea of the various letters, than by representing them on a cushion by the arrangement of pins.

In short, when a teacher is desirous of conveying to his blind
pupil an idea of any form, the pin-cushion presents an easy and
convenient method of doing so ; and although he may be able
quickly, and sometimes effectually, to convey the idea by drawing
with his finger upon the palm of his pupil's hand, yet when this fails,
as it very frequently does, either from the complicated character of
the form itself, or the misapprehension of the pupil, the pin-cushion
is a certain and an easy resource in all such difficulties. With it at
his command, he need not be afraid to attempt to teach any branch
of knowledge, however much its intelligibility may depend upon
pictorial illustrations, diagrams illustrative of optics, machinery,
and other scientific subjects, drawings of buildings, furniture,
implements, and other objects. Even profiles of distinguished

individuals may all be distinctly delineated, in a tangible form, by the same means.

In teaching history and geography, *maps* of a temporary kind may be hastily got up on the pin-cushion ; and the addition of a piece of twine greatly diminishes the labour. Every turn in the coast is indicated by a pin, and the twine is either made to turn round it, or the pin is stuck through the twine. A dozen pins in this way, may make a very respectable map of the coast of a country. Cities and towns may be represented by three, or four, or five pins stuck close together ; villages, by one or two, according to their relative sizes. Rivers may be indicated by rows of pins, if such should be required ; and mountains, by masses of pins stuck so close that all the heads are not able to go down.

It may appear to some that this is too tedious a process, considering the temporary character of such a map ; but it must be kept in mind, that as all knowledge ought to be communicated gradually, this pin-map may be the very best way in which geography can be taught, even to those who see. At first, the teacher may give, by a piece of twine and a few pins, a general idea of the *outlines* of the country. This being a simple form, and unencumbered by minute details, which are apt to distract the attention, becomes deeply impressed upon the mind of the pupil, and forms the basement upon which farther knowledge is to be reared. The teacher gradually adds to the map ; first, the capital, which he represents by three pins at first, and then leads up the river upon which it stands, or forms the bay in which it is situated. The next most important city or town is then added with the same accompaniments ; and thus while the teacher is gradually building the map, he is at the same time securing every step of the pupil's progress, by carefully abstaining from confusing his mind, by presenting to it objects which he perhaps is never called on to remember.

I might suggest to those who would wish to teach geography in this manner, that they might use a common map, laying it on a piece of paper the same size, and with a pin prick it at those points where he would wish to insert the pins. He may then lay it on the cushion, and be guided by those marks ; or he may have the cushion crossed with the lines of longitude and latitude either with ink or with threads. Two or three cushions may be made for the purpose, having the lines differing in number and inclination, so as to suit maps of any extent of spherical surface, and of any part of the world.

The pin-cushion is also useful in writing and teaching *music*. This may be done in two ways. Five cords are sewed upon the musical cushion to represent the lines, and pins are thrust either into the cords or spaces, and varied, either in their combination or position, so as to represent the variation of the time of the notes. Further variety may be obtained by melting a globule of sealing-wax upon the head of the pin, and this globule may be sharp, or round, or square, according to the caprice of the person who adopts the signs. The pin may be bent, or even decapitated, for the sake of further variety ; but we are bound to remark that decapitation is not altogether safe or advisable, as the only sure method of preventing the pins from being buried in the cushion, is to allow them to wear their heads.

There is at all times a very great convenience arising from simplicity of instruments and methods ; the multiplication of signs, therefore, ought as much as possible to be avoided ; and as common pins, without being altered or added to, and therefore not requiring to be kept in separate boxes, are quite capable of supplying all the signs requisite in the notation of music, I would recommend the second method as that which ought to be adopted, in preference to the first.

The second method consists in adopting the numerical notation of music (which we shall afterwards describe). In it we employ nearly the same signs which we use in arithmetical notation, with the addition of a few others, which are necessary to represent other signs peculiar to music. I need not here enter into the particulars of this branch of the subject, as it will more naturally occur after I have described the numerical notation itself.

MUSIC.

Printed music, for the use of the Blind, is of considerable importance ; but to have printed it in its ordinary character would have been impossible. The Blind could not distinguish such complicated characters, more especially if they were surrounded by five parallel lines. A new notation has been invented so simple, that any one could understand how to sing from it with only one lesson. The notes are represented by the numbers 1 2 3 4 5 6 7. The " rest " is represented by a 0. To give an idea of time, points are used after the figures ; one point doubles the time of the simple figure ; two points multiplies it by four ; and three points multiplies it by eight.

If more than this be required, a line after the figure indicates four of the points, and one or two points may follow it, so as to multiply the time of the simple figure by sixth-four. For example,

Demisemiquavers	1	2	3	4
Semiquavers	1.	2.	3.	4.
Quavers	1..	2..	3..	4..
Crotchets	1...	2...	3...	4...
Minims	1—	2—	3—	4—
Semibreves	1—.	2—.	3—.	4—.

It scarcely ever happens that six different kinds of notes occur in one piece of music ; frequently there are only two, the minim and the semibreve. In such cases the minim would be the simple figure, and the semibreve the figure with one point after it.

In the Appendix (No. IV.) will be found an exposition of the principles upon which this musical notation is founded, along with the details of its arrangements. I shall here only give a few specimens of sacred music printed on this plan.

YORK. *c.m.* *g major.* C. (.)

1.	3	5	4	6	3	5	2.
O	do	thou	keep	my	soul,	O	God;

2.	3	5		5	z		5.
Do		thou	de -	liv -	er		me.

1.	3	5	4	6	3	5	2.
Let	me	not	be	a - shamed, for			I

3.	4	3	2	2	1.
Do	put	my	trust	in	thee.

MANCHESTER. *c.m.* *f major.* ⅜ (..)

1.	3..2.	1..87	6.5.4.	4.3.
I	to the	hills will	lift mine	eyes,

8.	5.4.3.	6.7.83	3.2.
From	whence doth	come mine	aid;

23	4..3.	6..5.	5.4.3.	3.2.
My	safe - ty	com - eth	from the	Lord,

7.	8.4.3.	54 3.2.	1..
Who	heaven and	earth hath	made.

ANGELS' HYMN. *l.m.* *a major.* ¾ (.)

1	3 . 1	2 . 3	4̄ 3 2	1 .
All	peo - ple	that on	earth do	dwell,

1	3 . z	5 . 2	5 . z	5 .
Sing	to the	Lord with	cheerful	voice.

3	4 . 5	6 . 5	4 . 3	2 .
Him	serve with	mirth, his	praise forth	tell,

5	4 . 3	2 . 1	4̄ 3 2	1 .
Come	ye be -	fore him	and re -	joice.

ST. LAWRENCE. *c.m.* *f major.* C. (. .)

0 . 1 .	3 . 3̄4	5 : 6	3 . 2 .	1 .
Oh	thou my	soul bless	God the	Lord,

5 .	6 . 8 .	5̄ 4̄ 3	3̄ . 2 .	
And	not for -	get - ful	be	

0 . 5 .	1 . 2 .	3̄ 4 5 .	6̄ 5̄ 4 3	6 .
Of	all his	gracious	be - ne -	fits

8 .	5 : 6	3 . 2 .	1 ..	
He	hath be -	stowed on	thee.	

The advantage of translating music into figures consists not only in the ease with which we are able to read music at first sight by its means, but also in the small space which is required for its notation. For example, a whole tune, consisting of four common metre lines, in all its parts, treble, tenor, counter, and bass, may all be distinctly printed in a space not more than two inches long and half an inch broad.

FRENCH. *c.m.* *f major.* (·)

.1 34 51 23 4. 03 2 11 7,1. 05 87 65 5z 5. 03 21] 17 1.
.1 11 11 71 1. 01 7,16,5,5. 01 32 17, 32 2. 01 7,1 6,5. 5.
.3 56 33 55 6. 05 4 34 23. 03 55 z5 66 7. 05 43 42 3.
.8 84 86 58 4. 08 5 64 58. 08 85 67 z2, 5. 08 56 45 1.

This, when printed in large types for the Blind, is no larger than the common notation of the same tune for those who see.

Another great advantage consists in the facility with which music may be expressed, either vocally or by signs. It may be printed with the types used in the books for the Blind. It may be written with the *stamps* or the *Typhlograph.* It may be represented by *pins* on the pin-cushion, or with *knots* on a string.

Although no music books were ever to be *printed* for the Blind, they may be *written* with the stamps with great ease, three or four copies being written at the same time. All the signs required in this notation are to be found among the stamps used for common writing. It is intended, however, to have music books printed for the Blind immediately.

Even were no writing stamps to be had, tunes could be written on the cushion with pins, using the same signs as in the arithmetical notation.

Greater distinctness may be gained in writing music by pins on the cushion, if we stretch a cord along the place upon which we wish to write. When the figures 1 2 3 4 5 6 7 are written beneath this cord, they form the lower octave; when they are written above it, they form the higher octave.

The 8th figure is used to represent the *rest.* The 9th figure represents the point for marking time, and the 0, which is a single point stuck perpendicularly, represents the dotted note, or when stuck close to another note, indicates the semitone above it; in other words, it is a sharp. Flats do not require to be marked, as the sharp of the note below indicates the same tone.

The other signs usually written above music, such as the *bind*, the *pause*, &c., may all be indicated by pins *stuck into the cord*.

The writing of music on the cushion ought always to be adopted before writing it with stamps. The tune having been written on the cushion, and carefully examined that it be correct, may then be commenced on paper with the stamps. When one note is written on the paper, the pin representing it should be lifted out of the cushion, and in this way repetition or omission is prevented.

To the Blind who compose music, the pin notation must be most valuable, on account of the rapidity with which it may be written, the ease with which it may be revised, and even altered, without wasting paper or destroying materials.

The numerical notation of music enables us also to write upon string.

A large knot represents 1.

A double knot represents 2.

A twisted knot represents 3.

A plait represents 4.

A loop represents 5.

A loop with a knot in the middle, 6.

A side knot, 7.

A loop with the string drawn through it, 0.

A small knot the point for marking time.

Two sets of knots are used ; one small, the other large, for a higher and a lower octave. Both are formed in the same way.

When *one* small knot is placed close *before* a note, it sharpens it. If *two* be found in the same situation, the note is to be flattened.

When the notes are placed close together, they have only half the time of the same notes placed a little separate. If a small knot be placed a little in advance of the note, it doubles its time ; if another be placed a little in advance of that, the time is twice doubled. If a third be placed a little in advance of that, the time is doubled three times, and so on.

When one small knot is placed close *after* a note, or if any of the knots which increase the time be double, then the note before it is to be considered a dotted note.

Geography is of importance to the Blind for various reasons. In the *first* place, it adds to the general stock of knowledge possessed by the Blind ;—it corrects false ideas, both in reference to places and events ; and it cultivates the mind, by expanding its ideas, and illustrating its other studies. In the *second* place, it affords an additional variety in the exercises of the school : this is of much greater importance than is generally supposed. In the *third* place, the examination of proper maps cultivates the sense of touch. This has been most strangely overlooked in the education of the Blind. When we consider what delicacy of touch has been acquired by those who did cultivate it, and how much they must be dependent upon that sense for receiving all their ideas of form, it is evidently a great neglect.

The maps, globes, and other apparatus which have been used in the education of the Blind, are by far too gross and rough to be of any use in the cultivation of their sense of touch. The great object seems to have been to meet the obtuseness of the feeling by a magnitude of the parts, so that they might be perceived even by the most unpractised fingers. The consequence has been, that admidst all the acquirements which result from the education of the Blind, the cultivation of the sense of touch is neglected.

We have already remarked, in an early part of this little work, that the cultivation of the sense of touch does not consist so much in a greater sensibility in the nerves, as in acquiring the habit of receiving information by its means. The Indian, who can track his way through the pathless forest, has no better eyes than the bewildered European ; but he has learned to make a much better use of them. The position of a leaf, the growth of the trees, and many other circumstances which habit at first suggested, but which habit at length conceals even from his own reflection, enable him, as if by instinct, to preserve an undeviating course through the woody wilderness. So it is with the Blind. When their sense of touch is cultivated by habit, or by education, which is the same thing, that, which to others is perceived by the eye, is almost equally perceptible to their touch ; partly by the superior sensibility which is gradually attained, but more particularly by that powerful intercourse which has been established between the mind and the nerves of the fingers.

The examination of maps is well adapted to the cultivation of the sense of touch ; much more so than reading by the fingers. When the map is first presented to their feeling, there are *great general features* which are at once recognised, long before the more delicate indications are perceived. The mind, however, feels no dissatisfaction from this inability, and will, for some time, rest satisfied with that measure of knowledge of the form of the country which it has already obtained.

But when the finger has become familiar with the great outlines, it will soon begin to make further discoveries of the more minute forms and lines which were at first unnoticed ; and this process of discovery goes forward, without effort and without end, until the finger has acquired such a degree of sensitiveness as to enable it to feel even the most delicate indications of form and position. In reading by the fingers, the case is altogether different, because until the finger has been able to arrive at a certain degree of aptitude in distinguishing each letter, the mind is altogether uninformed, and feels a painful anxiety until it has ascertained what the letter is. When that is done, no further effort is required.

The maps published in Edinburgh are engraved in a very simple manner.* Upon a plate of type-metal the map is drawn reversely. The land is scooped out, and the water is allowed to remain. The rivers being raised, have their margins shelving downwards, and the mountains are cut still deeper in the already lowered land.

Impressions are taken from this plate at the common printing press ; and by adding patches of thick paper behind, the map is

---

* The Society of Arts awarded their honorary silver medal to Mr. Gall, junior, for this invention.—Another prize of five sovereigns was also awarded to him, for the Typhlograph, and the Arithmetical Pin Notation.

embossed in a manner the reverse of the plate. The sea is low
and the land high, while the rivers run in valleys ; and the hills
rise above the land in rugged imitations of their originals. In
short, the map is, in some degree, a very natural imitation of the
countries which it represents.

The representation of towns, and boundaries of provinces, may
either be produced by the press, or by the hand after they are
printed. They have been executed in both ways ; but those in
which they have been added by the hand, are best and most
distinct. The towns are produced by pressing a blunt bodkin at
the back, so as to elevate the paper without piercing it. The
boundaries are made by a series of punctures also on the other
side in lines corresponding with those which we wish to elevate.

Very good maps may be made by the pin alone ; and although
they cost a great deal of trouble, and can never be so plain and
beautiful as those which are embossed,—yet when circumstances
prevent the pupil from procuring them,—or when a map is wanted
which has not been embossed, the punctured maps must be very
useful. The method of making these will be described afterwards.

Those maps, which are already published, are as follows :—
Eastern Hemisphere, 1s. Western Hemisphere, 1s. Europe, 2s.
North America, 2s. Edinburgh, 2s.

PICTURES FOR THE BLIND.

The Blind can feel the shape of any image which they can
handle ; but not having any idea of perspective, it is only an
outline which can be understood. They readily perceive the
resemblance between the outline of Italy and a boot, and they can
also perceive the resemblance of any other outline which is full
and well defined. We are, therefore, able to give the Blind many
illustrations of different objects by means of the printing press, or
the pin-cushion, or another method which is now about to be
described.

The reader's attention has already been directed to the method
of writing by pin-stamps. In it, the lines of the letters are produced by the puncturing of the paper with pins. But not only

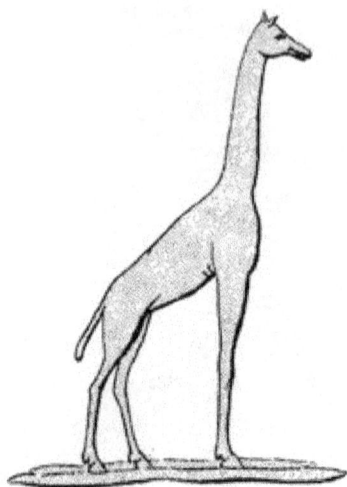

may letters be produced in this way,—any figure or diagram may be represented with great ease. On the other side of the paper which is to receive the representation, an outline is drawn with a pencil ; and we have only to puncture these lines with a pin or a needle, in order to make them quite perceptible to the finger. Two or three copies may be punctured at once.

We have seen copies of a little book on Geometry, in which the words were written with the stamps, and the diagrams punctured with a needle. Books of natural history, philosophy, geography, &c., may be made by the same means.

Maps especially may be executed in this manner, as we have already mentioned. The outlines are drawn reversed, on a piece of smooth and thick letter-paper. The coast is first punctured with a needle, and the sea is punctured in lines round the coast, gradually diminishing in strength, until it fades away, somewhat resembling the lines on the coast represented in maps. The rivers are punctured with the same instrument very finely, in two or three lines at the ocean, but gradually decreasing in breadth and strength, until they fade away at the source. The representation of the cities and towns is produced by a large blunt bodkin, which does not pierce the paper. The boundaries of the kingdoms or counties are represented by straight punctured lines, not close, but strongly marked ; and the mountains are produced by crushing the paper with a blunt piece of wood.

ORAL INSTRUCTION.

Whatever may be the extent of the literature which is yet in store for the Blind, it is important, that, in the meantime, we should have an easy and successful method of communicating oral instruction. It is rather remarkable that this also should have been long ago provided by the same individual to whom the Blind are indebted for the many efforts which are now made in their behalf. It is a plan, not indeed intended originally for the Blind, but for the young generally, with whom it has been eminently successful. It is peculiarly adapted, however, to the instruction of the Blind, and it will be found that no other method

D

can ever be so successful in rapidly communicating knowledge, and rendering the impressions on the mind both clear and lasting.

The system of oral instruction recommended by Mr. Gall, consists in condensing the knowledge which we wish to communicate into short and simple sentences. We then state one sentence at a time ; and after allowing the pupils to direct their whole attention to it alone, we catechise them upon it, asking them regarding the person who did it,—the action which he performed,— the person on whom it was done,—the manner, the time, and the place of the action, &c., according to what the sentence may be. The next sentence is then stated in a similar way, and in like manner catechised on.—The effect of this method of communicating knowledge is most surprising. When the questions are rapidly brought before the children, their spirits become quite exhilarated by the pleasant activity of mind produced during the exercise. They never tire of it ; the teacher is the first who tires, unless he catechises so slowly, that the pupils, not getting a sufficient supply of matter for thought, begin to meditate on something else ; and thus the exercise is destroyed ; and the children would much rather that the teacher did not ask questions at all, that the wandering excursions of their own minds may not be interrupted by questions which *distract* without *occupying* the attention.

The effect of this exercise, in conveying clear and permanent impressions to the mind, is still more advantageous. When the mind, in a *passive* state, wanders in half-attention over a long unbroken statement, its powers are diffused so widely, that the impressions thereby conveyed are of a dim and shadowy character. There is not point enough to make a deep impression, and in a short time it is nearly obliterated. But when the mind, in an *active* state, is called on to examine a short and simple statement at one time, without being distracted by the consideration of other matters, the whole energies of the children are concentrated upon that statement as into a focus ; and when they are further called on to analyze even that sentence, by *stating* the several ideas of which that sentence is composed, the very exercise of *expressing* the ideas, as well as thinking of them, gives a power and a precision to every corner of the sentence ; and so distinct and deep is the impression thereby made, that it remains uneffaced for months or for years afterwards.—It may be necessary to give an illustration of this method of communicating knowledge.

We shall suppose that the teacher wishes to communicate to the Blind the following passage from the History of England :—

" Henry VII. repressed many rebellions, and made the common people more civilized. He was a great and a wise king, and died at the age of fifty-two."

He ought to break it up into small pieces, and catechise upon each after announcing it. Thus,—

" Henry VII. repressed many rebellions."
Who repressed many rebellions ?
Which of the Henries was this ?
What were numerous during Henry's reign ?
What did Henry do to these rebellions ?

" He made the common people more civilized."
What did Henry VII. do to the common people ?
Who civilized the common people ?
What class of the people did Henry civilize ?

" He was a great and a wise king."
What was Henry's general character ?
Who was great and wise ?
What was he besides being a great king ?

" He died at the age of fifty-two."
How old was Henry when he died ?
Who died at the age of fifty-two ?

This exercise appears long, but in reality it is very short ; the question and answer occupy very little time, and it requires no study to fix the ideas on the mind—that object is accomplished at once, and the impression is lasting.

TEACHING LANGUAGES.

This method may also be applied with the greatest success in teaching languages to the Blind without books. In this instance we must be guided by nature, as she also teaches language without books. And as the child acquires language, by being led to express his thoughts before learning its grammatical rules, so must we endeavour to give a knowledge of whatever language we teach the Blind, by making them express their thoughts in it, and teach the grammar afterwards.

This is very easily accomplished by catechising on a sentence, and making the pupil answer in the words of the language. He is thus made, as it were, to *think* in the language, and this must be the most powerful way of communicating it.

To illustrate this method, I shall take an example from the Latin Testament :—

Mark iii. 1.—Et introivit (Jesus) iterum in synagogam : et erat ibi homo, habens manum aridam.

2. Et observabant eum, si sabbatis curaret ut accusarent eum.

3. Et ait homini habenti manum aridam : Surge in medium, &c.

The teacher reads the first sentence, translating each word thus :—*Et*, and,—*introivit*, went,—*iterum*, again,—*in synagogam*, into the synagogue.

He then reads the Latin words, calling on his pupils to give the English. Thus, the teacher says, *Et*,—the pupil answers, *And*. The teacher says, *Introivit*,—the pupil answers, *Entered*. The teacher says, *Iterum*,—the pupil answers, *Again*. The teacher says, *Synagogam*,—the pupil answers, *Synagogue*.

The teacher next pronounces the English word, and the pupil answers the Latin.—Thus :

Teacher, And.	*Scholar*, Et.
Teacher, Entered.	*Scholar*, Introivit.
Teacher, Again.	*Scholar*, Iterum.
Teacher, Synagogue.	*Scholar*, Synagogam.

If to know a word once, were sufficient to remember it, there
would be no need of anything further ; but we are all too well
aware that the remembrance of mere words is very difficult, and
soon fades, unless the impression be deepened. The following
plan, however, serves to deepen the impression without fatigue,
and make, the recollection permanent. The teacher next catechises
in English, and makes the pupil answer in Latin. In doing this
the pupil feels no difficulty, because the words are still fresh upon
his memory. But if the catechising were delayed even for half
an hour, the pupils would scarcely be able to answer. So firmly,
however, does the catechising deepen the impression, that the
fruits of five minutes' catechising will last for as many *weeks* as it
would have otherwise done for *minutes*. Take the following as
an example of the catechising :—

T. Who entered into the synagogue ?
S. *Jesus.*
T. What did Jesus do ?
S. *Introivit in synagogam.*
T. When did he enter the synagogue ?
S. *Iterum.*
T. What did he enter into ?
S. *In synagogam.*
T. Who was there ?
S. *Homo.*
T. Where was this man ?
S. *Ibi—in synagogam.*
T. What is said of this man ?
S. *Habens manum aridam.*
T. Who had the withered hand ?
S. *Homo.*
T. What had he ?
S. *Manum aridam.*
T. What had he withered ?
S. *Manum.*
T. What kind of a hand had he ?
S. *Aridam.*

T. What did the people do to Jesus ?

S. *Observabant eum.*

T. Whom did they observe ?

S. *Eum.*

T. What did they wish to observe about Jesus ?

S. *Si sabbatis curaret.*

T. What did they think Jesus would do to the man ?

S. *Curaret.*

T. When did they think Jesus would cure him ?

S. *Sabbatis.*

T. For what purpose did they watch him ?

S. *Ut accusarent illum.*

T. What did they wish to do to him ?

S. *Accusarent.*

T. Whom did they wish to accuse ?

S. *Illum.*

T. What did Jesus do when he saw them watching him ?

S. *Ait, &c.*

T. To whom did he speak ?

S. *Homini habenti manum aridam.*

T. What did he say to him ?

S. *Surge in medium.*

T. What was he to do ?

S. *Surge.*

T. Where was he to rise ?

S. *In medium.*

The above specimen exhibits the method of asking and answering the questions ; but in teaching it will often be necessary to repeat questions again and again, the answers to which are not sufficiently familiar to the mind ; for it must be remembered, that no passage should be left until it be completely taught.

The reader will also observe, that many answers must be given which are not grammatical. At first this is of no importance, the chief business being to give a knowledge of the words. When the pupil finds different forms of the same word, his mind is enabled to perceive the *root* which is common to both ; and when the mind is sufficiently at leisure, it will naturally revert to the difference. When, by the occurrence of these, a regular analogy is presented to the mind, it begins to anticipate the principle, and to perceive the character of these inflections. This is the best preparation which the pupil can have for entering on the study of the grammar of the language ; and to the blind pupil it is a valuable assistance, because instead of receiving difficult, dry, and to him unmeaning sounds to remember, he delights to find that the grammatical rules and inflections are by no means new, but are rather the welcome explanation of former difficulties ; while, instead of being a tax upon the memory, it is rather its assistant, by giving an orderly arrangement of what was previously in confusion.

By means of this method of teaching the Blind, the difficulties are so equally blended, that at no point do they ever become repulsive. At the first, when the mind is unoccupied by previous information, although all the words are new and unknown, they are easily remembered. In one lesson, eight or ten verses may be taught without fatigue. And afterwards, when the mind has to retain former words, as well as to acquire new ones, the difficulty is diminished by finding, that a great number of the words have already been learned during former lessons. The excitement produced by the lively exercise of catechising, more than reconciles the mind to what would otherwise be pure drudgery.

When the pupil has obtained some better knowledge of the language, which in a short time he will be able to do, the teacher will expect that all the questions *shall be answered grammatically ;* and when the pupil fails to do so, the teacher has a most favourable opportunity of shewing and explaining what is right and what is wrong.

In a short time, the teacher may *ask* the questions also in Latin, and thus the whole exercises are carried on in the same language. The progress of the pupil will thenceforward be doubled, for he not only improves by what he answers, but by what he hears.

Practical lessons in Latin may then be required from the pupil, drawn from the passage which he has been reading ; and after that, the scheme may be completed by making him give an amplified paraphrase, or abridged abstract of the passage, in words and phrases, differing as much as possible from the original.

From the success which has attended this method of teaching languages among those who see, and from its peculiar adaptation to the Blind, who in this way may both teach and learn languages without books ; it is hoped, that another means is thereby obtained for the acquisition of knowledge by the Blind ; and another facility added for the useful employment of the same interesting class of individuals, by their becoming the teachers of others, and therefore useful members of society.

APPENDIX.

No. I.

An ALPHABET for the BLIND.

The importance of a proper choice in the selection of an Alphabet for the Blind is evident from the fact, that the failure of the previous efforts on the Continent are almost altogether to be attributed to the character which they adopted.

The first point to be decided is, whether we shall adopt a known alphabet, or an arbitrary one. The advantage (and it is the only advantage which it was ever supposed to possess) of an arbitrary character is, that its forms may be adapted to the sense of touch, so as to make even small letters easily distinguished from each other. Even this advantage may be given to the common alphabet ; but supposing that it could not, it would have been decidedly better to have adopted a common known alphabet than to have encountered the more serious disadvantage which would to a certainty ruin any attempt to introduce a literature for the Blind, founded on an arbitrary alphabet.

1. In the *first* place, we must keep in view the perpetual sentence of banishment from the understandings and sympathies of the public generally, which, practically speaking, would be pronounced against it from its very birth. No man can never be expected to feel so much interest in a thing which he must learn before he can understand, as in that which is plain to his eyes and his understanding. If the Blind, therefore, must depend upon the interest which the public takes in the accomplishment of this object, it is

well that, in making the arrangements, we give some weight to
the probable operation of their feelings.   In single instances one
misfortune may be encountered without danger ; but when there
is one, even a small disadvantage of a general and perpetual
character, it gathers itself into a misfortune of the deadliest kind,
sufficient to blast an otherwise hopeful cause.

2. No one but professed teachers of the Blind would, in all
probability, ever undertake to learn it.   This would be a most
serious disadvantage to a literature which is intended, not merely
for Blind Asylums, but for every parlour and cottage where there
is a person Blind.   To attempt a literature only for the Blind who
are lodged in Asylums, would be to exert ourselves in behalf of
only a fractional part of the number of the Blind.   Parents and
friends will feel no difficulty in teaching an alphabet which they
themselves know, while an arbitrary character which they do not
know (suppose Chinese, Persian, or any which the reader has never
learned), will be exceedingly repulsive, more especially at the
commencement ; and it is there that the failure of benevolent
intentions generally takes place.

3. There is an awful insecurity attending any books which might
be printed in an arbitrary character, and as great an insecurity
attending the learning to read them.   It will be impossible to
get all to agree in their opinions regarding any arbitrary character
which may be proposed.   Those who learn to read one arbitrary
character will not be able to read books printed in another ; and
any improvement which may be made on any one of them must
destroy all the books which have been previously printed in that
character.   There is, in short, no standard of approximation by
which the framers can be guided.   The "a" of one may be like
the "z" of another ; and we would fall into a complete Babel of
confusion by assenting to the idea of adopting an arbitrary character, in preference to one which is known.

4. The adoption of an arbitrary character would ruin all the
prospects of the system of epistolary correspondence between the
Blind and their friends.   At present, the Blind write letters which
any one can read.   They themselves can read them with their

fingers, and the postmen can also read the addresses written in the same manner. The Blind, therefore, if an arbitrary character were used, could not send any letters unless to persons who not only had learned that particular alphabet, but who had either acquired sufficient expertness to enable them to read it, or had sufficient perseverance to induce them to translate the letters one by one, until they had got the substance of the communication. It is easy to imagine how few correspondents the Blind would have, and how impossible either to address their letter in the same character, or to send it to individuals who did not know the alphabet, with any prospect of its being received or read.*

Throwing aside the idea of an arbitrary character, we have still a choice between the capital letters, such as A B C D and the small letters, such as a b c d or *a b c d*.

In order to come to a proper decision upon this point, it is necessary to understand the principles upon which the tangibility of an alphabet is regulated.

When the finger is put down upon an embossed letter, the feeling is produced by part of the finger yielding to the elevation, and conveying to the nerve a feeling of resistance. This feeling may exist even when the object *does not really touch the finger*. Lay a small bead, or even the head of a pin upon the table, and press the finger upon it for a few seconds, until the skin has received an indentation by the pressure. Throw away the bead, and lay the finger upon the smooth table, the feeling will still remain ; and unless sight disprove it, the person would be apt to suppose that the bead was still under his finger. This sensation would continue so long as the indentation remained.

This is the reason why an *open* line is much more easily felt than one surrounded by others ; because the flesh of the finger cannot get round about it to make an impression. This is also the reason why *sharp points* are easily felt, and why rounded and blunt lines are very indistinctly perceived.

1. *Sharp and prominent* CORNERS are therefore important

* See Gall's Origin and Progress of a Literature for the Blind, p. 34.

requisites in the formation of a character for the Blind ; and any alphabet which possesses blunt and rounded lines must be unfit for their use.

2. *Diversity of* OUTWARD *form* is absolutely necessary for a blind alphabet ; for if the characteristics of a letter be in the *centre*, the finger cannot discover them.

Upon these principles, we see at once that the capital letters are very far from being fitted for the use of the Blind. When we reduce the alphabet to a small size, we can distinguish the letters from each other only *by the position of their* CORNERS. Now, it unfortunately happens that no fewer than six capital letters have their CORNERS (by which alone they can be distinguished), *exactly* the same. These are EHKNXZ. Each of these six letters appears to the fingers merely as an oblong square ; and the M can only be distinguished from them by the slight difference of its breadth. The BDRU cannot be distinguished from them, or from each other, except by the *bluntness* of some of the corners, for the *position* of the corners is not different. The AIJLW alone have their *corners* in different positions from all the others. OCGQS are merely rounded knobs without *corners*, and therefore are incapable of being distinguished by the finger, except by their want of form. The S, in the same manner, will almost appear an O, or a D, or a U, or an R. The F and P will appear almost the same. T will scarcely be distinguished from the V and Y, because the CORNERS of all the three are the same. Instead, therefore, of twenty-six different and easily distinguished forms, we have only nine which are different. They may be represented by the following letters : AHIJLOPTW ; and under one or other of these *all the others* are sheltered from observation.

A second great disadvantage in the capital letters consists in their perpendicular sides. This disadvantage will easily be perceived by comparing those letters which have perpendicular sides and those which have not. Take the OVCA. Although these letters were placed close to each other, the finger perceives the individuality of each, and is in no danger of supposing that part of one letter belongs to the one next it, because the finger gets in between the letters at the top or the bottom, although the letters themselves are quite close. There is economy of space here ; but take any of the letters which have perpendicular sides, they must be kept separate in order to be felt. Thus, M H N I. If these were placed close to each other, the finger could not feel any letter at all :—MHNI.

A third disadvantage consists in the breadth of the tops and bottoms. Letters for the use of the blind should have the tops or bottoms of the letters, in as many instances as possible, terminating in only one CORNER. This would give an *individuality* to each, because the finger would feel the top and bottom, and would know that there was a complete letter between. When there are two CORNERS at the top or the bottom, the finger does not easily perceive which of the corners belong to one letter, and which belongs to the one next it. For example, when we have such letters as these coming together, HINEMKXZ, the finger can scarcely feel anything more than a succession of points, all equally distant from each other ; and he is unable to say which of the corners belongs to one letter. It is as if it had been printed thus ⋮ ⋮ ⋮ ⋮ ⋮ which no person could read, nor could any one even tell how many letters it was composed of.

These reasons are scientific, and founded upon experience ; but there are two popular arguments which, to the general reader, must be more convincing. Let us consider whether we like to read the capital or the small letters ourselves ; which is the most legible, and which would take up least space when it is printed ? What would we think of a printer, who, in his anxiety to print a copy of the Bible in its very smallest size, would print it all in capitals ? And if we, in our anxiety to diminish the bulk of a Bible for the Blind, choose the capital alphabet instead of the small one, it is most evident that we would be still less successful. There is considerable difficulty in reading sentences printed in capitals ; and if we would but examine the reasons, we would find that they are almost the same with those which have been already specified.

When is it that words or sentences are always printed in capitals, and never in small letters ? In title pages—and why ? Because of the *uniformity* of the alphabet. Words printed in capitals have so few great distinguishing features, and are so monotonous in their character, that they are always preferred to the common alphabet in titles. If we were to print a title with types of the common alphabet, the words would have no resemblance to each other, and the symmetry would be totally destroyed. The reason why the capitals are best for titles, is the very reason why they are totally unfit for the Blind.

I have been thus particular in my remarks upon the fitness of the capital letters, on account of the preference which has been given to them by two individuals, whose experience in regard to the Blind is great, and whose anxiety for their welfare is unbounded. Actuated by the most correct views of the mischief which the adoption of an arbitrary character would necessarily entail upon the literature of the Blind, they have fallen into the opposite error of supposing that it was necessary, not merely that all should be able to read the books, but that the alphabet should be *exactly the same* as the common alphabet. If this had been necessary, the small letters, without any modification, would have been much better than the capitals ; but as a *modification* of the *small* letters would possess all the simplicity and superior legibility of an arbitrary character, without having any one of its disadvantages, it must be much better adapted to the use of the Blind than the capital alphabet.

The modification of the small alphabet, as prepared by Mr. Gall, possesses the two great characters required—simplicity and tangibility. The triangle is the simplest form which can be produced. Mr. Gall has therefore adopted the triangular modification. For the (a) or rather (*a*), he uses ◁ , for (*b*) he uses ▷, for (*c*) he uses <, for (*d*) he uses ◁, and so on. It will be observed, however, that the b and d have got a peculiar top, like a swallow's tail. This is not exactly in character with the principle of the alphabet ; but in the large alphabets it is necessary for the economy of space : for if the top were given in its full length, there would be too much space between the lines. This part of the letter is therefore aggravated by means of the broad top, so that it may be felt without being very long. In small alphabets this is not necessary, because the space required between the lines gives sufficient room for the extension of these top lines.

It is thus evident that every letter is stripped of every part which is not essential to its character, while every characteristic is so magnified as to distinguish its possessor from every other letter. *Corners* are given instead of *rounds*, and these corners are so arranged that no letter has them under the same arrangement.

It is pleasant to find that the same principle has been adopted in America ; and although the letters are not nearly so simple (and consequently can never be reduced to so small a size and yet retain their legibility), yet so great is the similarity, that those who have learned to read Mr. Gall's books are also able to read those from America. If the capital alphabet had been adopted here, this advantage would have been lost.

No. II.

TABLE for shewing the Method of Forming the Letters of the Alphabet by Means of the Typhlograph.

MOVEMENTS IN MAKING THE SINGLE LETTERS.

(a)—d *d* s r*   (n)—e h v

(b)—*y* o Q   (o)—d *d* v

(c)—a *a* v   (p)—*y* y y k v

(d)—d *d* s *z* p   (q)—d *d* s B p

(e)—F *a* v   (r)—e f G

(f)—k *k* y y *c* G S   (s)—T *u*

(g)—d *d* s B y *v*   (t)—*y* y p N

(h)—*y* y A h v   (u)—*C* q r

(i)—D *C* r   (v)—d s Q

(j)—D *C* B y *t*   (w)—*C* q q Q S

(k)—*y* y A g U x   (x)—*c t* t a *a* v

(l)—j m   (y)—d s B y *v*

(m)—e i h v   (z)—O *a x* N

---

* In the above references to the figures represented in the accompanying plate, it is supposed that when the line referred to has one extremity nearer the left hand than the other (not calculating the slope), then the left extremity is the beginning of that line. When none of the extremities are nearer than the other, it is supposed that the top is the beginning. When this supposition is reversed, the letter referring to that line is printed in *Italic.*—That is to say, when the letters of reference are printed in the *Roman* character, the line begins at the left hand, or at the upper extremity. But when the letters of reference are printed in the *Italic* character, the line begins either at the right hand, or at the lower extremity.

Index to the Movements in Writing by the Typhlograph.

a b c d e f g h i j

k l m n o p q r s t

u v w x y z A B C D

Unguided Movements.

E F G H I J K L M N

O P Q R S T U V W X

Facsimile of writing with the Typhlograph by a Blind Girl.

Commandment

MOVEMENTS IN MAKING THE CAPITAL LETTERS.

(A)—u i r

(B)—e B A z k *J* R *t*

(C)—J m

(D)—y *t* X u *e*

(E)—*d* L v

(F)—g E *j t* N

(G)—J m A B *v*

(H)—I A *u* T O *z* r

(I)—I A *s*

(K)—I A *u* u O* d *d J* R v

(L)—*k t* X *t*

(M)— { i B A *A* l B A *A* l r
      s i B A *A* l r

(N)—s i B A *A* k

(O)—n

(P)—e B A *z* k K

(Q)—n X w

(R)—e B A *z* k *J* R v

(S)—s h *J*

(T)—d M y *s*

(U)—e q *z* p

(V)—e q h

(W)—*I* A q *z* o h

(X)—e s s h *h* r

(Y)—e q *z z* y *v*

(Z)—*I* A B i *s*

MOVEMENTS IN MAKING THE FIGURES.

(1)—C A

(2)—c *J* N

(3)—*b* U *w*

(4)—*T* N

(5)—x *c C* o

(6)—d *v y*

(7)—O *T*

(8)—*b* H *w* W

(9)—*d* v A B

(0)—d *d* v

These directions for making the letters, particularly the capitals and figures, are only to be considered as suggestions to the teacher. Many of them might be much better delineated in other ways by the same instrument.

The small letters are those which are most elegantly formed ; and although, for convenience sake, it is better to use the same instrument to form the capitals, yet when elegance is required in both small and capital letters, cards may be cut for each of the capitals, and their places in relation to the other writing indicated by the notches in the slide-rest.

---

* This move (O) is not to be marked ; the pencil is merely to remove from the one extremity to the other, to begin the next move at its proper place.

In making the crossings of the t and A, there is a part of the typhlograph which supplies the line for guiding the pencil in forming them. In this also the notches of the slide-rest are necessary to shew where the crossings are required. They may also be made by leaning the pencil above the projection of the guide, and moving both pencil and guide so as to cross the letters which require it.

In writing by the Typhlograph, the pencil ought to be kept perpendicular ; but sometimes the elegance of the letters may be increased by changing that position, and running the point under the guide ; thus, in making the c, the under part of the letter should be made in this way, so that it may be made broader than the top.

Between some of the letters it may be necessary to make a line, the breadth of the hole in the guide, that the letters may not be too close. For example, when two o's come together, they must be separated in this way.

In the specimen of writing given in the preceding page, the *e* is connected with the *n* in this manner. This does not appear so handsome as when the writer is able to enlarge the *curve*. The girl who wrote the specimen, it may be remarked, has had only a few lessons, and scarcely any practice.

When the blind are taught to write with the Typhlograph, their experience in forming the letters is evident from the force with which they press the pencil against the sides of the guide ;—this gradually diminishes as they proceed in their practice. In a little while they are able to anticipate the line which the guide would direct them to make ; and at length their hand will be so completely schooled into the forms of the letters, that they will be able to write without the guide at all.

Those who have learned to write before they became blind, ought occasionally to practise writing with the typhlograph. Those who see are corrected in their writing by the eye ; but when they become blind, their writing is always apt to grow worse, for want of this discipline. The occasional use of the typhlograph will supply its place.

The Blind may write very small letters with great ease and precision. Indeed there is scarcely any limit to the reduction of the size. When the hand *tries* to form the letters large, the guide confines the movement to the size for which it is constructed ; the letters, therefore, are quite perfect, however minutely they may be formed. It would not be difficult for the Blind to write the Lord's Prayer upon a piece of paper not larger than a square inch ; and there is no doubt but that the Blind may yet exhibit specimens of penmanship which might be fairly entitled to comparison with the production of accomplished writers.

Neither is there any limit to the variety of character which the Typhlograph may be made to form. Any blind person may use a particular style of writing for himself, by using always the same guide. It is very difficult to make two guides alike in every respect. There is therefore almost a certainty that each is different from every other.

German writing may be made with even *greater* ease than the ordinary Italic form ; while the ease with which the guide may be made for such writing is an additional recommendation. An elongated hexagon, with a small projection in the middle of the right side, will make an excellent German-text guide.

No. IV.

The NUMERICAL MUSICAL NOTATION for the BLIND.

It will be necessary first to explain the principles upon which the numerical notation is founded, before describing the notation itself.

The octave in music possesses a definite and unchangeable character. When a cord by vibrating, produces a distinct musical tone, and when we make the vibrations become rapid by shortening it, the tone rises in the same proportion, until the rapidity of the vibrations is exactly doubled. Then there is a complete accord with the fundamental tone which was first produced. This is the first decided character which music assumes, and is called an octave. Within the octave, there is a kind of semi-octave, which is very perceptible in bass accompaniments. And between the fundamental tone or key-note, and the semi-octave, there is a minor semi-octave, less distinctly marked, but which accords both with the fundamental tone and the semi-octave. So that when these three are sounded at the same time, there is produced a perfect simple harmony, to which nothing can be added.

A more minute division of the octave gives us seven distinct notes, in which we recognise the fundamental tone as the first, the semi-octave as the fifth, and the minor semi-octave as the third.

These tones, however, are by no means regular; and it is only when we institute a mechanical rather than a musical division of the octave, that we find a regular and natural division into twelve tones or rather semi-tones.

In this secondary scale, we recognise the notes of the septenary scale, and we are better able to perceive their relative distances from each other, as well as the relation of the three choral notes to each other. Thus :—

Major

Tones	1	2	3	4	5	6	7	8
Semi-tones		2	3	4	6	7	9 10	11 12	

	2	3	5	6	7	9	10 11	12	Semi-tones
1		2	3	4	5 6		7	8	Tones

Minor

It is worthy of notice here, and may be useful in some cases, in arranging the notation, that although the minor key rises in a different succession of semi-tones, the abstract relation of the tones remains the same. For example, in the major key, the third full tone falls on the fifth semi-tone, but in the minor key it falls on the fourth. But if we consider the first of the minor key to be the sixth of the major key, all the notes are the same in both.

Arithmetical Pin Notation

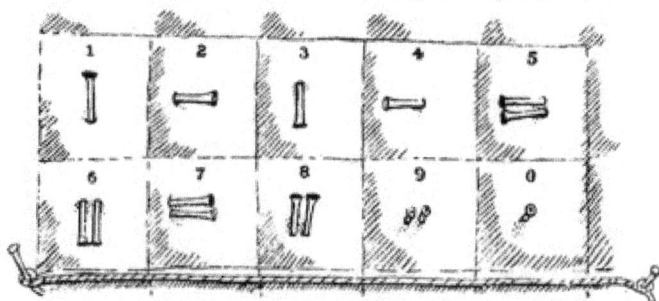

OTHER SIGNS
Formed by two or three Pins

In Teaching Arithmetic the Pupil may be assisted in keeping the lines of figures straight by having a Cushion quilted in Squares. This however ought to be used only for a short time.

On account of the irregularity of the ascent of the septenary. notes, musical instruments must be furnished with twelve tones instead of seven ; so that whatever of them may be selected for the fundamental or key-note, the other notes may be found on the semi-tones on which they ought to fall.   This renders it necessary, in the common notation, to mark a clef with a certain number of flats and sharps.   If no clefs were marked, no one could play the tune ; for that which with one clef would indicate an interval of two semi-tones, would, with another, indicate an interval of only one—and the most common tune might be played in twelve different ways—different in the relation of the notes to each other. In using the common line notation, therefore, we are forced to the difficult study of the clef in all its twelve different modifications ; and before being able to read a simple piece of music, we must examine and reason on the character of the clef, and the semi-tones which it brings into service.

Upon the same principle we find, that one tune may be written in twelve different ways, and yet, by making a corresponding alteration in the clef, no change would take place in the music itself, except in the elevation of the voice in singing it.

As the relative proportion of the notes must always remain the same, in whatever pitch the tune may be raised, it is evident, that for the Blind it is as well to represent the tune *itself* with 7 notes as to represent its *performance* upon 12.

For this purpose, we must take the key-note of the music the key-note of the notation also, calling it 1.   The six notes above, are 2 3 4 5 6 and 7.

In teaching the intervals, the pupil is greatly assisted by the choral notes, which are represented by 1 3 5 8, which the ear very readily remembers ; and when these are firmly impressed upon the memory, any of the others may easily be lighted on by their means.

This then being the foundation upon which the notation for the Blind is to be reared, it is only necessary to give them the figures representative of music, along with a system of time, and a few other symbols.   The Blind may then learn in less half the time, and with half the labour usually sacrificed by those who see.

1. The seven notes of music are represented by the first seven figures, 1 2 3 4 5 6 7, and a rest is represented by a cipher 0.

2. The change from one octave to another is represented by raising or sinking such notes above or below the line, or by attaching marks indicative of such a change. When only the 1 and 2 are used in the octave above, 8 and 9 may be used instead. When this is not sufficient, a comma turned upwards after such notes as are of the higher octave may indicate the same thing ; a comma turned downwards may indicate a transition to the lower octave.

3. In order to shew the elevation of the key-note, there must be placed at the beginning of the tune a letter indicating the note of the instrument upon which we are to modulate the key-note of the tune. We may alter the elevation of the tune by altering the letter.

4. To mark the time, it is only necessary to indicate the relative proportions which one note bears to the others, provided we indicate, at the commencement, the mark which is correspondent with the semi-breve.

5. The simple figure is considered the basis ; a dot added doubles the time ; two dots multiply it by 4 ; and three dots multiply it by 8. If a larger range of time be required, instead of four dots we may use a score, and after it may be placed another dot, or even two, to multiply the basis by 32 or 64. The largest note therefore would be represented by the figure itself, a score, and two dots ; although I can scarcely suppose that any tune would have in it two notes, the one 64 times the length of the other. In many tunes there are only two different kinds of notes, and in many more, only three ; in such cases there would be the greatest economy of space ; but even in those whose time varies, there would be an immense saving when compared with the common notation.

6. In describing the method of marking an octave higher or lower, the use of commas is mentioned ; but this is only necessary when the figure is simple, and has no point for marking time. When the points follow the figure, to mark an increase of time, they may be turned up to mark the higher octave, or turned down

to mark the lower. In all such cases, however, there must be prefixed to each line a point turned either up or down, to shew in what direction the figures in the line are supposed to be turned. Thus, if at the beginning of the line the point be turned upwards, and 7 occur in that line with a point turned downwards, this would indicate that the 7 of the octave below was to be used. Again, if the point be turned downwards at the beginning, and in the line there occur a 1 with the point turned upwards, this would indicate that the keynote of the octave above was to be used.

7. When dotted notes are required, a colon is used instead of a point; but where there is no point attached to the figure a semicolon is used—the comma of the semicolon indicating as usual the position. It would thus, when in its natural position, represent the lower octave, and when turned up, the higher octave.

8. Flats and sharps may be represented with common types by a parenthesis prefixed. The flat by the parenthesis turned *from* the figure—the sharp turned *towards* it.

9. Flats and sharps which occur in music, not in the clef, but accidentally, are generally caused by a change in the keynote; and the most frequent occurrence is upon the fourth of the major key, although the present form of notation prevents us from perceiving such analogies. When therefore this does occur upon the fourth of the major scale, the cause is, the changing of the key from the grand octave to the semi-octave; and as the note below the grand octave is 7, which is a semi-tone, when the 5 takes the place of 8 or 1, the 4 takes the place of 7, and must be semi-tone also. It becomes, if I may use the expression, half a 7 and half a 4, and may therefore be made a Z, which partakes of the shape of both.

10. The bars are indicated by spaces between the figures where they occur.

The numerical notation of music enables us to make out indices of tunes, not merely by the alphabetical arrangement of their names, but by the numbers composing their first lines; so that on hearing any tune, we could find out its name by such an index.

FRETTED TYPES.

PRINTING with fretted types is one of the most valuable inventions for which the Blind are indebted to Mr. Gall, as it has placed this interesting art upon a more stable and sure foundation than ever it was before. Although many advantages were expected from it, not only have they all been realized, but many more have been obtained which were never even thought of.

The fretted types are similar in every respect to the old ones; only, instead of having the lines smooth, they are composed of a succession of points, which, when the paper is pressed upon them, almost perforate it. The impression thus made is more *legible* and more *durable*, while it takes only about one-half of the labour to produce it.

The books are much *cheaper* than those which are produced in the old way. They are printed with *greater* ease and quickness than even common printing, because the types do not require to be inked.

Formerly it was impossible to print upon both sides of the paper. Now, however, by means of the fretted types, the paper may be printed on both sides. About one-fourth of the paper may thus be saved; and the lines being kept more asunder are made more legible, and, to the finger, less confused.

Formerly the lines were apt to fall in the middle when hard pressed by the finger. Now, the lines are supported by a series of arches, so that no pressure of the finger can make them fall.

Formerly the lines were smooth and blunt, so that a considerable pressure by the finger was necessary to produce a distinct indentation. Now they are rough and sharp, so that the finger is more distinctly indented, while a much slighter pressure is required to produce the effect.

No. VI.

Size of the TYPES for the BLIND.

In the specimens of printing at the end of the book, the reader will perceive an alphabet for the Blind on the *English* size of type. This is a size which the Blind are already able to read, and there is no doubt but that books will yet be printed upon types much smaller than even this.

Indeed, there can be no limit assigned to the reduction of the size of type, so long as we keep to the present alphabet, whose characteristics (as has been already mentioned) are altogether *external*.

But it is a dangerous error to suppose that the books should be printed upon the smallest type which the Blind can be taught to read. They should *at first* be printed very large, for although the bulk of the books may be an important matter for after consideration, it ought not to be allowed to affect that which is of still more importance at present. There must be Bibles for the Blind printed on various sizes of types ; but it would be best to print the large size first, and let the smaller sizes follow, for the following very important reasons :

1. We must provide in the meantime Bibles which *all the Blind* will be able to read. If it were only for children that we had to provide Bibles, there might be some doubt which size to adopt first. Children are able to read print which the adult Blind cannot feel ; but any print which the adult can read the children can read also. This is one reason therefore why the books should be printed on a large type first. The fretted type upon which the specimen at the end of the book is printed, can be read by any blind person, with more or less difficulty, *even at the very first.* A type much smaller could not be felt at first by many of the Blind, whose fingers are hardened by manual labour. It were cruel, therefore, as well as impolitic, to exclude from the first opening of God's Scriptures

to them, so large and so interesting a class of individuals as the *adult* Blind. Mr. Gall's efforts were not undertaken to give an additional interest to the platform of an Asylum examination. His eye rested on the dark chamber of the solitary Blind.

2. The great question now is not, How small print can the Blind be taught to read ? but the question is, *What size of print would the Blind* LIKE *to read ?* A very little consideration is sufficient to shew us, that unless the Blind can be made to take pleasure in reading, the books will remain unread. And although benevolent individuals may take great pains, and lay out great expense in procuring for them Bibles, unless this simple fact be considered and acted on, they will find, that, as in France, their labour and their money bought only a shadow. In endeavouring to save room, they will lose their books altogether. In endeavouring to save money, they will throw away all that they do expend.

The first object is to make readers, and to create a thirst for reading. For this purpose we must encourage them to read ; not by shewing them how small the books are which they cannot feel, but how easily they can feel the books that are provided for them. Even after they have learned to read, they must still be thus encouraged, if we wish them to derive any benefit from their learning. A blind man may be *able* to read, and yet it may require so great an effort, that he will feel no *pleasure* in doing so. It is only when the ability to read is attended with almost no effort, that the *pleasure* of reading commences ; large and easily felt print is therefore the only way in which we can accomplish this object, and avoid the cause which ruined the Parisian books. *They* could be read, and they are read to this day ; but they have always been confined to the inmates of the asylum and a few others, who had opportunities of cultivating their sense of touch, and patience and perseverance to enable them to overcome the difficulty. They are nevertheless a failure, *because they are not* FOR THE BLIND *as a whole.*

The Blind ought to be dealt with as we would deal with aged people, whose eyes are dim, or even as we would wish to be treated ourselves. We would not like to be provided with books printed upon a microscopic great primer, which brought the letters to become visible, but nothing more. We do not print novels or scientific works upon diamond types; and even the Bible would never be printed upon small types, until an edition had been provided upon a more comfortable size of letter, which could be read not merely by children, but by *all*.

No. VII.

The Price of BOOKS and PRINTING for the BLIND.

Books printed upon the same size of type with that of the specimen at the end of this book, and also a size smaller, may be printed with additions of 500 copies at the rate of one penny per sheet of small post; or in other words, one farthing for every leaf of common letter paper. When printed upon the small English type, such as that in the specimen, the expense would be about three-half-pence per sheet.

The whole New Testament, printed on the large type, would cost about 30s. or 33s. if printed only on one side. If printed on both sides, it would cost about 26s. Upon a smaller type, which will probably be the *medium* type for the Blind, the New Testament would cost about 25s. Upon the English type, it would cost about 12s. 6d. or 15s. Testaments may yet be printed on the triangular character, capable of being read by the Blind, for 5s. and bound into a single volume.

Upon these terms, benevolent individuals may benefit the Blind by printing parts of the Bible for their use. To print 500 copies of four pages, would cost rather less than £2 2s., and this sum might be greatly reduced by the sale of the copies, both to the Blind and to those who see.

No. VIII.

Mr. ST. CLAIR'S WRITING APPARATUS for the BLIND.

A very ingenious and simple apparatus has been invented by Mr. St. Clair (who is himself blind), by which he is enabled to correspond with his seeing friends.* It consists of a slip of tin plate, in which is cut a range of square holes.

Within these he is able to form the capital letters with considerable precision.

The great peculiarities of the capital letter point them out as well adapted to this plan of writing. Nearly the whole of them are squares, varied only in their internal structure, or in the obtuseness of some of their corners. The square hole therefore is in a great measure a guide for them all. The following is a facsimile of the writing which Mr. St. Clair produces by its means :—

JOHN ST. CLAIR

The ease with which the instrument may be made, and the facility with which the writing by its means may be learned, render it an important auxiliary in the education of the Blind.

---

* The Society of Arts adjudged to Mr. St. Clair a prize of three sovereigns for this contrivance.

No. IX.

SCHOOLS for the BLIND.

So great are the facilities now afforded to the education of the Blind, that

Religious knowledge	Algebra
Reading	Geometry
Writing	Geography
Grammar	History
Arithmetic	Languages
Book-keeping	Music

and almost every other department of science may be taught with great ease. Schools may be instituted in every town throughout the country ; or in places where there are few blind persons, a class may be attached to the parochial schools, in which all or any of the above branches may be taught. Even private individuals, who are interested in any blind persons, may become their teachers. The whole art is so simple, that any one may accomplish it.

Libraries may also be formed for the Blind, either in their own school, or in the clergyman's house. From them the Blind may procure books to read and to return, as in other libraries.

The establishment of such schools would greatly benefit the Asylums for the Blind ; as it would procure for them educated individuals as inmates, from all parts of the country, who would be therefore more useful members of the institution, and would require less care in being taught their trade.

Many of those trained in such schools would not require to be removed to any Blind Asylum. Their minds being cultivated, would soon strike out some useful occupation in their own locality. They would not only become independent of charity, but might even be able to occupy elevated situations in society. Many have already done so without having so great opportunities.

We have already instances of the Blind becoming Scripture readers to their neighbours ; and most useful readers they are, because they find a deeper interest, and a more affectionate welcome attend their visits, than would fall to the share of any other on a similar errand.

To the Blind themselves the ability to read the Bible is of great value. Even the comparative slowness with which at first the verses are read is not without its advantages. It gives the mind food for thought, and time for attention and reflection. The Blind are necessarily solitary, and any occupation, however trifling, is valuable. How important then to give them the Bible ! Never was there a better opportunity of presenting God's word as a message to man.

If there are advantages possessed by those who see over the Blind in reading, it must be confessed at the same time, that the Blind possess other advantages, which those who read with their eyes cannot have. They need no candle. They can read by night as well as by day. Even in bed, when sickness would prevent him from sitting up, the Blind person can take his Bible to bed with him, and read with his book beneath the bed-clothes.

The Blind may become deaf, and the Deaf may become Blind. In either case the books for the Blind, and the writing apparatus, must be of great advantage. One instance of the latter kind has already occurred, and already has the remedy been applied. One young woman, who was an inmate of the Glasgow Deaf and Dumb Asylum, became blind, and was thus shut out from all intercourse with society, except through the medium of the sense of touch. That young woman has been taught to read Mr. Gall's books with her fingers ; and thus, though nearly shut out from intercourse with man, she enjoys continual access to the word of God.

No. X.

The following address, *written and signed with the writing stamps*, was presented to Mr. Gall, by the pupils of the Belfast School for the Blind, accompanied with a handsome copy of the Bible.

RESPECTED SIR,

Permit us to convey to you our deep sense of the unspeakable benefits you have conferred upon us. We can now read and write. Our solitary hours, which were formerly employed in brooding over our deprivations, are now spent in drawing holy comforts from the Word of Life ; so that to us who sat in darkness light is sprung up. For these blessings, sir, we are, under God, indebted to your exertions.

We cannot express what we feel ;—we cannot repay what we have received. But we beg you to accept the accompanying small Bible, being the valueless representative of that which is above all value.

We have requested Mr. Collier, our teacher, to present it to you in our name.

We daily pray to God that he may bless you, and spare you to see many happy results of your benevolent labours.

Signed on behalf, and at the request of the pupils of the Belfast School for the Blind,

SAMUEL THELLAR.

August 1, 1835.

The following is Mr. Gall's answer :

Myrtle Bank, Trinity, Edinburgh,
13th August, 1835.

MY DEAR YOUNG FRIENDS,

I have most unexpectedly received, by the hands of your respected teacher, Mr. Thomas Collier, a very estimable token of your gratitude to me, as the humble instrument of providing the means by which you are now enabled to read and write.

This mark of your affection to myself, and of your estimation of the blessings of Literature, has afforded me great satisfaction. It is the first indication I have received of the kind, the "sheaf of the first fruits" of my labours for the Blind; which with humility and gratitude, I desire to "wave as a wave-offering before the Lord"; while I request you to join me in acknowledging Him as the author of the blessing, and alone entitled to the glory.

The closing intimation of your letter is peculiarly pleasing. I have long experienced the value of the prayers of the pious young; and your spontaneous daily supplications on my behalf, I esteem above all price. They are the most valuable, and most appropriate return that gratitude could dictate. Allow me earnestly to solicit their continuance; and that He who has put it into your hearts to do so, may hear and answer our prayers for each other, is the earnest desire of,

Your affectionate Friend and Wellwisher,

JAMES GALL

To the Pupils of the Belfast School
for the Blind.

THE END.

LONDON: WILLIAM CLOWES AND SONS, LIMITED, STAMFORD STREET AND CHARING CROSS.

a b c d e f g h i j k l m n
o p q r s t u v w x y z

JOHN I.

1 In the beginning was the
word, and the
word was with
god and the
word was god.
2 The same was
in the beginning
with god.
3 All things we-
re made by him:

and without hi-
m was not any
thing made that
was made.
  & in him was
life. and the
life was the light
of men.
  s and the light

shineth in dar-
kness and the
darkness compr-
ehended it not-
6 there was a
man sent from
god whose name
was John.

www.ingramcontent.com/pod-product-compliance
Lightning Source LLC
Chambersburg PA
CBHW020449270326

41926CB00008B/545

9783742833761